C000120584

GAY & LESBIAN
LONDON

Graham Parker

Gay & Lesbian London

Written by Graham Parker
Photography by Alison Henry
Cover photographs by Alison Henry
Edited by Ally Ireson
Design by Metro

Published in 2002 by
Metro Publications
PO Box 6336
London
N1 6PY

Printed and bound in Spain by Imago

© 2001 Graham Parker

British Library Cataloguing in Publication Data.
A catalogue record for this book is available from the British Library.

ISBN 1-902910 09-5

ACKNOWLEDGMENTS

Since Gay London was first published so much has changed that this new edition has been far less of a revision than an altogether new book. My thanks therefore go to all the busy people (bar staff, night club owners, shop managers etc) who have helped me to compile this book and answered all my often detailed questions. Among them special thanks go to the staff at Central Station, who have helped me track down several social groups when all else had failed. With things changing on the gay scene so quickly Andrew and Susi and other staff at Metro have done a sterling job of unearthing last minute changes, making sure this book is as up-to-date as possible, and even takes into account changes that are happening as we go to press.

My thanks also go to Alison Henry whose photographs illustrate this book and to Susi and Lesley at Metro for the maps and other design work. Lastly, my thanks go to my editor, Ally Ireson, whose attention to detail and valuable suggestions have proved a great help.

KEY

*	– late-night opening
TV	– TV/TS friendly
♀	– women's night or women only

Contents

INTRODUCTION

Being gay and lesbian has got the thumbs-up over the past decade. The likes of Lily Savage, Ellen DeGeneres, Brian and Anna on *Big Brother* and *Queer as Folk* have brought the message into everyone's living room. Even George Michael turned a rather compromising situation into a No.1 hit due to a widespread public vote of homo support. There are now 'out' MPs, lesbians and gays returning to active service in the armed forces, and partnership rights being won in court – as well as legislation decreeing that men from the age of 16 can indulge legally in gay sex.

But despite the new emerging generation of teenagers who are comfortable to speak out about their sexuality, there are still sinister undertones. The Clause 28 debate has still not been satisfactorily resolved, for some homophobia is a daily reality and AIDS charities are losing their battle to educate the masses as sexual health is ceasing to be 'fashionable'.

Still, London caters well for its gay and lesbian population. The main spotlight is on Soho's Old Compton Street, although there are smaller pockets where our brothers and sisters congregate. Earl's Court has risen from the ashes as a gay focus, decamping backpacking Australians and building up a network of gay eateries and drinking holes around the grand old dame called the Coleherne; while Stoke Newington and Hackney have definite lesbian leanings.

The structured scene is most visible, leading many to believe that being gay means wearing crop tops, sporting buzz cuts and listening to the 'right' music. But there really is more to it than butch and drag, Doris and Judy, Mykonos and Madonna. Professional groups draw lawyers, accountants and doctors who often don't step inside clubs; introduction agencies cater for many lesbians and gays who think of themselves as more than fitting into mainstream; and our community's lobbying groups focus on very many different aspects of the sexuality issue.

Gays and lesbians no longer all bat for the same team. This book is for those who want to pick and mix, exploring the options to complement their personality and taste – for those who value their sexuality, but are not dictated to by it.

ACCOMMODATION

Accommodation is one of the bugbears of living in London, whether you're visiting, homeless or just changing your address. There are homeless projects and hotels that deal specifically with gay men and lesbians, as well as a strong network of general accommodation-finding facilities, from the small ads in the gay press (see p.121-125) to gay agencies.

RESIDENTIAL ACCOMMODATION BUREAUS

Housemartins

⌨ *3 Plough Way, Surrey Quays, SE16*

☎ *020 7231 5656*   ✆ *020 7231 0535*

⌨ *24 Market Way, Chrisp Street Centre, Docklands, E14*

☎ *020 7531 3636*

⌨ *105 Blackheath Road, Greenwich, SE10*

☎ *020 8694 7989*

✍ *raymail@aol.com*

✍ *www.housemartins.org*

🕐 *Mon-Fri 9am-6pm, Sat 9am-5pm*

London's only gay estate agency chain is also one of the city's fastest-growing independent estate agents, covering east and southeast London. Housemartins' comprehensive services include residential and commercial sales and rentals, full property management, as well as supplementaries such as interior design, builders and decorators, property refurbishment, rental furnishing and removals. Financial services and mortgage advice is available through an in-house independent advisor, and the agency can also provide a list of local solicitors who offer excellent conveyancing services at competitive prices.

Lesbian and Gay Accommodation Outlet

⌨ *32 Old Compton Street, Soho, W1*

☎ *020 7287 4244* ✆ *020 7734 7217*

✎ *homes@outlet4homes.com*

✎ *www.outlet4homes.com*

🚇 *Leicester Square LU*

🕓 *Mon-Fri 10am-7pm, Sat noon-5pm*

Outlet is *the* housing resource for lesbian, gay and gay-friendly Londoners, set up in 1995 to offer a wide selection of long- and short-term accommodation. They coordinate a range of services including phone, internet and face-to-face interviews to match landlords and tenants to their ideal permanent house or flatmate, as well as having flats and studios to rent. To guide you through the mire, all shared accommodation on file has information on the age and sex of the other occupiers, their occupations, hobbies, household hours and general cleanliness of the property. They also offer mobile phone hire on a day to day basis, contracts, referencing and general advice.

London Lesbian and Gay Switchboard

⌨ *PO Box 7324, King's Cross, N1*

☎ *020 7837 7324 (24hrs)*

🕓 *24 hours daily*

The Switchboard (see p.89) runs an accommodation service based exclusively on flatshares. If you have accommodation to offer or are looking for a place to live, ring the main switchboard number (some patience – and a redial button on your phone – is essential). Landlords are charged a nominal fee, but for flatseekers the service is free.

Out To Flat

✎ *www.outtoflat.co.uk*

Both landlords and flatseekers can register over the internet.

Shares UK

✎ *www.sharesuk.com*

As well as a house- and flatshare service for the gay and lesbian community throughout the UK, Shares UK can also help to arrange holiday accommodation.

www.gayhotels.com

The first on-line, real-time booking service for gay and gay-friendly accommodation worldwide. Includes guest houses, hotels and apartments; as well as club, restaurant, gym and bar reviews.

GAY HOTELS

Centaurus B&B

⌨ *100 Old Street, EC1*

☎ *020 7251 3535* 📠 *020 7251 3536*

✉ *guy@centaurus.co.uk*

✉ *www.gayaccom.co.uk*

🚇 *Barbican or Old Street LU*

💷 *from £49.50 single per night, £39.50 double; lower rates for longer stays*

Close to the Barbican Centre (about 1½ miles east of Soho), Centaurus offers a very comfortable self-contained private guest suite with en-suite shower, private toilet, TV and video, radio-alarm, an iron and tea/coffee-making facilities.

Number Seven Guest House

⌨ *7 Josephine Avenue, Brixton, SW2*

☎ *020 8674 1880*   ✆ *020 8671 6032*

✎ *hotel@no7.com*

✎ *www.no7.com*

🚇 *Brixton LU*

💰 *singles from £49, doubles from £69*

Since it opened in 1992, this exclusively gay and lesbian guesthouse has won several *Pink Paper* awards as London's best hotel/guesthouse, due to its staff efficiency, facilities and ambience – it really feels like someone's home. The Victorian terrace house lies in a quiet, tree-lined avenue close to several Brixton gay nightspots and is ten minutes by tube from the West End. All rooms have an en-suite bath, direct-dial phone, colour TV, hairdryer, tea/coffee-making facilities and minibar. A full English breakfast in the garden conservatory is included in price, and there is free private parking, and laundry, fax and photocopying services available.

Philbeach Hotel

⌨ *30-31 Philbeach Gardens, Earl's Court, SW5*

☎ *020 7373 1244*   ✆ *020 7244 0149*

✎ *www.philbeachhotel.freeserve.co.uk*

🚇 *Earl's Court LU*

💰 *budget singles £35, standard singles £50, singles with shower £60, standard doubles £65, doubles with shower £90, standard triples £75, triples with shower £100*

Europe's largest gay hotel is now over twenty years old, but has recently been renovated. The Victorian building features 35 bedrooms (all with en-suite bathroom, direct-dial phone, tea/coffee-making facilities, fridge and colour TV) as well as a TV lounge, 24-hour reception, guest internet facilities, a bar available for private functions and the Wilde About Oscar award-winning garden restaurant (see p.164). The hotel is Transvestite /Transsexual friendly. Prices include a Continental breakfast. Philbeach is open over the Christmas period.

Prince William Hotel

⌨ *42-44 Gloucester Terrace, Paddington, W2*

☎ *020 7724 7414*

🚇 *Paddington BR/LU*

💰 *singles from £39, doubles from £55*

This welcoming gay-friendly, central London hotel has rooms en-suite, with satellite TV, a phone, and tea/coffee-making facilities as standard; its prices include continental breakfast. The hotel has recently undergone a major refurbishment.

Russell Lodge

⌸ *20 Little Russell Street, Bloomsbury, WC1*

☎ *Khaleda 020 7430 2489*   ✆ *020 7681 7604*

✎ *www.russell.lodge@virgin.net*

🚇 *Holborn/Russell Square/Tottenham Court Road LU*

💰 *singles £35, doubles £45, doubles with shower and WC £55, triples £65*

This 17th-century listed Georgian building close to the British Museum is an exclusively gay and lesbian guesthouse with 13 rooms, which plans to buy another property in a nearby street to extend. The hotel does Bed & (vegetarian) Breakfast, and has a common room with cable TV, laundry and dry cleaning facilities; as well as airport transfer and cab services, booking services for theatre, cinema, travel and restaurants, and fax and word-processing facilities. The hotel also administers a two-bedroom apartment near Leicester Square for long or short lets.

HOLIDAY APARTMENTS

Accommodation Outlet

⌸ *32 Old Compton Street, Soho, W1*

☎ *020 7287 4244*   ✆ *020 7734 7217*

✎ *holidays@outlet4holidays.com*

✎ *www.outlet4holidays.com*

🚇 *Leicester Square LU*

Outlet offer clean, comfortable and centrally located self-catering accommodation that caters for everyone's budget, with a range of double rooms with shared bathroom and kitchen and apartments with private bathroom and kitchen. Their prices are competitive and the properties are located no more than 5 minutes from their offices on Old Compton Street. Outlet offer additional services such as mobile phone hire, tour guides and left luggage. They plan to launch an international service in the near future.

Clone Zone

⌸ *64 Old Compton Street, Soho, W1*

☎ *020 7287 3530*   ✆ *020 7287 3531*

✎ *www.clonezone.co.uk*

🚇 *Leicester Square LU*

💰 *from £75 per night*

In the heart of London's gay village, these self-contained modern studio apartments are above the gay shop of the same name (see p.178 and are decorated to a high standard. The stylish double rooms have en-suite facilities, while the luxury apartment has both a kitchen and bathroom and sleeps up to four people. Staff in the shop are happy to advise you about the gay scene.

GAY-FRIENDLY HOTELS

K&K George Hotel

⌨ *1-15 Templeton Place, Earl's Court, SW5*

☎ *020 7598 8700*   📠 *020 7370 2285*

✉ *hotelgeorge@kkhotels.co.uk*

✉ *www.kkhotels.com*

🚇 *Earl's Court LU*

💷 *singles £160, doubles/twins £190, triples £210*

In a quiet residential street behind Earl's Court Road, this smart hotel is managed by the international K&K group and has 154 elegant rooms, all with en-suite bathroom, direct-dial phone, cable TV with radio, tea/coffee-making facilities, safe, minibar and hairdryers. Non-smoking rooms are available. A buffet breakfast is included in the price. There's also a secure car park, bar, bistro and a large, lush private garden.

Oxford Hotel

⌨ *13 Craven Terrace, Paddington, W2*

☎ *020 7402 6860*   📠 *020 7262 7574*

✉ *info@oxfordhotellondon.co.uk*

✉ *www.oxfordhotellondon.co.uk*

🚇 *Paddington BR/LU*

💷 *from £55 per night*

Ten minutes from Soho and close to Hyde Park, this budget hotel offers basic Bed & Breakfast accommodation at reasonable rates.

Rathbone Hotel

⌨ *Rathbone Street, Fitzrovia, W1*

☎ *020 7636 2001*   📠 *020 7636 3882*

🚇 *Goodge Street LU*

💷 *singles £180, twins £200, studios £230, suites £250*

Close to Soho and Oxford Street, this big, gay-friendly hotel feels like a stylish club, with chandeliers, sofas, and marble and rosewood panelling throughout the public rooms. All 72 guest rooms have temperature control, air-conditioning and pink marble private bathrooms, many with a whirlpool bath. The plush Peacock Cocktail Bar and Restaurant have top-quality cuisine, and breakfast is £10.75-14.75 on top of the price charged. Guests can eat out at a number of nearby restaurants and opt to have their bill charged to their room account.

Waverley House Hotel

⌨ *130 Southampton Row, Bloomsbury, WC1*
☎ *Paula 020 7833 3691*   📠 *020 7837 3485*
✉ *waverleyhs@aol.com*
✉ *www.aquarius-hotels.com*
🚇 *Russell Square LU*
💷 *singles £79, twins/doubles £99, suites £189*
Central, gay-friendly hotel with comfortable accommodation.

HOMELESS PROJECTS

Albert Kennedy Trust

⌨ *Unit 305a, 16-16a Baldwin Gardens, EC1N*
☎ *020 7831 6562*   📠 *020 7405 6929*
✉ *london@akt.org.co.uk*
✉ *www.akt.org.co.uk*
🚇 *Chancery Lane LU, Farringdon BR/LU*
Named after the homeless 16-year-old in Manchester who was provoked
to commit suicide by his family's and friends' homophobia, this registered charity helps homeless gay, lesbian and bisexual teenagers achieve
independence and self-confidence by placing them in independent lodg-
ings or with suitable foster families who provide positive gay role
models. Their aim is to tackle violence in the home, rejection, homophobia, racism and loneliness. Since 1989, the Trust has made over 100
placements and helped more than 450 other teenagers by offering
accommodation, counselling, safe sex information and vocational help.
Volunteers are always needed to work in marketing, office management,
fundraising, career recruitment or service provision, which includes
outreach and advice work. They also provide a befriending service,
housing and benefit advice and referral to other agencies.

London Connection

⌨ *12 Adelaide Street, Covent Garden, WC2*
☎ *020 7321 0633*   📠 *020 7839 6277*
🚇 *Charing Cross BR/LU*
🕐 *Mon, Tues, Thurs & Fri 8am-3pm, Wed 8am-1pm & 6pm-9pm*
This project offers a range of facilities to 16-25-year-old homeless and
unemployed people, including showers, laundry, counselling, youth club
activities; advice on education, jobs, housing and training; courses in
personal development and computing, and cheap food in the café. The
Lesbian & Gay Youth Group meets once a week offering a mixed social
evening with discussion groups and cinema trips (Thursdays 6pm-9pm).

Stonewall Housing Association

⌸ *Unit 2a, Leroy Business Centre, 436 Essex Road, Islington, N1*

☏ *020 7359 5767   Helpline 0808 800444 (Fri 10am-1pm)*

🚇 *Angel LU*

🕓 *Mon-Fri 10am-5pm*

The SHA provides short-term accommodation for both lesbians and gays, with three shared houses in north London. A drop-in surgery is held on Thursdays from 2pm-3.30pm at St Giles, 64-68 Camberwell Church Street, Camberwell SE5.

GAY HOSTELS

The London House

☏ *020 8959 3661*

💰 *£25 per night, £80 per week*

A roomshare with free breakfast and use of TV, kitchen, telephone, shower and washing machine.

FURTHER GAY-FRIENDLY ACCOMMODATION

Kwik Lets

⌸ *184 Broadhurst Gardens, West Hampstead, NW6*

☏ *020 7328 7170*

London in Style

☏ *020 7341 9330*

Rainbow Bedsits

⌸ *448 Uxbridge Road, W12*

☏ *020 8743 9999*

Aston's Studios

☏ *020 7370 0737*

Bailey's Hotel

☏ *020 7373 6000 (daytime)*

George Hotel

⌸ *58-60 Cartwright Gardens, Bloomsbury, WC1*

☏ *020 387 8777*

Grange Hotels London

⌸ *58 Rochester Row, SW1*

☏ *020 233 7888*

Lonsdale Guest House

⌸ *15 Lonsdale Road, E11*

☏ *020 8532 2586*

Oakfield Hotel

☏ *020 8859 8989*

ARCHIVES AND RESEARCH

The love that dare not speak its name hasn't had a hell of a lot written about it until recently. The following organisations are guarding gay and Lesbian history for future generations.

Hall-Carpenter Archives

⌨ *BM Archives, London, WC1*

☏ *020 7955 7223*

⌕ *www.aim25.ac.uk*

Named after gay writers Marguerite Radclyffe Hall and Edward Carpenter, these archives were founded by the Campaign for Homosexual Equality (CHE) in 1982, and are founded on a collection of press cuttings dating back to 1937. Today, the archives contain material relating to gay and lesbian history, with over 40,000 press cuttings from British national and local publications. The collection is divided between Middlesex University in Barnet, where press cuttings, banners, posters and leaflets are stored; the National Sound Archive, with oral history recordings dating back 60 years; and the British Library of Political and Economic Science at the LSE which houses the largest core collection. This comprises the organisation records of a number of community-based national and local groups such as the CHE, Albany Trust and Gay Liberation Front. Some prominent gay activists, such as Peter Tatchell and John Chesterman, have also donated personal campaign collections. The photograph collection from Gay News is also there, as well as periodicals, including most British and Irish newspapers and many newsletters from lesbian and gay groups throughout the UK.

ID Research Ltd

⌨ *2nd Floor, Swiss Centre, 10 Wardour Street, Soho, W1*

☏ *020 7864 1300*

⌕ *admin@idresearch.co.uk*

ID Research was established in January 1999, and is the first exclusively gay social and market research company in the UK. Its aim is to provide clear information about the lesbian and gay population to inform both social debates and commercial initiatives. As the largest and most comprehensive body of research on any lesbian and gay community ever undertaken, its first census was distributed in late 2000 and drew on a target sample of 25,000 gays and lesbians, with findings published in spring 2001. The census collated data about where gays and lesbians live, their backgrounds, specific needs, how they spend their time and money, which magazines or newspapers they read, who they turn to when they first realise that they are attracted to a member of the same sex, how they were treated when they 'came out', whether they have experienced discrimination, etc. To take part in the next census, e-mail or phone to register and a questionnaire will be sent out in the autumn. ID Research also offers efficiency studies, bench-marking studies, satisfaction surveys, sample recruitment, organisational development, literary reviews and consultancy.

National Lesbian and Gay Survey

🖃 *20 Park Street, Totterdown, Bristol, BS4 3BL (send a SAE)*

An archive and mass observation project started in 1985, this survey collects confidential written observations from lesbians and gays on various topics, for which they write four directives a year. The archive is stored at the Mass Observation Archive at the University of Sussex and is used by students and researchers completing dissertations. Volunteers are always needed to supply their written thoughts.

Sigma Research

🖃 *Unit 64, Eurolink Business Centre, 49 Effra Road, Brixton, SW2*

☎ *020 7737 6223*   ✎ *020 7737 7898*

✐ *michael@sigmaresearch.org.uk*

✐ *www.sigmaresearch.org.uk*

A social research group specialising in the policy aspects of HIV/AIDS, Sigma was set up in 1987 to study the patterns of sexual behaviour of gay and bisexual men in England and Wales. During the 1990s, Sigma published more than 70 research reports, papers and book chapters that extended understanding of HIV issues, by tracking trends in condom use, and investigating public sex venues, alcohol and immunity, risk behaviour and AIDS. All of the papers Sigma publishes are available free of charge.

Stormbreak Limited Research and Consultancy

🖃 *74 Kinveachy Gardens, Charlton, SE7*

☎ *Tony 020 8855 4982*   ✎ *020 8855 4985*

This organisation specialises in the pink economy and uses both qualitative and quantitative research methodologies. They are interested to hear from gay men and women interested in becoming interviewees and from men and women who would like to join a panel of interviewees.

 CAFÉS

Gay cafés are now opening their windows to the world, allowing gay boyz to look out... but also the world to look in and show that they really have nothing to be afraid of. The café scene has burgeoned over the past few years, with an emphasis on continental decor and quality food as opposed to the limp lettuce leaf culture of old.

Costa Bar

Blush

⌨ *8 Cazenove Road, Stoke Newington, N16*
☎ *020 7923 9202*
🚈 *Stoke Newington BR*
🕐 *Daily 5pm-midnight*

Opened in 2000, Blush is the latest addition to the burgeoning Stokey lesbian and gay scene. It's a stylish bar-café over two floors with a relaxed atmosphere and no posing. There's a good selection of food at the weekend (noon–5pm), and a big, sunny and secluded beer garden for the warmer months. On Sundays there's live music from 5pm.

The Box

⌨ *32-34 Monmouth Street, Covent Garden, WC2*

☎ *020 7240 5828*

🚇 *Covent Garden/Leicester Square LU*

🕐 *Mon-Sat 11am-11pm, Sun noon-10.30pm*

This chic café/bar opened in early 1994 and had a major refurbishment in 2000, which has helped maintain its popularity as a West End meeting place. The decor is contemporary with an open, airy feel, music in the background (getting louder in the evenings), and a good range of bottled beer. The excellent freshly prepared food they serve (daily noon-5pm) includes some very tempting desserts. It's mixed during the day, and the summer sees a few tables outside on the pavement. The only downers are staff with attitude and a never-ending supply of saucers to put your change in. The downstairs bar serves over 70 cocktails served in front of chart videos, and there are monthly art exhibitions. Discount tickets are available to the top gay clubs – Atelier, Collection, F25, Trade and Heaven. The recent refurbishment included designer unisex toilets. See also Pubs and Bars p.122.

Café Goya

⌨ *85 Acre Lane, Brixton, SW2*

☎ *020 7274 3500*

🚇 *Brixton LU*

🕐 *Mon-Sat 5pm-11pm, Sat & Sun 11am-5pm*

This gay-friendly café-bar is halfway between Brixton and Clapham, and therefore a bit of a hike from the tube. That said, it turns on the charm with three floors of rooms that can accommodate anything from an intimate first date to a large work send-off, and the café runs a full event-planning service. It's a good laid-back after-work place, and its stripped floorboards, bright yellow walls, gilt mirrors and candelabras add a touch of theatricality, depending on your outlook. Food is reasonably priced, with starters such as soup at £2.95, ginger and pork meatballs for £4.25 and mixed meze at £4.95; and main courses like lemon baked aubergine, chargrilled chilli pork chops or grilled darn of salmon between £7.95 and £9.95. First & third Wednesday: Fried Green Tomatoes – women-only bar (7.30pm-11pm; free).

Citron Express

⌨ *6a Laystall Street, Clerkenwell, EC1*

☏ *020 7833 8113*

🚇 *Farringdon BR/LU*

🕐 *Mon-Fri 9am-6pm*

This tiny gay-run sandwich bar/café caters to the City-borders lunchtime office trade, with home-made food and an emphasis on the Mediterranean. You can buy dishes to take away or sit at one of the wooden tables and munch on roasted aubergine and courgette, risotto with asparagus and ham, minestrone or mushroom soup, and penne with sundried tomatoes, among other specialities. The café also operates the Citron Express catering company, for all occasions – office meetings, parties, buffets and private functions – and a delivery service for those too busy to leave their desks.

Costa Coffee

⌨ *39 Old Compton Street, Soho, W1*

☏ *020 7734 4639*

🚇 *Leicester Square/Piccadilly Circus LU*

🕐 *Mon-Sat 8am-11pm, Sun 9am-11pm*

Does Old Compton Street need another coffee shop? Costa seems to think so, and the shop embodies a persuasive argument. The ground floor is always packed, with a coterie of muscle boys perched on tall stools sightseeing out of the window. Downstairs has inviting sofas and deep armchairs amidst a decidedly Mediterranean decor. They do a range of coffee, tea and chocolate and a small but tasty selection of cakes and pastries.

First Out Café-Bar

⌨ *52 St Giles High Street, Soho, WC2*

☏ *020 7240 8042*

🚇 *Tottenham Court Road LU*

🕐 *Mon-Sat 10am-11pm, Sun 11am-10.30pm*

First Out was London's first gay café, opening in the early 1980s on a scruffy row of shops behind Charing Cross Road. Over the years, they've refined the formula and First Out is one of the capital's best café-bars. Stylish but unintimidating, smart but not overpriced: the perfect venue for a first date. They serve tasty vegetarian food – along the lines of pasta, spinach and mushroom lasagne, salads and celestial desserts like chocolate mousse or chocolate madness cake – and there's gay art on the walls and a bar downstairs that gets very smoochy at night. See also Pubs and Bars (p.124)

Freedom Café*

- 60 Wardour Street, Soho, W1
- 020 7734 0071
- Leicester Square/Piccadilly Circus LU
- Daily Mon-Sat 9am-11pm, downstairs club until 2am

This affable but lethally hip café-bar is more mixed than it used to be because of its late license, and it's a friendly young crowd who come for the arty décor and up-to-the-minute music, the great daytime food, and designer drinks and cocktails. The in-house art department revamps the interior every couple of months, and organises haute couture glamour parties in the downstairs theatre. See also Pubs and Bars (p.125).

The Fridge Café-Bar*

- Brixton Hill, Brixton, SW2
- 020 7326 5100
- Brixton LU
- Mon-Thurs 10am-2am, Fri 10am-Mon 2am

The massively popular Fridge club opened this café-bar so Saturday night revellers could kick on from Love Muscle and continue partying the following day. It's a light, arty place with bleached floorboards and funky background music. Their small menu is a blend of Spanish, Italian and English cuisine and features fresh home cooking (daily 10am-5pm), with lamb and spinach burgers, Thai curry, salads, a couple of pasta dishes, and snack food during the evening. With a capacity of 300, the venue features regular entertainment, with stand-up comedy and performance art in the downstairs club/cocktail bar.

Garden Café

⌨ *111-117 Lancaster Road, Notting Hill, W11*

☎ *020 7792 1200*

🚇 *Ladbroke Grove LU*

🕐 *Mon-Fri 9am-9pm, Sat 10am-midnight, Sun noon-5pm*

London Lighthouse's revamped in-house café is open to members of the public as well as users of the centre, and serves inexpensive subsidised meals in airy, comfortable surroundings with huge modern paintings on the walls and large windows that overlook a paved garden. The menu includes a range of sandwiches and pastries, as well as three-course evening meals for just £5. The Love Club (Mon 2.45pm-5.30pm) allows gay men and their friends to socialise and find out more about the work of the Lighthouse (see p.76). Saturday: Vita's – women-only dance lounge (8pm-midnight).

Greenhouse Café-Bar

⌨ *2a Sunny Hill Road, Streatham, SW16*

☎ *020 8677 7562*

🚇 *Streatham/Streatham Hill BR*

🕐 *Mon-Sun 9am-4pm*

This sunny suburban café is only open at weekends, but serves fresh uncomplicated dishes like roast pork or chicken, all-day breakfasts and a range of home-made cakes to a friendly mixed local crowd. Their Sunday roasts are particularly worth the trip. Above the Greenhouse is the Prohibition Bar private drinking club with its small shop (see p.143).

Old Compton Café*

⌨ *34 Old Compton Street, Soho, W1*

☎ *020 7439 3309*

🚇 *Leicester Square LU*

🕐 *Mon-Fri noon-3pm & 5.30pm-11.30pm, Sat 5.30pm-midnight*

It may be too brightly lit at night, freezing cold in winter and too busy for words, but this café is the heart of late-night gaydom. Tasty Latino waiters squeeze between tiny tables with lattes and cappuccinos, and the food counter bristles with salads, hot meals and cakes. In summer you can sit out on the semi-pedestrianised street, breathing in traffic fumes and watching the parade of gay boys in clothes too small for them.

Old Compton Café

Patisserie Valerie

🖼 *44 Old Compton Street, Soho, W1*

☎ *020 7437 3466*

🚇 *Leicester Square LU*

🕐 *Mon-Sat 8.30am-7pm*

OK, so it's not exclusively gay or even gay-run. But it's hysterically gay-friendly and has the best mouth-watering Belgian pastries in the world – or at least London. Now on two floors, the Old Compton Street branch has a window that displays such sinful pleasures as white chocolate cake, glazed apple tarts, fresh cream éclairs and the like. The ground floor is always packed out with gay boys and girls, people's mothers and tourists. Also at 8 Russell Street, Covent Garden, WC2

The Regent

🖼 *65 Graham Street, Islington, N1*

☎ *020 7608 2656*

🚇 *Angel LU*

🕐 *Mon-Sat noon-midnight, Sun noon-11.30pm*

The Regent (formerly The Angel) is now a gay-friendly, fashionable café serving 101 Belgian bottled beers. The decor is stylish, the food good and the music jazz. Still a great bar, but no longer one with a specific gay identity.

SW9*

🖼 *11 Dorrell Place, Brixton, SW9*

☎ *020 7738 3116*

🖥 *www.outsideuk.com*

🚇 *Brixton BR/LU*

🕐 *Mon-Thurs 9am-11.30pm, Fri & Sat 9am-1am*

This stylish after-work and pre-club venue is tucked up a side alleyway by M&S and used to be the Brixtonian Backyard. A refurb in mid-2000 has resulted in a stylish venue with huge plate-glass windows, subtle lighting and pristine decor, and an after-work and pre-clubbing crowd that feels comfortable with itself. It's atmospheric here – jazz sounds play during the day as gay boys who don't have offices to run sip latte, then the beat picks up later as the poor working stiffs pile in. There's seating outside year round. Food is served from 8.30am to 1.30pm, including an extended breakfast, with Continental, English, all kinds of eggs (£3.50-4.95), and a menu that's big on pasta, burgers and steaks, and alternatives such as saffron risotto (£6.25), Toulouse sausages and mash (£6.95). There are cocktails at £3.45, cheap draught beer and cider, as well as a weeknight Happy Hour (5pm-8pm).

 CLUBS

Candy Bar

In the late Seventies, in the wake of the 1967 reform of the law criminalising homosexuality, gay clubs were born. Bang appeared at the height of disco fever in 1976, with Heaven opening its doors in 1980. After several years of boomtime, the first reports of AIDS in the early 1980s applied the brakes and the scene stagnated, but the financial craziness of the late Eighties precipitated a resurgence. In the early 1990s, all-night parties became legal, with nights like Trade.

Gay boys and girls have never had it so good. The first post-AIDS generation just want to party all night, and the scene is well set up for it. Since the heady days of Bang and Heaven, the scene has evolved into something much more diversified, with men and women – straight and gay – bumping and grinding on the dancefloor.

One aspect of gay clubs hasn't changed however – the queue. There's one to enter, one to check your coat in, one to use the loo, one to get a drink – you can't avoid them. One handy innovation on the gay scene is the flyers or press ads you can use to get into gay clubs cheaper. Always check for these in a central London pub or café before sloping off to a club.

333

🖳 *333 Old Street, EC1*

☎ *020 7739 5949*

🖉 *www.info@queernation.org*

🚇 *Old Street LU*

The former London Apprentice pub now caters for sexy gay, straight and bi people who don't conform to the norm, hosting the capital's biggest monthly night – One Nation. The main room spins house and garage, the basement R&B, hip-hop and 2-Step, and the upstairs floor good old-fashioned disco and funk. First Friday: Denime – cutting-edge music (10pm-5am; £10, £5 before 11pm), second Friday: One Nation – garage and house sounds, with hip-hop and disco/funk rooms (10pm-5am; £8, £5 before midnight), Sunday: LA3 – cruise night (10pm-4am).

The Backstreet

🖳 *Wentworth Mews, off Burdett Road, Mile End, E3*

☎ *020 8980 7880*

🚇 *Mile End LU*

🕐 *Thurs-Sat 10pm-3am, Sun 9pm-1am; entrance charge*

With a membership of 5,000, the world's most popular men-only leather club is an intimate, dark cruise joint that's been running for over fourteen years – think Tom of Finland and you've got the ambiance. Rubber and leather queens travel from all over for the club's strict dress code – you'll be turned away if you don't stick to it.

Benjy's 2000

🖳 *562a Mile End Road, Mile End, E3*

☎ *020 8980 6427*

🚇 *Mile End LU*

🕐 *Sun 9pm-1am (last admission midnight)*

💰 *£2*

This former ballroom makes a glitzy but attitude-free venue for young boyz after a cheesy Sunday night out but who don't want to schlepp up to the West End. It's a huge place with a big dancefloor that gets packed out for its commercial disco and dance sounds, and has two bars with a separate lounge area and lots of seating, and the occasional PA.

The Block

- 28 Hancock Road, Bow, E3
- 020 8988 0257
- www.the-block.co.uk
- Bromley-by-Bow LU

It started life in Shepherd's Bush, moved to Islington and has ended up the East End. This warehouse-style dress-code club is infamous, sleazy and hugely popular with a hard crowd who like the feel of leather and rubber against their skins, as well as skinheads, and uniform/construction-wear lovers – no trainers allowed. Plenty of dark corners to explore. Wednesday: underwear night (10pm-3am; £3), Thursday: Bear leather and demin night with rock and retro (10pm-3am; £5), fourth Thursday: Gummi Hanky Code – (9pm-3am; £5), Friday, Saturday & Sunday: dress code cruise (10pm-6am, Sun 'til 3am; £5).

Brompton's

- 294 Old Brompton Road, Earl's Court, SW5
- 020 7370 1344   020 7370 3176
- bromptonsclub@aol.com
- www.bromptons-club.com
- Earl's Court LU
- Mon-Thurs 11.30pm-2am, Fri & Sat 10pm-2am, Sun 5.30pm-midnight
- free, £3 after 10.30pm

Always busy, always friendly, always cruisy – especially at weekends when it's positively heaving with a mixed age range of guys and plenty of rough boys who come on after the Coleherne in their denim, leather or western gear. It's a big place with room for 400 men, with a large dance floor, real ale, the more intimate and quiet Warwick bar upstairs (see p.149), and a state-of-the-art sound system for those who like their music loud. Popular with tourists. Regular cabaret and PAs, as well as DJs and strippers.

Café de Paris

- 3 Coventry Street, off Leicester Square, Soho, W1
- 020 7734 7700
- www.salvation-london.com
- Leicester Square LU
- First Sun of every month 5pm-midnight
- £9, £5 members and before 7pm

The faded glory of the Café de Paris – Noël Coward and Shirley Bassey trod the boards here in the 50s – has been revamped and updated for the new millennium for a sophisticated, heavy-partying crowd at the lush Salvation dance night.

Candy Bar* ♀

📠 *23-24 Bateman Street, Soho, W1*

☎ *020 7437 1977*

🚇 *Tottenham Court Road LU*

🕐 *Mon-Tues 5pm-1am, Wed-Sat 5pm-3am, Sun 5pm-midnight*

The basement of the UK's first seven-night-a-week lesbian club/bar hosts some super club nights in its laid-back, funky space. Monday is karaoke night (called Opportunity Knockers), Tuesday has a DJ playing funky soul, Wednesday sees Nicki Lucas playing US Jazz, Thursday has DJ Kinky playing R&B and Garage, on Fridays and Saturdays there's House, and on Sundays DJ Lush plays Indie & Retro tracks.

Charlie's TV

📠 *9 Crosswall, off Minories, Tower Hill, EC3*

☎ *020 8363 0948*

✍ *www.thewayoutclub.com*

🚇 *Tower Hill LU/DLR*

🕐 *Sat 9pm-4am*

💷 *£10, £8 before 11pm*

Wayout.com has got to be the most outrageous night in London, with gays, straights, TVs, TSs and their friends dressing to compete with Liz Taylor. You're guaranteed a warm welcome, especially if you're in a dress. Weekly stage extravaganzas and events, cabaret and dance.

Candy Bar

Chats Palace

⌨ *Brooksby Walk, Homerton, E9*

☏ *020 8986 6714*

🚉 *Homerton BR*

🕐 *Fri 8pm-2am*

💷 *£3*

Intimate venue with a good vibe. Everything She Wants is the 70s/80s disco night for women-only and their guests.

The Clinic

⌨ *13 Gerard Street, Soho, W1*

☏ *020 7734 9836*

🚉 *Piccadilly Circus LU*

🕐 *Fri 10pm-4am*

💷 *£5*

A relaxed mixed crowd pours in for the weekly night Illegal Nature, with its deep house, disco and electrochill.

Cloud 9

⌨ *67-68 Albert Embankment, Vauxhall, SE1*

🚉 *Vauxhall BR/LU*

Just behind the Crash Bar, London's coolest underground club attracts pretty poseurs and muscle boys to its two mixed nights. Dress to excess. Friday: Enlightenment – psychedelic trance (10pm-6am; £8, £10 after 11pm), Saturday: Catch 23 – (10pm-6am; £8).

Crash Bar

⌨ *Arch 66, Goding Street, Vauxhall, SE11*

☏ *020 7820 1500*

🚉 *Vauxhall BR/LU*

🕐 *Mon-Thurs 10.30pm-3am, Sat 10.30pm-6am*

Raunchy crowded men-only cruisefest popular with muscle boys, plenty of crotch watching, top DJs spinning upfront house and garage, a dark-room for more intimate amusement, and plenty of dark corners to cruise some of the raunchiest guys in town; two chill-out areas, four bars, two dancefloors and VIP room. Monday: Barracks – army theme night (£4), Tuesday: The Rig – cruise night for greased-up boys (free, £3 after midnight), first & third Wednesday: Red Hanky – cruise night for those into FF, second & fourth Wednesday: Score – for sports wear fans (free, £4 after 11.30pm), Thursday: Men's Room – cruise night (free, £4 after midnight), Saturday: Crash – house night (£10, £8 before 11.30pm).

The Cross

⌨ *King's Cross Goods Yard, cnr York Way and Goods Way,*
King's Cross, N1

☎ *020 7251 8778*

✎ *www.club-fiction.net*

🚇 *King's Cross BR/LU*

🕐 *Fri 11pm-late*

💰 *£12, £8 before 11.30pm*

Next to Bagleys, the DTPM people host the packed Hi-NRG Fiction club night for a hip and happening mixed crowd with funky progressive house and 90s anthems, two bars, three dancefloors and an outdoor area.

The Depot

⌨ *4 Carlisle Street, Soho, W1*

🚇 *Tottenham Court Road LU*

🕐 *Fri 9pm-2am*

💰 *£5, £3 before 10pm*

The end-of-the-week Eyeslash! night combines sophistication and tack in a vibrant night of music and colourful cabaret, pure self-indulgent fun.

The Dome Club

⌨ *1 Dartmouth Park Hill, Tufnell Park, N19*

☎ *020 8446 1606*

🚇 *Tufnell Park LU*

🕐 *First & third Fri 10pm-3am*   💰 *£5/£7*

Club Kali at the Dome Club offers its mixed gay and lesbian crowd an eclectic assortment of Bollywood, Bhangra, House, Arabic and R&B. The atmosphere here is relaxed and friendly and DJ Ritu insures that the music is innovative and original.

The End

⌨ *16a West Central Street, Bloomsbury, WC1*

☎ *020 7419 9199*

✎ *www.the-end.co.uk*

🚇 *Tottenham Court Road LU*

🕐 *Thurs 10pm-3am*   💰 *£5*

Groovy, laid-back lounge-style mixed basement venue that hosts Atelier, a funky lounge-lizard night with DJs and a more clubby ambiance later on. Very media, fashion, film and TV, dahling, with Philippe Starck-designed seating, computer generated visuals and London's most power-ful sound systems. The hippest night out in the capital.

Exilio

🖳 *LSE Building, Houghton Street, London, WC2*

☎ *07956 983230*

🚇 *Holburn LU*

🕐 *Saturdays 10pm-3am* 💰 *£6*

Exilio will lift your soul! Latin, Salsa and Merengue music blasts out of this hotel basement while cheap beer is served a plenty. Attracts a mixed age group of women and queenie men who are veterans of the dance classes. Whether your footwork is fancy or not is irrelevant if you don't want to take part yourself you can just sit and watch the performance.

Fabric

🖳 *77a Charterhouse Street, Farringdon, EC1*

☎ *020 7251 8778*

✍ *info@dtpm.net*

✍ *www.dtpm.net*

🚇 *Farringdon BR/LU*

🕐 *Sun 10pm-late*

💰 *£12, £7 before 10pm*

DTPM moved from Bar Rhumba to the End, then on to Fabric, which offers a stunning sound system and great visuals. Garage, Latino, house, R&B, disco – London's best polysexual club night in three rooms.

Fluid

🖳 *Charterhouse Street, Farringdon, EC1*

☎ *020 7253 4222*

🚇 *Farringdon BR/LU*

🕐 *Sun noon-6pm* 💰 *£5*

Playground packs two floors with DJs spinning hard house and trancy sounds for a stylish post-Trade chill-out crowd.

Form

🖳 *4-5 Greek Street, Soho, W1*

☎ *0798 997 8362*

🚇 *Tottenham Court Road LU*

🕐 *Thurs 8pm-1am* 💰 *Free*

The weekly Chill Bitch is a mixed gay chill-out lounge party with laid-back sounds encompassing afro, house, jazz, soul and disco.

The Fridge

⌂ *Town Hall Parade, Brixton Hill, Brixton, SW2*

☎ *020 7326 5100*

🖰 *www.fridge.co.uk*

🚇 *Brixton LU*

🕐 *Sat 10pm-7am* ✆ *£13*

The Fridge has cut back on its gay nights, but Saturday's Love Muscle still packs in a capacity 1,110 sweaty muscle men and cute puppies. Offers up weekly PAs, strippers and dance clutchbag music, go-go boys, lights and lasers, a chill-out room and food all night in the café-bar. One of the best dance nights out in London.

The Garage

⌂ *20-22 Highbury Corner, Islington, N5*

☎ *020 7607 1818*

🚇 *Highbury and Islington LU*

Smallish, grungy venue with two queer nights, featuring regular PAs. Fortnightly: Club V – indie and queercore night (9pm-3am; £5), Fortnightly Saturdays: More Science Less Arts – homo breakbeat and drum & bass (9pm-3am; £5).

Heaven

⌂ *Under the Arches, Villiers Street, Charing Cross, WC2*

☎ *020 7930 2020*

🖰 *www.heaven-london.com*

🚇 *Charing Cross BR/LU or Embankment LU*

Legendary gay club opened in 1979 in a former rollerdisco under Charing Cross station. Its main dancefloor has a sensational laser show, the country's best DJs, and PAs over the years from Madonna, Kylie and the Village People; the Dakota Bar and Star Bar have mixes of soul, funk, house and swing sounds. The entire place is packed with thousands of young, cruisy hard bodies – boys who spend too long down at the gym and in Diesel. Not the trendsetter any more, but still one of the best nights out. Monday: Popcorn – 80s & 90s pop, dance, indie and hard (10.30pm-3am; £4), Wednesday: Fruit Machine – fun mixed night with glam Powder Room drag bar and commercial sounds (9.30pm-3am; £4, £1 before 11.30pm; TV/TS friendly), Friday: There – indie and hard dance mixed night (10.30pm-5am; £10, £5 with voucher), Saturday: Heaven – mixed gay night – the best club night in town with garage, house, Euro… you name it (10pm-5am; £12, £5 before 11pm).

The Hoist

⊡ *Arch 47c, South Lambeth Road, Vauxhall, SW8*

☎ *020 7735 9972* ✆ *020 7735 7000*

✍ *www.thehoist.co.uk*

🚇 *Vauxhall BR/LU*

London's most infamous dress code bar is the best leather club in town, and appropriately, occupies a large dungeon under Vauxhall station, with exposed brickwork, stocks, benches and cages for those who like it rough. It's run by two former Mr Leather finalists who keep an eye on the strict leather/uniform/army/rubber/topless dress code. Also hosts many fetish and party nights organised by SM Gays and Bear Hug. Changing facilities. Concessions to Gummi, SM Gays, Saidie Maisie Club and SM Bisexuals members. Third Thursday: SM Gays (8pm-midnight; £5), Saturday: men only (10pm-3am; £5), first Sunday: Whack – leather, rubber, uniform and industrial wear CP night (5pm-late; £5).

Imperial Gardens

⊡ *299 Camberwell New Road, Camberwell, SE5*

☎ *020 7252 6000*

✍ *www.lbhradio.com*

🚇 *Oval LU*

🕐 *Sat 10.30pm-6am*

✆ *£8-£13*

If you think this is the sort of place that Regina Fong would hang around, you couldn't be more wrong. It's a porn cinema, cruising gallery and playroom where the monthly FIST night has moved to. The dress code is rubber, leather, uniform, PVC and skin gear; music is cutting-edge, the playroom sleazy and the live shows push the limits.

Jacque of Clubs ♀

⊡ *47 Ossory Road, Southwark, SE1*

☎ *020 7252 0007*

🚇 *Elephant & Castle BR/LU, then 53 bus*

🕐 *Sat 9pm-4am*

Halfway down the Old Kent Road is London's best lesbian club night – Cheekies. Women-only, but men can come in as guests.

Liquid

- 52 Wandsworth High Street, Wandsworth, SW18
- 020 8871 3910
- Wandsworth Town BR
- Thurs 9pm-2am   £8

The world's largest drag agency donned its stilettos in December 2000 with the clubnight House of Drag, a cross-dressing fest for men and women where anything goes – girl drag, boy drag, muscle and fetish drag… you name it. A sophisticated mix of tacky high camp and butch femme.

London Astoria

- 157 Charing Cross Road, Soho, WC2
- 020 7734 6963
- www.g-a-y.co.uk
- Tottenham Court Road LU

Attitude-free commercial disco G.A.Y. – presided over by the omnipresent DJ Jeremy Joseph – is the biggest gay clubfest in Europe, housed in an old theatre over three floors. The music is an eclectic mix of vintage trash, happy house and current chart music that gets the young, fun-loving beautiful boyz a-dancing, and there are really big-name PAs from the likes of Steps, All Saints and Geri Halliwell. It's all big and brash, with 2,000 boys under one roof. Mega-trashy, fluffy fun. Friday: Camp Attack – huge 70s and 80s pop party (11pm-4am; £3), Saturday: G.A.Y. – pop party with top name PAs (10.30pm-5am; £8).

London Astoria 2

- 165 Charing Cross Road, Soho, WC2
- 020 7734 6963
- www.g-a-y.co.uk
- Tottenham Court Road LU

Jeremy Joseph's midweek Pink Pounder club nights on the huge basement dancefloor of the Astoria make for a really cheap and cheerful weekday bop. The music is equally as happy but harder than at the weekend, with a sundry collection of musclemen, gay foreigners and young boyz out for a cruisy time. Monday: Pink Pounder – campy dance (10.30pm-4am; £3, £1 with flyer), Thursday: G.A.Y. – commercial pop and dance (10.30pm-4am; £1).

Madame Jo Jo's

- 8-10 Brewer Street, Soho, W1
- ☎ 020 7734 2473
- Leicester Square or Piccadilly Circus LU
- Tues 10pm-4am £7

Plush theatre bar that has set the standard for cross-dressing for years, although these days it's a bit too much like a clichéd idea of gay life – all feather boas and sequins à la Cage aux Folles. The only gay night at the moment is Steers club night, mixing the latest house from across the Atlantic and the UK. Flamboyant and outrageous.

Mass

- St Matthew's Church, Brixton Hill, Brixton, SW2
- ☎ 020 7737 1016
- Brixton LU

This converted church opposite The Fridge makes a deliciously warped venue for fetish and cruise nights. Last Friday: Torture Garden – mixed fetish club (10pm-6am; £12), Saturday: Sleaze – mixed gay/straight night of high-energy trance and disco/soul (10pm-6am; £10, £8 before 11pm).

Orange Bar ♀

- 22 Kingsland Road, Dalston, E2
- ☎ 07947 652755
- Old Street LU
- Fri 8.30pm-2am £6

Club Ace women's club night.

The Phoenix

- 37 Cavendish Square, behind BhS, Marylebone, W1
- ☎ 020 7491 0888
- Oxford Circus LU

Busy basement club that packs in a young and unpretentious crowd every weekend – lower key than Heaven or G.A.Y. but with less attitude and more laughs. Serves up no-frills charty tunes and remixed favourites to a young crowd of weekend disco dollies. There are regular cabarets and strippers. Thursday: Hybrid – indie, psychedelic, trance cutting-edge tunes (10pm-2.30am; £3), first & third Friday: Juanchito Gay – salsa, pachanga and boogaloo (10.30pm-3am; £5), second & fourth Friday: Amore – women-only night (10.30pm-3am; £5), Saturday: Energize – handbag and happy house (10.30pm-3am; £5).

Plastic People

⌨ *147 Curtain Road, EC1*

☎ *020 7739 5725*

🚇 *Old Street LU*

🕐 *Sun 5pm-midnight* 💰 *free before 7pm, £4 thereafter*

Lets Go Swimming is a new mixed gay party at Plastic People. DJ's Rob Mello, Cosmo, Nikki Lucas and Zaki, play whatever they like to an attitude free crowd.

Reflections

⌨ *8 Bridge Road, Stratford, E15*

☎ *020 8519 1296*

🚇 *Stratford BR/LU/DLR*

🕐 *Mon-Thurs 9pm-2am, Fri & Sat 9pm-5am,*

Sun noon-1am; free Fri & Sat £2.50 after 10.30pm

Intimate club for local East Enders, with regular cabaret.

Reflex

⌨ *184 London Road, Kingston, Surrey*

☎ *020 8549 9911*

🖱 *www.reflexnightclub.com*

🚇 *Norbiton BR, buses 57, 87, 213, N77 or N9*

🕐 *Fri & Sat 10pm-3am* 💰 *£5, £3 before 11pm*

Basement disco with Saturday Night Fever-style illuminated dancefloor with disco anthems from the 70s and 80s, and the latest commercial handbag sounds. Its friendly, packed with cute boys, has some PAs, and a car service offers both collection from home and return journey in the price (book ahead). Upstairs there's a Roman theme bar called the Forum, which is a good place to chill-out if the disco gets too crowded.

The Rhythm Factory

⌨ *16-18 Whitechapel Road, Whitechapel, E1*

☎ *020 7247 9386*

🚇 *Aldgate East LU*

Classy venue with good-looking mixed crowd funking to cool, sexy and innovative deep house, a great vibe and top DJs. Fortnightly Saturdays: Up! – innovative, progressive, house (10pm-6am; £8, £6 before 10pm).

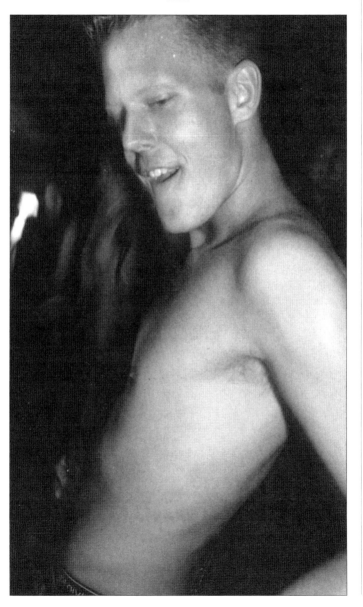

The Rock

🖥 *Hungerford House, Victoria Embankment, Charing Cross, WC2*

☎ *020 7976 2006*

🖋 *salvation-london.com*

🚌 *Embankment LU*

🕙 *Sun 5pm-till midnight*

💰 *£4 before 7pm or with flyer/advert, £5 members, £7 guests*

Salvation hosts Splash at this ultra modern club over looking the river Thames. The DJ's play some of the newest sounds to a crowd of around 600 fashionable gay men. One of the sexiest ways to end the weekend.

Rumours at Minories ♀

⌨ 64-73 Minories, London, EC3

☎ 020 7702 1658

🚇 Aldgate / Tower Hill LU

🕐 Sat 9pm-2am 🏷 £6

An excellent mix of music, DJ Linda knows how to warm up a crowd then keep them there. This very successful 500 capacity nightclub has gone from once to three times a month (check press for dates). Lots of fun with a good mix of mostly young girls. Pub price drinks at the two bars, plenty of hanging-out space and pleasant coat check girls. The dance floor gets busy quickly – be prepared for long queues at the toilets, but an excellent night out in all.

The Scala

⌨ 275 Pentonville Road, King's Cross, N1

☎ 07956 549 246

🖋 www.popstarz.co.uk

🚇 Kings Cross LU

In an old cinema with swanky marble interiors and rambling rooms, the long-running Popstarz night shoehorns in bucketsful of post-adolescent boyz who love indie and retro. The many bars and rooms include the Love Lounge with disco, funk and motown; a VIP chill-out lounge; the Big Beat Bar with house sounds; the Common Room with traditional indie/alternative sounds; the Rubbish Room with 70s and 80s handbag; and the Glass Bar for a chill-out. Friday: Popstarz – alternative music party with gay indie (10pm-5am; £8, free with flyer or web advert before 11pm).

Shillibeer's ♀

⌨ Carpenters Mews, North Road, Holloway, N7

☎ 020 7607 0519

🚇 Caledonian Road LU

🕐 Sat 8pm-2am

🏷 £6, £3 before 9.30pm

This warehouse conversion is all exposed brickwork and high ceilings, and bills itself as a cocktail lounge and restaurant. It hosts the monthly Gia club night for women, with live music and DJs. On Gia night the restaurant is open from 8pm-10pm, with the two-course meal option good value at £13.95. At 10pm the music goes up and the lights go down. The mixed age group crowd, are all up for a boogey, and the drinks are well priced with a good range of wines on offer. A successful, fun night.

Sound On Sunday

⌨ *Sound London, Swiss Centre, Leicester Square, W1*
☏ *020 7287 1010*
✎ *www.sound-on-sunday.com*
🚇 *Leicester Square LU*
🕐 *Sun 6pm-1am*
🌑 *£2 before 8pm (free with flyer or advert), £3 after 8pm*

Sound on Sunday offers a mix of dance, pop and chart music to a lively mixed crowd of gay boys and girls. DJ's include Steve 'B' and Dusty 'O', along with other guest DJ's. Sound is a fabulous way to enjoy a Sunday evening with free vodka jellies throughout the night and a late bar open until 12.30am.

The Spiral

⌨ *138 Shoreditch High Street, Shoreditch, E1*
☏ *020 7613 1351*
🚇 *Liverpool Street BR/LU*
🕐 *Wed-Thurs 10pm-2am, Fri-Sat 10pm-4am, Sun 10pm-3am*
🌑 *£4 non-member, £2.50 members*

Friendly gay club on two levels, with karaoke, chill-out nights and a piano bar. The club is small and intimate with a capacity of 150 and events on most nights – Wednesday is men only night and the piano bar is on Sundays.

Substation South

⌨ *9 Brighton Terrace, Brixton, SW9*
☏ *020 7737 2095*
🚇 *Brixton BR/LU*

Small, dark venue decked out in industrial chic for cruisy boyz who like their music as hard as their men. Hosts London's longest-running underwear night, when truly anything goes, and has a fistful of other specialist nights that make the most of the dimly lit and raunchy ambience. The hottest night of the week is undoubtedly Dirty Dishes house night. Popular with black boyz. Monday: Y-Front – underwear night (10pm-3am; £3), Tuesday: Massive – big men (10pm-2am; £3), Wednesday: Bootcamp – leather, rubber, demin and boots, Thursday: Blackout – cruise in the dark (10.30pm-3am; £3), Friday: Dirty Dishes – hard house and cruisy guys (10.30pm-5am; £5), Saturday: Queer Nation – New York house and garage sounds (10.30pm-6am; £7), Sunday: Marvellous – indie, retro and two-tone night (10.30pm-3am; £3, free before 11pm).

T2 Bar

⌨ *84-86 Wardour Street, Soho, W1*
☎ *020 7405 5475*
✉ *factor25@lineone.net*
🚉 *Piccadilly Circus LU*
🕐 *Fri 10pm-4am*
💷 *£8, £5 before 11pm*

Drawing a more varied crowd at the T2 Bar than their Sunday night at the Rock, Factory 25 pull in a smart set of young 'n' trendies, muscle boys and the merely aspirational, for their glam and trashy night of disco/house crossover. Two bars.

The Tube

⌨ *5-6 Falconberg Court, Soho, W1*
☎/✉ *020 7287 3726*
✉ *www.tube-club.co.uk*
🚉 *Tottenham Court Road LU*

What was Substation Soho is now a late-night six-nights-a-week gay club and men's cruise bar behind G.A.Y. Very busy after 11pm. Tuesday: Babe – commercial house and handbag (10.30pm-3am; £3, £2 before midnight), Wednesday: Mamma Mia – the best of 60s, 70s and 80s (10.30pm-3am), Friday: Babe – commercial house and handbag (10pm-4am; £4), Saturday: Wig Out – indie and trash retro night (10.30pm-6am; £7).

Turnmills

⌨ *63b Clerkenwell Road, Clerkenwell, EC1*
☎ *020 7250 3409*
🚉 *Farringdon BR/LU*

For over ten years this rambling club has been hosting Trade for the city's most mouth-watering muscle-bound men, stripped to the waist and raring to go. The two dance rooms play funky, hard sounds, and sexy house/disco. The upstairs Chill Out Room has coffee and cocktails, the Anthems Room plays house and classic tunes, and the Lite Lounge offers funky house. Saturday: Trade – techno/house all-nighter (4am-Sun 1pm; £10 members, £15 non), Sunday: Hype – wild happy house party (10pm-5am; £10, £6 before midnight, £8 before 1am).

Twenty Three

　📮　*23 Romilly Street, Soho, W1*

　☎　*020 7734 2323*

　🚇　*Leicester Square LU*

　🕐　*Last fri of every month 6.30pm-midnight*

　💷　*£3*

Cuir Royale is a relaxed and intimate evening of food, wine and music. The event is held in the rather grand 'leather lounge', deriving its name from the suede walls and leather sofas rather than anything kinky. A stylish way to spend a Friday evening, designed for those who want a change from the club scene.

The Underground

　📮　*Central Station, 37 Wharfdale Road, King's Cross, N1*

　☎　*020 7278 3294*

　🚇　*King's Cross BR/LU*

　🕐　*Mon-Wed 10.30pm-2am, Thurs till 3am,*
Fri-Sat till 4am, Sun noon-midnight

　💷　*£3-£5*

Sleazy basement club that runs a series of steamy sex nights for men into rubber, sportswear, big men and the like. Lots of dark corners to lose yourself in. Monday TCP – for tattoos, crops and piercings (10pm-2am; £3), Tuesday Beautiful Bend – kooky club night (10pm-2am), Thursday: Glory Hole – floozy night for naughty boys (11pm-3am; £4), Friday: Strictly Handbag – high-energy camp (5pm-4am; free, £3 after 10pm), Saturday: disco (10.30pm-5am; £3), First, third & fourth Sunday: Shoot! sportswear fetish club (6pm-midnight; £5), Second Sunday: Gummi – rubber night with a strict dress code (6pm-midnight; £5).

Underground West Central Bar

　📮　*29-30 Lisle Street, Soho, WC2*

　☎　*020 7479 7981*

　🚇　*Leicester Square LU*

The basement of West Central makes for a fun, no-frills night out, kicking off on a Tuesday night, and packing in young boys for the ever-popular Shinky Shonky night of old tunes and high-camp on Fridays. Thursday: Gaya – funky global music (10.30pm-3am; £4), Friday: Shinky Shonky – retro club night with cabaret (10.30pm-3am; £5), Saturday: Fairylea – campy gay disco (9pm-3am; £5).

Velvet Room

⌨ *143 Charing Cross Road, Covent Garden, WC2*

☎ *020 7734 4687*

🚇 *Tottenham Court Road LU.*

🕐 *Mon-Sat 12noon-2am, Sun 1pm-midnight*

💲 *Thurs-Sat; £1, £2 guests*

Cool, funky, rockin' and with more glitzy fashion than you see in the pages of *Vogue*. LowDown organises the Off the Hook mixed club night, with underground garage, soul, ragga and hip-hop. Popular with black gay boyz.

Voltz

⌨ *The Roebuck, 25 Rennell Street, Lewisham, SE13*

☎ *020 8852 1705*

🚇 *Lewisham BR/DLR*

🕐 *Thurs 8pm-2am, Fri & Sat 8pm-3am, Sun 8pm-midnight*

💲 *£3*

Lewisham's only nightclub is in the basement of the Roebuck pub, just off the High Street. Very rough and ready, friendly and intimate, with pool table, a raised dais as a dancefloor, and wooden floorboards. Think small nightclub in Norfolk.

West One Four

🖃 *3 North End Crescent, West Kensington, W14*

☎ *020 7603 7006*

🚇 *West Kensington LU*

🕓 *Mon-Wed & Fri 8pm-midnight, Sat 8pm-1am*

💲 *£7*

Since the closure of the women's night here, there are no special gay nights. The club is still gay friendly though, and has regular live music.

XXL

🖃 *London Bridge Arches, 51-53 Southwark Street, SE1*

✍ *www.fatsandsmalls.com*

🚇 *London Bridge BR/LU*

🕓 *Sat 10pm-3am*

💲 *members £6, non £8*

London's bear and chubby community must be like pigs in shit at the moment, with so many chunky nights going on. XXL is the latest, and caters for all sizes and shapes and tastes – beefy hairy hunks and their leaner admirers. There's no dress code, but they challenge you to wear what you dare. Dare to live large.

BALLROOM & OTHER DANCE CLASSES

Why do gay boys and lesbians like ballroom dancing so much? Is it the lure of low lights and sequins? Happy memories from childhood of *Come Dancing*? The desire to re-enact sultry scenes from the *Strictly Ballroom*? Whatever the reason, ballroom is big in London, and anyone who mentions the Gay Gordons will be given a very stoney look indeed. On the outer fringes of the genre, there is also a sprinkling of tea dances, country & western nights and even disco classes, to help you put your best foot forward.

The Ballroom Club

⌖ *55 Princes Gate, Exhibition Road, South Kensington, SW7*

☎ *020 7589 4635*

🚇 *South Kensington LU*

🕐 *Wed 7.30pm*   💲 *£8*

Glen and Heather offer mixed lesbian and gay class tuition in ballroom, Latin American and social dancing in a friendly but no-nonsense atmosphere at the swanky Polish Club. Come along to improve your techniques – but not to pick up a Fred or Ginger lookalike: everyone's too busy watching their whisks and chassées to notice how moonstruck you look.

The Dance Studio

⌖ *1 Selborne Road, Walthamstow, E17*

☎ *020 8521 4901*

🚇 *Walthamstow LU*

🕐 *Tues 8.30pm-11pm*   💲 *£7*

A class for gay and lesbian north east Londoners to improve their *Come Dancing* style, focusing on Latin American and ballroom for beginners and intermediates.

Duke of Cambridge (Duke's)

⌖ *349 Kennington Lane, Vauxhall, SE11*

☎ *020 7793 0903*

🚇 *Vauxhall BR/LU*

🕐 *Tues 8.30pm-10.30pm*   💲 *£5*

This venue opposite The Royal Vauxhall hosts the Lines and Bears country & western evening, with instruction followed by a general social dance for chubbies and their admirers.

Rivoli Ballroom

🏠 *350 Brockley Road, Crofton Park, SE4*

☎ *020 8692 5130*

🚉 *Crofton Park BR*

🕐 *First Sat 7.30pm-midnight*

💷 *£5*

One of the last great ballrooms in London, the Rivoli is a riot of red velvet and gilding. It's also one of the few gay-friendly mainstream tea dance venues in the capital, with a gathering of 50-year-old+ dancers who've been doing it for years, and younger enthusiasts who don't raise an eyebrow as two gals or two blokes sashay by.

Salsa Rosada

🏠 *7 Wakefield Street, Bloomsbury, WC1*

☎ *Stephanie 020 7813 4831*

🚉 *Russell Square LU*

🕐 *Wed 7pm-8pm (beginners), 8pm-9pm (intro intermediates), 9pm-10pm (intermediates)*

💷 *£6 an hour*

These hot and spicy dancing classes for gay men and women take you from barely being able to move to mastering a large repertoire at a confident intermediate standard. They have formed a demonstration team to perform at gay festivals and events.

The White Swan (BJs)

🏠 *556 Commercial Road, Limehouse, E1*

☎ *020 7780 9870*

🚉 *Aldgate East LU or Limehouse BR/DLR*

An East End institution, the White Swan turns its back bar over to dancing enthusiasts every Sunday with a medium-sized dance and a fun, but cruisy, men-only crowd. On Sundays Jo Purvis' Original Tea Dance has a large, loyal following (5.30pm-midnight; £5), starting off with ballroom sounds, then moving onto classic disco. The waltzes kick off at 5.30pm, with free tea and sandwiches until 7pm.

 # EVENTS

ondon's gay calendar offers something for lesbians, gays and bisexuals of all persuasions – whether drag queens, S&M freaks, Christians, the sporty or just those who want to blow their whistle and show how proud they are.

Mardi Gras

Monthly London Fetish Fair

⌨ *Shillibeer's, North Road, Islington, N7*

☏ *020 7700 1858*

With 500 shoppers and 35 fetish stalls, this market takes place in the large warehouse space of Shillibeer's, and sells all manner of perverted produce – from metal nail extensions, piercing jewellery and spiked collars right through to adult toys, whips and floggers. There's also club wear, babywear, combat and latex gear, as well as kinky books, artwork and homewares such as barbed wire-spiked wine goblets.

ANNUAL EVENTS

END MARCH

Gay and Lesbian Film Festival

⌨ *National Film Theatre, South Bank, Southwark, SE1*

☏ *020 7928 3232*

✐ *www.llgff.org.uk*

The two weeks at the end of March have, since 1986, witnessed the best of worldwide gay film, TV and video at the NFT. Most of it tends to be contemporary narrative features, documentaries; full-length features and shorts, although there is also usually some archive material highlighting a gay icon or director.

APRIL

Lesbian and Gay Christian Movement Annual Conference

⌨ *Oxford House, Derbyshire Street, Bethnal Green, E2*

☏ *020 7739 1249*

✐ *lgcm@lgcm.org.uk*

✐ *www.lgcm.org.uk*

This national conference in central London started in 1976 to provide a Christian pow-wow as well as workshops exploring homosexuality and the Bible, fostering, adoption and bereavement.

MAY

Royal Vauxhall Tavern Sports Day

🖃 *Royal Vauxhall Tavern, 372 Kennington Lane, Vauxhall, SE11*

☏ *020 7582 0833*

This now celebrated annual event in the large open (Church of England-owned) patch behind the pub is a day-long charity benefit, with different pubs and clubs from around London forming teams for the sack race, handbag throwing competition, running races, egg and spoon race, drag race, skipping race, yard of ale race and the tug of war. There's a beer tent, indie and rave tents, a barbecue and a big screen outside showing the different acts who perform inside the pub throughout the day. The day starts at about 11am and goes right through to 6 or 7pm, with the bar opening at noon.

Soho Pink Weekend

🖃 *Old Compton Street, Soho, W1*

☏ *020 7837 7324 (Lesbian & Gay Switchboard)*

The gay ghetto's own celebrations not only raise large sums for charity but give the West End a camp eyeful as well. Organised by the managers of Old Compton Street's bars and cafés, the fest kicks off with a carnival parade through Soho, leading to jollity in St Anne's Gardens on Wardour Street, with stage acts, a *Blind Date* send-up, a best costume competition and dog show. The event is organised by gay businesses in Soho and doesn't have a central office, ring the above number for details.

LATE MAY

Pink Angel Festival

🖃 *Central Station, 37 Wharfdale Road, King's Cross, N1*

☏ *020 7278 3294*

✍ *www.pink-angels.com*

For one fun-packed weekend over Spring Bank Holiday weekend, this local group kicks into action, organising a host of quiz nights, cabaret, parties, karaoke and pool competitions across a slew of pubs and bars to raise HIV awareness. The original list of six Islington bars and clubs has swelled to include The Edward VI, Route 73, Central Station in King's Cross and Walthamstow, The Duke of Wellington, Bar Fusion, The Chapel, The Ram Bar, The Joiner's Arms and the Oak Bar. The event also receives support from Liquid Lounge, Regulation, Gay's the Word and Waterstones.

Mr Gay UK

- ⌨ *Walk 34, Middleton Road, Leeds, LS27*
- ☎ *0870 122 1166*
- ✎ *terry@mrgayuk.co.uk*
- ✎ *www.mrgayuk.co.uk*

This competition to find the hunkiest, most shaggable gay man in the UK starts in late January, with fifteen heats around the country and hundreds of muscle-bound lads trying for the title. Thirty mouth-watering contestants are weeded out, ready to compete in two departments: in their everyday or fantasy wear (with army uniforms, Red Indian garb etc.), and their swimwear or underwear. A panel of judges is responsible for debating (and salivating over) a winner, who receives £5,000. There is no set schedule over the coming year for the successful hunk, apart from attending London Pride and handing over next year's title, but there's usually some photo work in the pipeline for the winner. The final event has been held at various locations around the country in recent years.

JUNE

National Lesbian Beauty Contest

- ☎ *07956 400029*
- ✎ *pride@easynet.co.uk*

This contest turns its head on the average girlie beauty contest, with the panel on the lookout for attitude and entertainment value as well as visual pleasures. Contestants come from all over the country for the London-based Grand finale, competing in categories such as femme, drag, bitch, witch, butch, and woman of colour. Each contestant does a 2-minute turn on stage – singing, dancing, poetry etc. to persuade the judges and audience.

Walk for Life

- ⌨ *Crusaid, 73 Collier Street, N1*
- ☎ *020 7833 3939*
- ✎ *www.crusaid.org.uk*

Europe's largest HIV/AIDS fundraising event, the AIDS awareness Walk For Life started in 1989 in London, but now involves 20 cities in the UK and five in Europe. More than 6,000 take the 10-kilometre walks to raise money for Crusaid's hardship fund and local HIV services. London's walk follows the course of the Thames, starting at Royal Festival Hall at noon and ending at Shepherds Market in Mayfair. Celebrities like Joanna Lumley, Jayne McDonald, Jackie Clune, Anita Roddick, Edwina Currie, the Leeds Rugby League Team and George Michael have walked in the past.

Mardi Gras

London Mardi Gras Arts Festival

🖃　*10 Wardour Street, W1D*

☎　*020 7494 2225*

✉　*info@londonmardigras.com*

✉　*www.londonmardigras.com*

More than 50 gay and lesbian events throughout London combine to form this festival, including conceptual art installations, musical concerts, films, theatre, cabaret, workshops, readings and takes place at venues such as ULU, The ICA, Soho Theatre, Piccadilly Theatre, The Prince Charles Cinema, 108 Gallery and Gallery Westland Place. The happenings take in everything from club nights to film premieres.

JUNE/JULY

Mardi Gras (Lesbian, Gay, Bisexual and Transgender National Pride)

🖃　*10 Wardour Street, W1D*

☎　*020 7494 2225*

✉　*info@londonmardigras.com*

✉　*www.londonmardigras.com*

Since the organisation called Pride collapsed with large debts, its place has been taken by Mardi Gras – formed by a group of gay business men to provide the same opportunity for celebration, but on a sounder financial footing. The show kicks off at 11am – usually at Hyde Park – for a Saturday march/parade that meanders through central London and down Whitehall past Downing Street to make the gay and lesbian voice heard. The main venue has varied from Finsbury Park, Kennington Park, Brockwell Park, Victoria Park and Clapham Common, but always features a vast area of beer tents, market stalls, a funfair, cabaret tent, crèche facilities, sports demonstrations, food and drink trailers. The three stages see a day of entertainment that culminates in an evening concert on the main stage with international acts like Kylie Minogue, and Mel B performing. Previous sponsors include Ford, Virgin, and Eurostar. Tickets cost £15 and are available from Ticketmaster and many gay pubs and bars.

EARLY JULY

Sex Maniacs' Ball & Erotic Awards

🖃　*Sexual Freedom Coalition, BCM Box Lovely, London, WC1N 3XX*

✉　*www.sex-maniacs-ball.com*

Raided by police in 1996, this is probably the wildest night out that London has to offer. It's sexy, frivolous and fun, catering for 1500 exhibitionist revellers who claim that "people are seeking others for honest, meaningful pleasure, spiced with gender play and glimpses of bisexuality". The evening has the Erotic Oscar awards, fetish fashion shows, SM stage shows, cabaret performances, and raises a bit of money for charity on the side.

Tennis London International Championships

36 Prince George Road, Stoke Newington, N16

020 7739 5567

tennislondon@bigfoot.com

www.maiko.demon.co.uk/tennis

Organised by Tennis London International, this warm-up for the Gay Games is the leading lesbian and gay tennis tournament in the UK, and one of the premier events in the growing international GLTA tournament circuit. The tournament is held outdoors in Battersea Park on medium-paced hard courts, and draws around 250 professionals and amateurs, over half coming from abroad. Accommodation is organised by TLI.

JULY

Miss Lesbian Beauty

020 7737 4043

The kind of contest that oppressed women for years is back, but with a post-modern twist – celebrating women and the beauty of a range of lesbian identities. Amy Lamé hosted the first event at The Café de Paris in 1997, with twelve contestants competing in three traditional rounds, parading in Daywear, Eveningwear and Swimwear in front of celebrity judges such as Rhona Cameron and Graham Norton. Tickets are available in advance from the Candy Bar and Retro Bar. The event is usually held every two years, ring above number for further details.

UK Gay Sports

Pool and Track, Chingford Road, Walthamstow, E17

020 8496 4661

www.gaysportsfestival.org.uk

The biggest gay and lesbian UK sports event of the year took place for the first time in 2000, and featured hundreds of men and women taking part in 16 different sports, including football, cycling, cricket, hockey, badminton, track events and bridge. The meeting is organised by the British Gay and Lesbian Sports Federation. The next event is scheduled for 2002.

AUGUST

Crusaid Summer Garden and Pool Party

▥ *Crusaid, 73 Collier Street, N1*

☎ *020 7833 3939*

✍ *office@crusaid.org.uk*

✍ *www.crusaid.org.uk*

The highlight of the year for HIV/AIDS fundraiser Crusaid (see p.68) takes place in the tropical gardens of an Earl's Court house, with an afternoon of drinks, buffet, entertainment, music and swimming. All proceeds go to the charity.

LATE AUGUST

National Bisexual Conference

▥ *BM Bicon, London, WC1*

✍ *bicon@bi.org*

✍ *www.bi.org/~bicon/*

Around 250 bisexuals and their partners attend this weekend-long residential conference, for three days of discussions focusing on bisexuality, biphobia, non-monogomy and relationships, transgender issues and campaigning action – as well as making new friends, partying and finding out what their sexuality is all about. The conference changes venue from year to year – see their website for further details.

OCTOBER

Stonewall Equality Show

▥ *46 Grosvenor Gardens, SW1*

☎ *020 7881 9440*   ✆ *020 7881 9444*

✍ *info@stonewall.org.uk*

✍ *www.stonewall.org.uk*

This prestigious annual concert at the Royal Albert Hall – the largest ticketed lesbian and gay event in Europe – raises money for lobby group Stonewall as well as raising its profile and the issues it campaigns for. Headliners who have taken part in the past include Kylie Minogue, Marc Almond, Michael Barrymore, Sir Ian McKellan, Stephen Fry, Sandi Toksvig, Julian Clary and Lily Savage, The Pet Shop Boys, Elton John, the Ab Fab girls, Alison Moyet and D-Ream. They also award an equality award each year to a prominent member of the gay community.

Skin Two Rubber Ball & Fetish Weekend

⌧ *63 Abbey Business Centre, Ingrate Place, London, SW8*

☎ *020 7498 5533*   ✆ *020 7498 5565*

✐ *rubberball@twpublishing.co.uk*

✐ *www.skintwo.com/rubberball*

The Skin Two Rubber Ball is the climax of the world's wildest fetish weekend. The event starts with a Friday club night at a major London venue. On Saturday and Sunday there is the Skin Two Expo, which is a design and fashion fair for those interested in all things kinky, with lots of exhibitors selling their wares, as well as regular performances, bars and cafés. There is usually a smaller clubbing event over the weekend, but the real partying begins on Monday with the Rubber Ball drawing in thousands of outrageously clad clubbers for a night with top DJ's and spectacular performance. The 2001 Ball was the events' 10th anniversary and the money raised was used to help the Crusaid charity.

NOVEMBER

Mr Black Gay UK

⌧ *Unit 46, Eurolink Business Centre, 49 Effra Road, Brixton, SW2*

☎ *020 7738 5274*   ✆ *020 7738 7945*

✐ *info@blackliners.org*

✐ *www.blackliners.org*

The Blackliners HIV/AIDS charity organises the antidote to the mainly WASP Mr Gay UK, with a contest to find the UK's tastiest gay black man. It's open to all black and Asian men and draws around sixty contestants from all over the country. Contestants introduce themselves and answer a few general questions as well as parade around the stage with not very much clothing. The winner snaps up two long-haul plane tickets and gets to promote the Mr Right On campaign for safer sex. The 2001 event took place in Birmingham, but it will return to London in future years.

Erotica Festival

⌧ *Earl's Court Olympia*

☎ *01708 768 000*

This erotic fair has raunchy male and female performers, and sells such must-haves as PVC and leather, piercing, tattoos and lingerie.

Glitterball

✍ *www.absolutelyglittered.co.uk*

🍷 *Buy tickets on door for £12.50*

This annual charity event is a hedonistic, polysexual night of glamour and glitz. The 2001 event took place at The Fridge and was presented by Kelly Wilde from *Disco Inferno*, with support from a host of show biz names. Get your tuxedo or ballgown dry cleaned and adopt your most recherché pose as you dance to the capital's top DJs, watch some blinding cabaret and lap up the go-go dancers. Proceeds go to HIV/AIDS charities.

DECEMBER

World AIDS Day – Dec 1

⌨ *New City Cloisters, 188-196 Old Street, EC1*

☎ *020 7814 6726*

✍ *www.worldaidsday.org*

With its signature red ribbon, World AIDS Day was originally set up in 1988 as a global event to acknowledge the epidemic and discuss the halting of it – now it is accompanied by snappy strapline like 'Shared Rights, Shared Responsibilities' or 'One World: Solidarity in Adversity'. The UK alone clocked up 4,500 different nationwide happenings in 1995, and London's contributions include photographic and painting exhibitions, fundraising nights in clubs and pubs, a Candlelight Vigil in Covent Garden's Piazza, services in various cathedrals, health conferences, and the Concert of Hope at Wembley Arena. Critics complain that the event should be a personal time to honour dead friends, not a good-time orgy with the vague acknowledgement of the disease – make your own mind up.

House of Drag

⌨ *Liquid Nightclub, 52 Wandsworth High Street, Wandsworth, SW18*

☎ *020 7209 3068*

✍ *www.houseofdrag.com*

The first House of Drag took place in 2000, but looks sure to become an annual favourite, with the most decadent cabaret and uninhibited patrons in town. There are performances from drag divas and go-go gods, and buckets of muscle drag, femme drag, boy drag, girl drag, fetish drag, androgynous drag, sexy drag... and the odd tuxedo. The establishment provides changing facilities.

 GYMS

The gay gym network allows you to flex your pecs, pump your body or otherwise enhance what nature gave you to make the most of those nights at G.A.Y. or Heaven. The list below also encompasses opportunities to take some punishment from a personal trainer, as well as gyms that offer tailored one-to-one programmes.

Earl's Court Gym

🏠 *254 Earl's Court Road, Earl's Court, SW5*

☎ *020 7370 1402*

🚇 *Earl's Court LU*

🕐 *Mon-Fri 6.30am-10pm, Sat 10am-10pm, Sun 10am-6pm*

💷 *Membership: monthly £73 peak/£48 off-peak, annually £480 peak/£340 off-peak*

A few yards away from Earl's Court underground station, this modern, clean and busy mixed gym is spread over three floors. The constantly updated gym equipment includes aerobic equipment, rowing machines, twenty Gym 80 resistance training machines and the most comprehensive range of free weights in central London. Fitness instructors individually customise training programmes free of charge, and there is a series of exercise classes covering specific parts of the body; as well as yoga, fat burning, body conditioning and aerobics. Sunbeds cost £7.50 per session. The reception desk sells a range of sportswear and food supplements.

London Central YMCA Club

▱ *112 Great Russell Street, Bloomsbury, WC1*

☏ *020 7637 8131*

🚇 *Tottenham Court Road LU*

◷ *Mon-Fri 7am-10.30pm, Sat & Sun 10am-9pm*

❧ *Joining fee £90; annual membership £440 peak/£320 off-peak, £15 a day taster*

The YMCA is the best gym in London, with a huge variety of physical education facilities ranging from weights, handball, racquetball and volleyball to yoga, tai chi, tap dancing, ballet and canoeing. There are also additional non-sport classes as varied as drawing, photography, flamenco, sculpture, piano, massage, juggling and pottery. The gym is spectacular itself, with dozens of free weights, sunbeds, rowers, bikes and a sauna, as well as badminton and squash facilities.

Oasis Sports Centre

▱ *32 Endell Street, Covent Garden, WC2*

☏ *020 7831 1804*

🚇 *Covent Garden/Tottenham Court Road LU*

◷ *Mon-Fri 6.30am-10pm, Sat & Sun 9.30am-6pm*

❧ *Membership: monthly £39, annually £420 (no joining fee)*

Not a gay gym, but the men's locker rooms tell a different story. Simply the best place in London to cruise beautiful bodies. It's recently been refurbished, so everything from its saucy changing rooms and all-year-round heated outdoor swimming pool and sundeck, to the poolside café, indoor pool, tanning sunbeds, sauna, 3 squash courts and cutting-edge gym looks great. Oasis also have a health and beauty clinic and provide laundry facilities.

Paris Gym

▱ *Arch 73, Goding Street, Vauxhall, SE11*

☏ *020 7735 8989*

🚇 *Vauxhall BR/LU*

◷ *Mon-Sat 10am-10pm, Sun 3pm-8pm*

❧ *Membership: £7 per day, monthly £46, annually £460*

This exclusively gay men's gym behind The Vauxhall Tavern has extensive free weights, Hammerstrength machines, steppers, cycles, treadmills and a Skywalker, as well as a sauna and sunbed.

Physical Culture Fitness

⊞ *Studios 21-22 The Arches, Winthorpe Road, Putney, SW15*

☏ *020 8780 2172*

✎ *www.physcult@globalnet.co.uk*

🚇 *East Putney LU*

🕐 *Mon-Fri 10am-10pm, Sat 10am-9pm, Sun 10am-5pm*

❧ *Membership: 6 months £199 (no joining fee)*

A well-equipped gym and one-to-one training centre.

Soho Athletic Club

⊞ *First floor, 12 Macklin Street, Covent Garden, WC2*

☏ *020 7242 1290*   📠 *020 7242 0899*

🚇 *Covent Garden LU*

🕐 *Mon-Fri 7am-10pm, Sat 10am-10pm, Sun noon-6pm*

❧ *Membership: monthly £58 peak/£40 off-peak,*
annually £440 peak/£325 off-peak

The gay sport and fitness centre of London is a friendly upmarket all-round health centre, with a supervised gym, aerobics and exercise classes, health and sports injury treatment, nutritional and dietary advice, regular health and bodybuilding seminars, complementary therapies and a café. When you first join, a personal trainer sets out a programme and takes you through your first workout. In the gym there are Unique Resistance machines, free weights, bikes, treadmills, a large stretch area, rowing machine, T-bar row, chest press machine, dumbbells, barbells and attachments; and staff can arrange you to have a training partner for extra motivation, or a personal trainer. Sunbeds cost £8 per session (course of five £35), and second floor studio and therapy rooms offer reflexology, sports and holistic massage, boxercross, reiki healing, protectorsize, and aromatherapy, as well as hair removal, martial arts and yoga. The SAC also has a social side with a softball team during the summer months, weekend war games and adventure weekends. The Revival Café serves health food during gym hours.

SWIMMING POOLS AND GYMS WITH GAY NIGHTS

The following offer gay and lesbian nights, but do check first as they tend to move around without warning.

Camberwell Leisure Centre

⊞ *Camberwell Green, Camberwell, SE5*

☏ *020 7703 3024*

🕐 *Fri 8.15pm-9.15pm*

Men's nude swimming.

Wavelengths

⊞ *Giffin Street, Deptford, SE8*

☏ *020 8694 1134*

🕐 *Thurs 9pm-10pm*

HEALTH

AIDS, pages 66-82
COUNSELLING & SUPPORT, pages 83-93

- Drugs And Alcohol Help
- Private Health Clinics & Other Health Organisations
- NHS Sexual Health Clinics
- Complementary Therapies
- Health Services For Rent Boys

Gays and lesbians are as vulnerable to health problems as the hetro population, and given the evident temptations of the scene some will find themselves exposed to even greater risks. Below are organisations which can help with all manner of health problems from drug dependency to mental health. No book dealing with gay health can avoid the issue of HIV/AIDS, refer to the seperate sub-section with its own introduction for further details concerning the disease and current treatment.

DRUGS AND ALCOHOL HELP

Drugs and alcohol abuse play a substantial part in the lives of many gay men, and can lead to a weakening of the immune system or risky sexual behaviour, which puts your health seriously at risk. The following agencies offer not only practical assistance with monitoring your intake, but also provide counselling and advice to help curb the habit.

Alcoholics Anonymous

Paterson Wing, St Mary's Hospital, Paddington, W2
☎ *020 7886 6666*
🚇 *Paddington BR/LU*

There are gay and lesbian meetings in London for those who want to stop drinking using the AA's 12-step programme almost every day. Ring for details.

Beresford Project

36-42 Hare Street, Woolwich, SE18
☎ *020 8854 9518*   📠 *020 8317 1786*
🚇 *Woolwich Arsenal BR*
🕐 *Mon-Wed & Fri 9am-5pm, Thurs 9am-7pm*

This project provides a service to drug users in southeast London, with a team of nine specialist clinical workers experienced in drug and alcohol misuse. The services include counselling, referral for detoxification, HIV and hepatitis pre-and post-test counselling, and a needle exchange (Mon, Wed & Fri 1.30pm-6pm). A drop-in service operates from 1pm-6pm, when you can consult one of the clinical workers face-to-face.

Lesbian, Gay and Bisexual Alcohol Project

⌂ *34 Electric Lane, Brixton, SW9*

☎ *020 7737 3579* ✆ *020 7737 2719*

✉ *info@acaps.co.uk*

✉ *www.acaps.co.uk*

🚆 *Brixton BR/LU*

🕐 *Mon-Fri 9.30am-5.30pm*

This organisation provides a free service to gay, lesbian and bisexual people who have drink problems, offering support, training and counselling. The project has gay and lesbian counsellors on hand to talk about alcohol abuse and its relation to HIV problems, and also runs alcohol awareness courses, workshops and education sessions. The volunteer counsellors give both daytime and evening sessions.

Narcotics Anonymous

☎ *020 7730 0009 (daily 10am-10pm)*

NA deals with people who have drug problems, and run specifically gay and lesbian meets. Ring for details.

Newham Alcohol Advisory Service

⌂ *7 Sebert Road, Forest Gate, E7*

☎ *020 8519 3354*

🚆 *Forest Gate/Wanstead Park BR*

🕐 *Mon-Fri 9am-4pm*

This service gives advice on alcohol abuse and its affect on the body and mind, as well as the links between HIV and alcohol abuse. It can provide counselling for individuals, lesbian and gay couples and families.

Phoenix House

⌂ *Featherstone Lodge, 1 Eliot Bank, Forest Hill, SE23*

☎ *020 8699 7152* ✆ *020 8291 9442*

🚆 *Forest Hill BR*

🕐 *Mon-Fri 9am-5pm*

This national charity gives substance misusers the opportunity to rebuild their lives by providing a range of services. From four different sites in southeast London, the residential rehabilitation clinic for drug and alcohol misusers offers a range of services from group therapy, counselling and health education to acupuncture and legal and housing advice. They can also provide hostel or bedsit accommodation to those able to live independently, and encourage the learning of practical and life skills to help maintain a drug-free future, which encompasses arranging college and training courses. Although not specifically aimed at the gay community, Phoenix House has workers specially trained to deal with issues of sexuality.

Project LSD

▣ *Unit 131, Aberdeen House, 2-24 Highbury Grove, Highbury, N5*
☏ *020 7288 1111*
LSD Line 020 7439 0717 (Wed 6pm-9pm)
🚇 *Canonbury/Highbury Islington LU*
◷ *Mon-Fri 9am-5pm*

A confidential service provided by Project LSD (literature and service on drugs) gives support and streetwise information on drugs, from poppers and Ecstacy to acid and speed. They are always looking for volunteers to help with counselling and their helpline.

Steroid Users' Support Service

▣ *CLASH, 11 Warwick Street, Soho, W1*
☏ *020 7734 1794*
🚇 *Piccadilly Circus LU*
◷ *first Fri 6pm-9pm*

This gay men's service offers steroid information, a needle exchange, information on injecting technique, free condoms and sexual health advice.

Stockwell Project Drugs Service

▣ *1-3 Stockwell Gardens, Stockwell, SW9*
☏ *020 7738 7784*   ✎ *020 7738 6056*
🚇 *Stockwell LU*
◷ *Mon & Wed 2pm-5pm, Tues 10am-1pm, 2pm-5pm Women-only,*
Thurs 10am-5pm (drop-in), Fri appointments only

A drug advice agency working with long-term users affected by HIV/AIDS in Lambeth and the southern part of Southwark, the SPDS can refer you to other services, give counselling and advice on diet, harm reduction and housing, and prescribe detox treatments. All work is done on a one-to-one basis and there is a gay male worker available. Once a week are sessions with a benefit worker, a solicitor from the Release legal project and a representative of the Drug Dependency Unit for fast-track assessments. There is also a drop-in room with free tea and coffee, and a needle exchange.

PRIVATE HEALTH CLINICS & OTHER HEALTH ORGANISATIONS

Boy Blue

🖃 *The Old Fire Station, 84 Mayton Street, Holloway, N7*

☎ *020 7609 4059*

✍ *boyblue@fsmail.net*

🚇 *Holloway Road LU*

Boy Blue is a sexual health project for gay and bisexual young men under 25, with a full range of sexual health services, including HIV testing and counselling, hepatitis A, B & C screens and vaccinations, free condoms and lube, and screening transmitted infections. Wednesday 5pm-8pm: sexual drop-in clinic for men.

Depression Alliance

🖃 *35 Westminster Bridge Road, SE1*

☎ *020 7633 0557*   📠 *020 7633 0559*

🚇 *Lambeth North LU*

🕙 *Mon-Fri 6pm-9pm; free*

A gay and lesbian self-help group for those suffering from depression. Send SAE for free information pack.

Face2Face Sex Advice

☎ *020 7816 4566*

Free confidential one-hour appointments conducted in either English, French or Spanish. Ring for further details.

Freedom Health

🖃 *16-17 West 12 Shopping Centre, Shepherd's Bush, W12*

☎ *020 8354 0742*

✍ *www.freedomhealth.co.uk*

🚇 *Shepherd's Bush LU*

This private general practice offers services tailored to the gay community.

NHS SEXUAL HEALTH CLINICS

The following NHS hospitals' Departments of Genito-Urinary Medicine offer a free and confidential service on all aspects of HIV and sexual health, including HIV counselling, testing and advice, screening and treatment of sexually transmitted infections, psychosexual counselling, safer sex advice, and free condoms and lube. You can usually walk into the department without an appointment, but it is indicated where you do need to ring ahead – as is where same-day HIV testing is available.

Central Middlesex Hospital Patrick Clements Clinic

Acton Lane, North Acton, NW10
020 8453 2221
Harlesden BR/LU
Mon-Wed 9.30am-noon & 2pm-4pm, Thurs 2pm-6pm, Fri 9.30am-noon

Charing Cross GUM Department

Charing Cross Hospital, Fulham Palace Road, Hammersmith, W6
Hammersmith/Baron's Court LU
020 8846 1576
Mon-Fri 9.30am-12.30pm & 2pm-5pm
Wed 2pm-7pm: Bernhard Clinic for women

Chelsea and Westminster Hospital, John Hunter Clinic

369 Fulham Road, West Brompton, SW10
020 8846 6171
Fulham Broadway LU
Mon, Tues, Thurs & Fri 8.30am-4.30pm, Wed 11.30am-4.30pm

Ealing Hospital Pasteur Suite GUM Department

Uxbridge Road, Southall, Middlesex, UB1 3HW
020 8967 5555
HIV treatment 020 8967 5554
Hanwell BR
Mon 9am-12.30pm, Tues 9am-12.30pm & 2pm-7pm,
Wed & Thurs 9am-12.30pm & 2pm-5pm
Same-day result HIV testing; appointment needed.

Greenwich District Hospital GUM Department

⌨ *Vanbrugh Hill, Greenwich, SE10*

☏ *020 88312 6056*

🚇 *Greenwich BR*

🕐 *Mon & Thurs 9am-12.30pm & 1.30pm-7pm, Tues 8.30am-12.30pm & 1.30pm-5pm, Wed 9am-12.30pm & 1.30pm-5pm, Fri 9am-12.30pm & 1.30pm-4.45pm*

Same-day result HIV testing (appointment needed), plus HIV treatment and care, hepatitis B screening and vaccination, STD treatment and screening.

Guy's Hospital GUM Department, Lloyd Clinic

⌨ *2nd floor, Thomas Guy House, St Thomas's Street, Southwark, SE1*

☏ *020 7955 4511*

🚇 *London Bridge BR/LU*

🕐 *Mon & Fri 9am-3pm, Tues & Thurs 11am-5pm, Wed 2pm-5pm*

Tues 5pm-7.30pm: After Five gay men's clinic

Same-day result HIV testing. Couple, relationship, and alcohol counselling.

Hammersmith Hospital Department of Infectious Diseases

⌨ *Du Cane Road, East Acton, W12*

☏ *020 8740 3315*

🚇 *East Acton LU*

🕐 *Tues 9am-noon, Thurs 1pm-5pm*

Same-day result HIV testing.

Homerton Hospital GUM Department

⌨ *Homerton Row, Homerton, E9*

☏ *020 8985 7575*

🚇 *Homerton BR*

🕐 *Mon 9.30am-12.30pm & 2pm-5pm, Tues 9am-noon & 1.30pm-4.30pm, Wed 2pm-7pm, Tues 9am-noon, Fri 9.30am-3.30pm*

King's College Hospital GUM Department

⌨ *Caldecot Centre, 15-22 Caldecot Road, Camberwell, SE5*

☏ *020 7346 3453*

🚇 *Elephant & Castle LU, Denmark Hill BR*

🕐 *Mon & Thurs 9am-6pm, Tues 10am-6pm, Wed & Fri 9am-4pm*

The Grove Clinic offers a fast-track service for sex workers with sexual health screening, counselling, advice and free condoms. Appointment needed. Dietician trained in HIV field; medication available free; acupuncture clinic; HIV mental health team. Wednesday 4pm-7pm: Rainbow Clinic for gay men (appointment only).

Lewisham Hospital GUM Department, Alexis Clinic

⌨ *Lewisham High Street, Lewisham, SE13*
☎ *020 8333 3216*
🚉 *Ladywell/Catford/Catford Bridge BR*
🕐 *Mon & Tues 9.30am-11.30am, Wed & Thurs 2pm-5pm, Fri 1pm-4pm; ring for an appointment*

Mortimer Market Centre

⌨ *Mortimer Market, off Capper Street,*
Tottenham Court Road, Bloomsbury, WC1
☎ *020 7530 5050*
🚉 *Tottenham Court Road LU*
🕐 *Mon, Wed & Thurs 9am-5pm, Fri 9am-1pm*
Emergency walk-in: Monday-Thursday 9am-7pm, Friday noon-3pm. Axis sexual health clinic for gay/bisexual men under 26: Thursday 7pm-9pm; drop-in or appointments.

Newham General Hospital GUM Department

⌨ *Glen Road, off Prince Regent Lane, Plaistow, E13*
☎ *020 7363 8146*
🚉 *Upton Park LU*
🕐 *Mon & Fri 9.30am-11.30am, Tues & Thurs 1.30am-5.30pm,*
Wed 1.30am-3.30pm

Queen Mary's University Hospital Dept of Sexual Health, Roehampton Clinic

⌨ *Roehampton Lane, Roehampton, SW15*
☎ *020 8789 0799*
🚉 *Barnes BR*
🕐 *HIV clinics Mon pm, Tues am; ring for appointment*

Regent's Park Clinic GUM Department

⌨ *184 Gloucester Place, Regent's Park, W1*
☎ *020 7402 2208*
🚉 *Baker Street LU*
🕐 *Mon, Tues, Thurs & Fri 9am-6pm, Wed 9am-8pm,*
Sat 9am-5pm, Sun 10am-4pm
HIV results in 15 minutes: £60, 2-hour results, £50; appointment needed.

Royal Free Hospital GUM Department, Marlborough Clinic

⌨ *Pond Street, Hampstead, NW3*

☎ *020 7830 2047*

🚇 *Belsize Park LU*

🕒 *Mon, Tues & Thurs 9am-10.30am*

Same-day result HIV testing.

Royal London Hospital Ambrose King Centre GUM Department ♀

⌨ *Royal Hospital Centre, Whitechapel Road, Whitechapel, E1*

☎ *020 7377 7312*

🚇 *Whitechapel LU*

🕒 *Thurs 7pm-9pm: East One Clinic for men, Fri 10am-5pm: Audre Lorde Clinic for women*

St Ann's Hospital Centre for Health Care GUM Department

⌨ *St Ann's Road, Tottenham, N15*

☎ *020 8442 6536*

🚇 *Seven Sisters LU*

🕒 *Mon-Fri 9am-11.30am (walk in), Mon & Thurs also 4.30pm-8.30pm, Fri 1.30pm-4.30pm (men only), same-day result HIV testing Mon-Thurs only, Tuesday 5.30pm-8.30pm: Zone 15 men's sexual health check-ups*

HIV testing, Hep A&B vaccinations, information and advice, counselling and support. Ring for appointment.

St Bartholomew's Hospital GUM Department

⌨ *First floor, Horder Wing, West Smithfield, Clerkenwell, EC1*

☎ *020 7601 8090*

🚇 *St Paul's Thameslink BR, St Paul's LU*

🕒 *Mon, Thurs & Fri 9am-9.30am, Tues & Wed 2pm-7pm*

St George's Hospital GUM Department

⌨ *Blackshaw Road, Tooting, SW17*

☎ *020 8725 3353*

🚇 *Tooting Broadway LU*

🕒 *Mon & Thurs 9am-5.45pm, Tues 2pm-4.15pm, Wed 9am-11.45am & 2pm-4.15pm, Fri 9.30am-11.45am & 2pm-4.15pm*

Same-day result HIV testing by appointment on Monday and Thursday, 9am-noon.

St Mary's Hospital, Jefferiss Wing

⌨ *Praed Street, Paddington, W2*

☎ *020 7886 1225*

🚇 *Paddington BR/LU*

🕐 *Mon 8.45am-7pm, Tues & Fri 8.45am-6pm, Wed 10.45am-6pm,*
Thurs 8am-6pm, Sat 10am-noon
Special service for male prostitutes.

St Thomas's Hospital, Harrison Ward

⌨ *First Floor, Lambeth Wing, Lambeth Palace Road, Lambeth, SE1*

☎ *020 7928 9292 ext 1677*

🚇 *Waterloo BR/LU*

🕐 *Mon-Fri 9am-6pm*

Victoria Clinic for Sexual Health

⌨ *South Westminster Centre, 82 Vincent Square, Victoria, SW1*

☎ *020 8746 8700,*

✎ *sorted@chelwest.org*

🚇 *Victoria BR/LU*

🕐 *Mon, Tues & Thurs 9am-7pm, Wed noon-4.30pm, Fri 9am-4.30pm*
Same-day result HIV result service, Monday-Thursday morning;
appointment needed. Walk-in sexual check-ups Friday 5pm-9pm; no
appointment needed.

Whipps Cross Hospital GUM Department

⌨ *Whipps Cross Road, Leytonstone, E11*

☎ *020 8535 6535*

🚇 *Leytonstone LU*

🕐 *Mon 2.30pm-6.30pm, Tues 9am-12.30pm & 1.30pm-5pm,*
Wed 2pm-5.30pm, Thurs 9am-12.30pm, Fri 1.30pm-5pm
HIV counselling and testing. Ring for times.

Whittington Hospital Archway Sexual Health Clinic

⌨ *Archway Wing, Highgate Hill, Archway, N19*

☎ *020 7530 2800*

🚇 *Archway LU*

🕐 *Mon & Wed 9am-5pm, Tues 1.30pm-7pm,*
Thurs 9am-7pm, Fri 8.30am-4pm

COMPLEMENTARY THERAPIES

There is only one complementary therapy practice run by and for gay men and lesbians in London. They offer a friendly, non-judgmental service with fully qualified practitioners.

Lavender Hill Homeopathic Centre

⌨ *33 Ilminster Gardens, Battersea, SW11*

☎ *020 7978 4519*

🚇 *Clapham Junction BR*

☺ *Mon-Sat 10am-5pm; ring for appointment*

The fully qualified gay and lesbian staff in this small complementary therapy practice specialise in homeopathy, osteopathy, healing and shiatsu, and there are also counsellors. Initial two-hour consultations are charged at £35, with further hour-long sessions at £20.

HEALTH SERVICES FOR RENT BOYS

Rent boys put themselves at risk not just sexually but also emotionally, many having been ostracised or distanced by their families (the average age in London is just under 18 years), with many having had contact with the penal and care systems. The following projects can give practical advice on safer sex, housing and medical issues, and also offer a supportive framework to make choices about their lifestyle.

CLASH (Central London Action on Street Health)

⌨ *11 Warwick Street, Soho, W1*

☎ *020 7734 1794*

🚇 *Piccadilly Circus LU*

☺ *Mon-Fri 9am-5pm*

This HIV prevention and health outreach service works with young men and women who sell sex, and with drug users and homeless people. The Gay Venues Outreach Team provides information on sexually transmitted diseases, safer sex, HIV, hepatitis and drug use. CLASH can arrange appointments and drop-in services, and run clinics with both male and female doctors and nurses.

Streetwise Youth

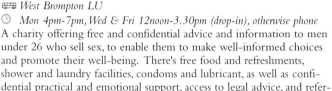

⌨ *11 Eardley Crescent, Earl's Court, SW5*
☎ *020 7370 0406* 📠 *020 7244 0037*
✉ *mail@swy.org.uk*
🚇 *West Brompton LU*
🕐 *Mon 4pm-7pm, Wed & Fri 12noon-3.30pm (drop-in), otherwise phone*

A charity offering free and confidential advice and information to men under 26 who sell sex, to enable them to make well-informed choices and promote their well-being. There's free food and refreshments, shower and laundry facilities, condoms and lubricant, as well as confidential practical and emotional support, access to legal advice, and referral on issues like housing, drug and alcohol use.

Working Men's Project

⌨ *Jefferiss Wing, St Mary's Hospital, Praed Street, Paddington, W2*
☎ *020 7725 1524;*
24-hour answerphone 020 7725 6666 ext 1185
🚇 *Paddington BR/LU*
🕐 *Mon, Tues, Thurs & Fri 8.45am-6pm,*
Wed 10.45am-6pm, Sat 10am-noon

This free sexual health service is for men who sell sex to other men, and supplies help in all matters of sexual health, including the screening and treatment of STDs, hepatitis B vaccinations, HIV testing, general sexual health screening, free medical treatment and medicines; a nurse is also available and they dole out free condoms, dental dams and lubricants. Advice workers provide information on housing, drug and employment issues. See also King's College Hospital (above).

AIDS

AIDS was first identified in 1981. Around 2.6 million people worldwide are dying from the disease each year, and an estimated 37 million people are living with HIV/AIDS. Add to that the 17 million who have already died of the virus, and you get the full grim picture. In the 1980s, the average life expectancy of AIDS sufferers was just five years, but new drugs have increased this to up to 20 years, and treatment breakthroughs in the US show promise in producing immunity cells to the HIV virus. But there is still no official cure.

In Britain, there are around 30,000 people living with HIV and AIDS (about a third of whom aren't aware of their status) according to the National AIDS Trust and Public Health Laboratory Service. London has around 62% of the total. Happily, deaths from AIDS have dropped by 70% in the UK since new treatments became available, but the prevention message is still not coming across as clearly as hoped. Red Ribbon International states that over half of all new infections occur in people aged 25 and under; and, according to Crusaid, 10% more people have HIV in the UK in 2000 than in 1999.

Despite this worrying increase, support for the cause is waning: AIDS is no longer as bankable as it once was – Body Positive closed down in 2000, London Lighthouse has been under threat of closure for several years, and many other organisations are crying out for funding.

www.aidsmap.com

The National AIDS Manual website is Europe's biggest HIV site, and provides a massive bank of treatment information, factsheets on drugs, on practical issues and on information regarding UK clinical trials, experimental drugs, alternative treatments, and contact details for clinics.

National AIDS Helpline

☎ *0800 567 123 (24hrs)*
Bengali, Gujarati, Hindi, Punjabi and Urdu 0800 282445 (Wed 6pm-10pm)
Cantonese 0800 282446 (Tues 6pm-10pm)
Arabic 0800 282447 (Wed 6pm-10pm)
Minicom for the hearing-impaired 0800 521361 (daily 10am-10pm)
If you have any questions about AIDS or HIV, this helpline offers confidential information, advice and referrals.

HIV/AIDS MAGAZINES AND NEWSPAPERS

The following publications are aimed at people with an HIV+ diagnosis.
+ve (see p.115)
AIDS Education and Research Trust (AVERT) (see p.115)
HIV and AIDS Treatment Bulletin (see p.74)
HIV and AIDS Treatment Directory (see p.117)
AIDS Treatment Update (see p.117)
National AIDS Manual (see p.69)
Positive Nation (see p.118)
Sigma Research (see p.11)

HOUSING ADVICE PROJECTS

See also Blackliners, The London Lighthouse and the Terrence Higgins Trust, all in this section.

FLAGS Support and Housing

▣ *The Basement, 706 Fulham Road, SW6*
☎ *020 7371 9574*
This organisation supply housing for HIV/AIDS sufferers who can live independently in the boroughs of Hammersmith, Wandsworth and Fulham. Strictly by referral through your local social services, THT, Positively Women, Blackliners or the London Lighthouse.

Strutton Housing Association

▣ *City Cloisters, 196 Old Street, EC1*
☎ *020 7608 4300*
The main housing provider in London for those with HIV/AIDS manages 250 self-contained, furnished properties in 22 boroughs. They only accept referrals through local councils and other relevant bodies.

La Verna House Project

⌨ *Capital House, 20-22 Craven Road, Paddington, W2*

☏ *020 7724 5840*   ✆ *020 7706 1327*

La Verna provides supported housing for homeless people with an HIV+ diagnosis, and whose symptoms may be aggravated by housing problems. They also give practical and emotional support and help with independent living skills.

FUNDRAISERS AND POLITICAL GROUPS

Community Health South London

⌨ *Elizabeth Blackwell House, Wardells Grove, Avonley Road, New Cross, SE14*

☏ *020 7635 5555, ext 5423*

This local NHS trust for the boroughs of Lewisham, Lambeth and Southwark has an HIV-oriented team with six specialist nurses who work with those infected to help them make informed choices about their health. Approximately half their patients are gay men to whom they can offer an extensive referal service.

Crusaid

⌨ *Crusaid, 73 Collier St, Islington, N1*

☏ *020 7833 3939*   ✆ *020 7833 8644*

⌕ *www.crusaid.org.uk*

⌕ *office@crusaid.org.uk*

Started in 1986 to help sufferers of HIV/AIDS, registered charity Crusaid is the UK's leading voluntary sector HIV/AIDS fundraiser. As well as sponsoring services and awarding individual hardship payments, it runs the Crusaid Medical Centre at the Chelsea and Westminster Hospital for both research and treatment. Their methods for fundraising include a charity shop for bric-à-brac in Pimlico (19 Upper Tachbrook Street, SW1), and annual events such as Walk for Life (see p.44).

Fashion Acts

⌨ *30 Elgin Crescent, Notting Hill, W11*

☏ *020 7229 7348*   ✆ *020 7221 8795*

⌕ *fashion.acts@virgin.net*

Established in 1988 to raise money for those affected by HIV and AIDS, this organisation pools the fashion industry's resources by coordinating a calendar of fashion-related activities.

National AIDS Trust

⌨ *New City Cloisters, 188-196 Old Street, EC1*

☎ *Derek 020 7814 6767*

This independent voluntary organisation promotes a wider understanding of AIDS and supports efforts to prevent its spread and improve the quality of life of those infected. The charity is responsible for policy development between the government and voluntary groups in the AIDS sector, and coordinates World AIDS Day, runs a mail-order service, promotes a business charter on HIV, and produces a number of HIV/AIDS publications (see p.173), and *AIDS Matters*.

National Long Term Survivors Group

⌨ *BM LTSG, London, WC1N 3XX*

☎ *01449 780211*

This support group welcomes straight and gay men and women infected with the virus for at least five years. They get away for four weekends a year, when they conduct a series of workshops, and enjoy aromatherapy and reflexology. It isn't a purely gay and lesbian group, but mainly gay. £150 per weekend, including food, accommodation and all therapies.

Positive Discounts

⌨ *PO Box 347, Twickenham, TW1 2SN*

☎ *Kevin 020 8891 2561*

✍ *hello@positive-discounts.org.uk*

✍ *www.positive-discounts.org.uk*

The card is a discount programme that enables its members to obtain discounts throughout the UK and in other countries. Although The Card is not gay-specific, there is a special Pink Discount Directory that lists lesbian and gay businesses that offer discounts. Other products and services are also available, including holidays and travel insurance for same sex couples and those with pre-existing medical conditions, including HIV.

PRACTICAL HELP

AIDS Mastery Workshop

⌨ *The Northern Lights Trust, BM NLT, London, WC1*

☎ *020 7306 3303*

✍ *nltrust@hotmail.com*

✍ *www.info@aidsmasterynorg.uk*

This organisation offers weekend workshops for people living with or affected by HIV/AIDS.

Basement Project

📟 *4 Hogarth Road, Earl's Court, SW5*

☎ *020 7373 2335*

🚇 *Earl's Court LU*

This project for 16-30 year-olds advises young people on housing, legal matters, benefits, education, health and employment. Their programme includes issue-based open access groups, counselling, and a needle exchange.

Bisexual Sexual Health Action (BSHA)

📟 *PO Box 10048, London, SE15 4ZD*

UK-wide bisexual group working on HIV/AIDS.

Blackliners

📟 *Unit 46, Eurolink Business Centre, 49 Effra Road, Brixton, SW2*

☎ *020 7738 5274*   📠 *020 7738 7945*

Helpline 020 7738 5274 (Mon-Fri 10am-6pm)

📧 *info@blackliners.org*

📧 *www.blackliners.org*

🚇 *Brixton LU*

This HIV/AIDS charity was formed in 1989 to provide counselling, support and advice to African, Asian and Caribbean people affected by HIV/AIDS – it is now the largest Black charity in the country. It also offers housing, immigration and welfare advice and a drop-in service at River House (see below). They also run a primary prevention health scheme and an emergency hardship fund.

Brothers & Sisters

📟 *Honourary Secretary, 25 Cruikshank Street, WC1*

☎ *minicom 020 7689 6867*

📠 *020 7837 5561*

📧 *DEAF@bfclub.freeserve.co.uk*

🕐 *Meeting first Fri of month from 8.30pm*

This project provides information, advice, counselling and support to hearing-impaired people living with HIV/AIDS, their families, carers and friends.

CARA

⊞ *95 Sirdar Road, Notting Hill, W11*
☎ *020 7727 1623*   ✎ *020 7792 8004*
🚇 *Latimer Road LU*
🕐 *Mon-Fri 9.30am-5pm*

CARA – Gaelic for 'friend' – is a community of friendship that offers non-judgmental support and care to men and women living with and affected by HIV/AIDS. Wednesday is a women-only day.

Central London Action on Street Health (CLASH)

⊞ *11 Warwick Street, Soho, W1*
☎ *020 7734 1794*   ✎ *020 7287 1368*
🚇 *Tottenham Court Road LU*

The Gay Venues Outreach Team targets gay pubs and clubs to promote sexual and mental health within the community. They offer a free condom scheme, referrals to other agencies and the monthly Sussed drop-in (first Fri 6-9pm) for advice and information about HIV/AIDS.

Chalk Farm Oasis AIDS Support Centre

⊞ *Salvation Army Hall, Haverstock Hill, Chalk Farm, NW3*
☎ *020 7485 2466*
🚇 *Chalk Farm LU*
🕐 *Mon 4pm-10pm*

This Salvation Army support centre caters for those affected by HIV/AIDS, giving advice on benefits and bereavement support and running a social and recreational programme.

CHAPS (Community HIV and AIDS Prevention Strategy)

⊞ *c/o THT, 52-54 Gray's Inn Road, Holborn, WC1*
☎ *020 7831 0330*
🚇 *Holborn LU*
🕐 *Mon-Fri 9.30am-5.30pm*

CHAPS is a partnership of community-based organisations coordinated by the Terrence Higgins Trust, running HIV prevention initiatives for gay and bisexual men.

Children with AIDS Charity

⊞ *9 Denbigh Street, Victoria, SW1*
☎ *020 7233 5966*

This group supports HIV-affected families with a transport service and hardship and holiday funds. Its education programme is at the forefront of AIDS awareness and prevention.

Terrence Higgins Trust

Eurocom Homecare

☎ *020 7511 5508*

✍ *www.eurocomgroup@aol.com*

London's leading gay specialists in HIV care. They offer regular house-cleaning or a one-off springclean by fully trained, friendly and experienced gay and lesbian staff. Eurocom work in conjunction with local authorities.

Foundation for AIDS Counselling, Treatment and Support (FACTS)

🏠 *23-25 Weston Park, Crouch End, N8*

☎ *020 8348 9195*   📠 *020 8340 5864*

✍ *tim@factscentre.demon.co.uk*

🚌 *Finsbury Park LU and then a W7 bus.*

🕐 *Mon-Thurs 10am-9pm, Fri 10am-6pm, Sat 11am-5pm, Sun 11am-3pm*

This registered charity offers a free primary care and outpatients clinic to people affected by AIDS.

Gay Men Fighting AIDS (GMFA)

🏠 *Unit 42, Eurolink Business Centre, 49 Effra Road, Brixton, SW2*

☎ *020 7738 6872*   📠 *020 7738 7140*

✍ *gmfa@gmfa.demon.co.uk*

✍ *www.demon.co.uk/gmfa*

This volunteer-led organisation for gay men works to prevent transmission of the virus, to fight prejudice towards sufferers, and to ensure the welfare of those affected. Their activities include providing information on the net, producing a newsletter, group training and promoting their message through the media. Their workshops cover topics such as assertiveness, SM sex and relationship development, and they run campaigns on a range of topics.

The Globe Centre

🏠 *159 Mile End Road, Stepney, E1*

☎ *020 7791 2855*   📠 *020 7780 9551*

✍ *info@theglobecentre.co.uk*

✍ *www.theglobecentre.co.uk*

🚌 *Stepney Green LU*

🕐 *Daily 10am-6pm*

A support centre for people with HIV/AIDS in the East End that has been going since 1990, the Globe Centre attracts people from all over London for its range of support services, including information on welfare rights, combination therapies, legal issues and housing. The centre operates a drop-in (Mon-Fri noon-5pm) and has a café and internet access.

Harbour Trust

⌨ *25 Hare Street, Woolwich, SE18*

☎ *020 8854 1788* ✆ *020 8316 2008*

✉ *office@harbourtrust.demon.co.uk*

✉ *www.harbourtrust.demon.co.uk*

This small community-based organisation caters for people affected by HIV/AIDS in the Bexley, Greenwich and Bromley boroughs and has a diverse client group of around 160 people.

Healthy Life Programme

⌨ *Health Promotion Service, St Pancras Hospital, 2 St Pancras Way, NW1*

☎ *020 7530 3424*

This six-week course provides an introduction to the gym and working out for HIV-positive gay men. It offers support and information on fitness, diet, nutrition, drugs and treatments, and stress management.

Healthy Options Team

⌨ *564 Mile End Road, Mile End, E3*

☎ *020 8983 4888*

Run by Tower Hamlets Healthcare NHS Trust, this user-led service gives drug users help and advice. There is a general drop-in (Mon-Thurs 2pm-4pm), with on-site HIV testing and a needle exchange.

The Helios Centre

⌨ *5-9 Tavistock Place, WC1*

☎ *020 7713 7120*

🚇 *Russell Square LU*

🕐 *Mon 7.30pm*

The Helios Centre is an alternative therapy and spiritual centre with lesbian and gay practitioners offering help with psychological and physical problems. The centre offers anyone with HIV free natural therapy treatment.

HIV I-Base

⌨ *3rd Floor East, Thrale House, 44-46 Southwark Street, SE1*

☎ *020 7407 8488 0808 800 6013 (treatment info line)*

✉ *admin@i-base.org.uk*

✉ *www.i-base.org.uk*

🕐 *Mon-Fri 10am-5pm*

This organisation produces printed material concerning HIV/Aids treatment, including *HIV Treatment Bulletin (monthly), Positive Treatment News* (3-times a year), *An Introduction To Combination Therapy* (twice yearly), and *Pediatric HIV Care* (annually).

Hospice Information Service

⌨ *St Christopher's Hospice, 51-59 Lawrie Park Road, Sydenham, SE26*

☎ *020 8778 9252* ✎ *020 8659 8680*

🚆 *Sydenham BR*

🕓 *Mon-Fri 9am-5pm*

Part of the establishment that did pioneering work in the hospice movement, HIS trains and educates, runs several HIV/AIDS residential units, and publishes a quarterly directory of hospice and palliative care.

The House

⌨ *33 Eaton Road, Enfield, Middlesex, EN1*

☎ *020 8363 2141* ✎ *020 8363 6197*

✐ *thehouse@dircon.co.uk*

🚆 *Gordon Hill BR or Enfield Town BR*

🕓 *Tues-Fri 9am-5pm, Sun lunch drop-in*

This AIDS charity offers a range of emotional and practical support to people with HIV/AIDS, and to their parents, families and friends.

Immune Development Trust

⌨ *90 Islington High Street, Islington, N1*

☎ *020 7704 1555*

✐ *info@idt.org.uk*

✐ *www.idt.org.uk*

🚆 *Angel LU*

🕓 *Mon-Fri 9am-5pm*

This healthcare charity comprises a group of 150 holistic practitioners who treat people with immune-related illnesses. Phone to arrange an initial consultation to determine which therapy is applicable.

International Community of Women living with HIV and AIDS

☎ *020 7704 0606*

✐ *info@icw.org*

Jewish AIDS Trust

⌨ *Walsingham House, 1331-1337 High Road, Whetstone, N20*

☎ *020 8446 8228* ✎ *020 8446 8227*

✐ *admin@jat-uk.org*

✐ *www.jat-uk.org*

This Jewish community charity provides face-to-face counselling for people with AIDS their family, partners and friends as well as financial support for those facing hardship.

The Junction

⌂ *207a Anerley Road, Anerley, SE20*

☎ *020 8776 5588*

A day centre for HIV/AIDS sufferers in the borough of Bromley.

London East AIDS Network (LEAN)

⌂ *35 Romford Road, Stratford, E15*

☎ *020 8519 9545*   ✆ *020 8519 6229*

⌂ *60 St Mary Road, Walthamstow, E17*

☎ *020 8509 3440*

⌂ *6 Mildmay Road, Ilford, Essex, IG1*

☎ *020 8478 7619*

🕓 *Mon-Wed & Fri 10am-4pm; closed Thurs*

This charity has three offices that provide a range of services to people affected by HIV/AIDS throughout East London, giving advice and support on housing, welfare and benefits.

London Ecumenical AIDS Trust

⌂ *St Paul's Church, Lorrimore Square, Walworth, SE17 3QU*

☎ *020 7793 0338*

🚇 *Kennington LU*

🕓 *Mon-Fri 9am-5pm*

This independent charity attempts to mobilise the gay community's response to AIDS in a non-theological way, and accepts referrals from state agencies. They offer practical homecare, information, training and health promotion to the Christian and Jewish communities.

London Lighthouse

⌂ *111-117 Lancaster Road, Notting Hill, W11*

☎ *020 7792 1200*   ✆ *020 7229 1258*

⌂ *47 Tulse Hill, Brixton, SW2*

☎ *020 8678 6686*

✍ *enquiries@london-lighthouse.org.uk*

✍ *www.london-lighthouse.org.uk*

Set up in 1986 in a converted school, this residential and support centre is committed to improving the quality of life of people living with HIV by providing health and social care services. There is a day care centre for ten people and a residential unit with 23 beds, providing convalescence and care for the terminally ill. The informal drop-in centre (daily 9am-9pm) and beautiful 80-100 seat café are open daily. Volunteers are always needed to help with fundraising, mail-outs, gardening, serving in the café and working on reception.

Mainliners

⌨ *38-40 Kennington Park Road, Kennington, SE11*

☎ *020 7582 3338   Helpline 020 7582 5226*

🚇 *Brixton LU*

🕐 *Mon-Fri 10am-5pm*

A drop-in agency that promotes self-help and provides information, health education and services to HIV sufferers who are also drug and alcohol abusers. They also offer emotional support, acupuncture and other complementary therapies, and publish a regular newsletter.

Mildmay Mission

⌨ *Hackney Road, Bethnal Green, E2*

☎ *020 7613 6300   ✆ 020 7729 5361*

🚇 *Old Street LU, then 55 bus*

🕐 *Mon-Fri 9am-5pm*

This independent Christian charitable residential and day centre for HIV/AIDS sufferers has a 32-bed residential unit with 24-hour nursing and a daycare centre with 12 family rooms.

NAZ Project

⌨ *Palingswick House, 241 King Street, Hammersmith, W6*

☎ *020 8741 1879 (Mon-Fri 9.30am-5.30pm)   ✆ 020 8741 9609*

🚇 *Ravenscourt Park LU*

🕐 *Mon-Fri 9am-5pm*

This HIV/AIDS and sexual health service for south Asian, Turkish, Arab and Irani communities offers non-judgemental education, support, counselling and interpreting services.

Outset

⌨ *Drake House, 18 Creekside, Deptford, SE8*

☎ *020 8692 7141   ✆ 020 8469 2532*

This national charity has a range of training courses for people with physical problems or disabilities – including HIV/AIDS – and train around 700 a year in information technology and business administration skills.

Positive Partners and Positively Children

⌨ *Unit F7, Shakespeare Commercial Centre, 245a Coldharbour Lane, Stockwell, SW9*

☎ *020 7738 7333*

🚇 *Oval/Brixton LU*

🕐 *Mon-Fri 9.30am-5.30pm*

An organisation that offers support and self-help to those affected by the virus, PPPC arranges mixed support groups, information and advice on HIV/AIDS, complementary therapies, massage, and grants for children under 18 years.

Positive Place

⌨ *52 Deptford Broadway, Deptford, SE8*

☎ *020 8694 9988   minicom 8694 2230*

✉ *posplace@charity.vfree.com*

🚉 *Deptford BR or New Cross BR/LU*

🕐 *Mon & Tues 1pm-4pm, Fri 10am-1pm*

This support and care centre for those in south east London who are affected by HIV/AIDS provides a free and confidential service including practical advice and medical care.

Positively Women

⌨ *347-349 City Road, WC1*

☎ *020 7713 0222*

🚉 *Angel LU*

🕐 *Mon-Fri 10am-4pm*

Provides a free and confidential counselling and support services to women affected by HIV/AIDS.

Project for Advice, Counselling and Education (PACE)

⌨ *34 Hartham Road, Holloway, N7*

☎ *020 7700 1323   Helpline 020 7697 0016*

✉ *www.pacehealth.org.uk*

🚉 *Caledonian Road LU*

🕐 *Mon-Fri 10am-5pm*

This charity was set up in 1985 to promote lesbian and gay emotional, physical and mental well-being through therapy, advocacy and education for people in the London area.

The River House

⌨ *PO Box 22443, W6 9FE*

☎ *020 8576 5875   ✎ 020 8846 9745*

🚉 *Hammersmith LU*

🕐 *Mon-Fri 10am-5pm, Sun noon-4pm*

This drop-in centre for people with HIV/AIDS in Hammersmith, Fulham, Ealing and Hounslow provides a safe, friendly environment where people can meet for emotional and practical support.

Route 15

⌧ *35 Romford Road, Stratford, E15*

☎ *020 8519 9545*

🚇 *East Ham LU*

🕐 *Mon-Fri 10am-5pm*

This registered charity lends support to care-givers of those with HIV/AIDS, whether partners, friends, family, volunteers or paid carers.

Eddie Surman Trust

⌧ *359 Southwyck House, Clarewood Walk, SW9*

☎ *020 7738 6893* ✆ *020 7733 8422*

positiveline 0800 169 6806

🕐 *Mon-Fri 11am-10pm, Sat & Sun 4pm-10pm*

A gay trust helping those living with HIV/AIDS to deal with fear and suicidal feelings brought on by a positive diagnosis. The Trust offers advice and information, small grants and housing advice.

Terrence Higgins Trust

⌧ *52-54 Gray's Inn Road, Holborn, WC1*

☎ *020 7831 0330* ✆ *020 7242 0121*

National helpline: 020 7242 1010 (daily noon-10pm)

Counselling helpline: 020 7835 1495

Legal line: 020 7405 2381 (Wed 7pm-9pm)

Aids Treatment Phoneline: 0845 947 0047

(Mon & Wed 6pm–9pm, Tues 3pm-6pm)

✉ *info@tht.org.uk*

✉ *www.tht.org.uk*

🚇 *Chancery Lane LU*

🕐 *Mon-Fri 9.30am-5.30pm*

Europe's leading HIV/AIDS charity has seven centres throughout the UK that supply HIV prevention information and direct support to people at risk. Their health promotion activities include producing a wide range of booklets for those living with HIV, treatment support groups for those taking combination therapy, sexual counselling, legal advice and a hardship fund to help with bills and essential purchases. The THT library has the best AIDS and HIV reference information in London.

UK Coalition of People Living with HIV and AIDS

⌨ *250 Kennington Lane, Kennington, SE11*

☏ *020 7564 2180* ✆ *020 7564 2140*

✍ *info@ukcoalition.org*

✍ *www.ukcoalition.org*

This nationwide self-help organisation is run by and for people living with HIV and AIDS. The Coalition runs several projects, including Positive Futures, which aims to enhance quality of life by assisting with access to training, education and employment. The Advocacy Project offers advice on welfare and related issues.

Waltham Forest HIV/AIDS Support Group

⌨ *PO Box 2274, London, E11*

☏ *020 8521 7441*

Set up by a group of gay and straight HIV+ people to provide practical support for people in the borough, it allows for a safe space for HIV+ people to meet and socialise, share information about drugs and treatments, and get advice about housing and community care problems.

Wandsworth Oasis AIDS Support Centre

⌨ *Salvation Army, 9 Ram Street, Wandsworth, SW18*

☏ *020 8874 9229*

🚇 *Wandsworth Town BR*

🕐 *Tues-Fri 4pm-9pm & Sat 2pm-7pm*

Working in partnership with the Salvation Army, the Oasis centre provides help and support to anyone affected by HIV/AIDS. It hosts quilt-making workshops, organises a range of social events, gives information about benefits, and runs a self-help group. Their drop-in lounge has TV and video, music, newspapers, and free tea and coffee.

YOUTH GROUPS

Health Initiatives for Youth (HIFY-UK)

⌨ *2 Willesden High Road, Willesden, NW10*
☎ *0800 298 3099*
🚇 *Willesden Green LU*

Launched to combat the lack of HIV/AIDS services available to young people in the UK, HIFY-UK offers one-to-one support, advocacy, group work and workshops for HIV+ people of all sexualities under 27. It runs education workshops for young people and for professionals who work with young people.

Teen Spirit

☎ *020 7833 4828*
🚇 *Russell Square LU*
🕐 *Thurs 6pm-9pm*

A project for HIV+ people of all sexualities, aged-between 13 and 19.

BEREAVEMENT PROGRAMMES

Cruse Bereavement Centre

⌨ *126 Sheen Road, Richmond, Surrey, TW9 1UR*
☎ *020 8940 4818*   ✉ *020 8940 7638*
Cruse Bereavement Line 020 8332 7227 (Mon-Fri 9.30am-5pm)
🚇 *Richmond BR/LU*
🕐 *Mon-Fri 9.30am-5pm*

National charity Cruse – founded in 1959 – has nearly 200 branches throughout the UK, offering confidential counselling for the bereaved.

Lesbian and Gay Bereavement Project

⌨ *Vaughan M Williams Centre, Colindale Hospital, Colindale Avenue, NW9*
☎ *020 7403 5969*
🚇 *Colindale LU*
🕐 *Mon-Thurs 10.30am-4.30pm*

This project offers practical support and advice, as well as a helpline for the bereaved.

HIV INFORMATION SERVICES

Each London borough's HIV information service offers advice and assistance to those affected by HIV/AIDS – from information about benefits, employment and housing to advice about money, the law or patients' rights.

Barnet AIDS Educational Unit *020 8359 2000*
Bexley Social Services *020 8303 7777*
Brent HIV Team *020 8937 1234*
Bromley Social Services *020 8464 3333*
Camden Social Services HIV Unit *020 7974 6666*
City of London Social Services *020 7332 1224*
Croydon Social Services *020 8654 8100*
Ealing Social Services HIV/AIDS Unit *020 8992 5566*
Enfield HIV/AIDS Social Services *020 8886 0031*
Greenwich Social Services HIV/AIDS Unit *020 8854 8888*
Hackney HIV Resource Centre *020 8356 4034*
Hammersmith and Fulham Social Services *020 8748 3020*
Haringey HIV Services Central Office *020 8808 1694*
Harrow Social Services HIV Team *020 8424 1252*
Hillingdon Service Coordination *01923 824 182*
Hounslow Corporate HIV/AIDS Unit *020 8583 2000*
Islington iCARE and HIV Prevention Unit *020 7359 7829*
Kensington and Chelsea Social Services *020 8960 8418*
Kingston and Richmond Health *020 8547 0011*
Lambeth Planning and Health Liaison Unit *020 7926 1000*
Lewisham Social Services HIV/AIDS Unit *020 8695 6000*
Merton HIV/AIDS Unit *020 8545 4547*
Newham HIV/AIDS Coordination *020 8534 4545*
Redbridge Directorate of Personnel Services *020 8708 5287*
Richmond Social Services *020 8891 1411*
Southwark Social Services *020 7525 3937*
Sutton Housing and Social Services Department *020 8770 4417*
Tower Hamlets HIV Drugs and Alcohol Section *020 7364 5000*
Waltham Forest HIV Unit *020 8527 5544*
Wandsworth Social Services *020 8871 6000*
Westminster Social Services *020 7641 6000*

COUNSELLING & SUPPORT

Taking care of your emotional health is just as important as making sure your body is in good nick. The following are a list of organisations that offer support and run courses specifically for gay men and lesbians, or who can refer you on to someone who can help. The list encompasses services for mental-health, gender identity, personal development, adoption, parenting, eating disorders, physical abuse and spiritual healing; as well as telephone helplines.

Al-Anon

Hinde Street Methodist Church, Hinde Street, Mayfair, W1

☎ *020 7403 0888 (10am-10pm daily)*

Support group for those affected by someone else's drinking.

Alcohol Counselling and Prevention Services (ACAPS)

34 Electric Lane, Brixton, SW9

☎ *020 7737 3579*

⌨ *www.acaps.co.uk*

Counselling, information and support groups for lesbians and gay men and bi-sexuals with drink problems.

Alcohol East

☎ *020 8257 3068*

A free and confidential service specifically for lesbians and gay men who have concerns or problems about alcohol.

At Ease

28 Commercial Street, Aldgate East, E1

☎ *Helpline 020 7247 5164 (Sun 5pm-7pm)*

Weekly counselling and legal advice line for gay and lesbian members of the armed services and their families.

Beaumont Trust

☎ *Helpline 07000 287 878 (Tues & Thurs 7pm-11pm)*

Funded by the Beaumont Society (see p.190), this charity attempts to promote a greater understanding of gender disphoria to professional people through a biannual gender conference.

Yoga @ Kairos

Careline

☏ *Helpline 020 8514 1177; Mon-Fri 10am-4pm & 7pm-10pm*

This is a confidential telephone counselling service offers help to people worried about relationships, sexuality and AIDS. Its volunteer counsellors hold details of agencies and social and support groups for gay people.

Edward Carpenter Community (ECC)

▨ *BM ECC, London, WC1N 3XX*

☏ *0870 321 5121*

This gay men's non-profit-making group is committed to caring, personal growth, creativity, trusting and sharing, and creates a safe environment for men to express themselves freely. They organise country retreats and a course for gay men living with HIV/AIDS.

Changes

▨ *London Friend, 86 Caledonian Road, King's Cross, N1*

☏ *020 7837 3337; also minicom*

🚇 *King's Cross BR/LU*

🕓 *Second and fourth Mon 6.30pm-8.30pm*

Lesbian group for those coming to terms with their sexuality.

Covent Garden Meditation Centre

⌨ *45 Shelton Street, Covent Garden, WC2*

☎ *Narga Raja 020 8981 1225*

🚇 *Covent Garden LU*

🕐 *Fri 6.30pm; £70 for a six-week course*

This meditation evening for gay men attracts between eight and fifteen men in search of inner peace. They also organise a summer retreat outside Norwich with over 50 people from all over the country attending.

Croydon Friend

⌨ *PO Box 464, London, SE25 4AT*

☎ *Helpline 020 8683 4239 (Mon 7.30pm-9.30pm);*
020 8690 6195 (Tues & Fri 7.30pm-9.30pm)

Croydon Friend offers a telephone befriending and information service for gay men and women in and around Croydon and South London.

East London Out Project

⌨ *56-60 Grove Road, Walthamstow, E17*

☎ *020 8509 3898*

Counselling and advice service for lesbians, gays and bisexuals over the age of 18, offering a weekly housing advice surgery, and gay men's and lesbian social and support groups.

FFLAG

⌨ *FFLAG, PO Box 153, Manchester, M60 1LP*

☎ *01392 279546*

✎ *Jenny@fflag.org.uk*

✎ *www.fflag.fsnet.co.uk*

Dedicated to supporting parents and their gay, lesbian or bisexual offspring, FFLAG provides a central point for exchange of information between gay parents groups and local parent contacts to encourage acceptance and understanding.

Gay and Lesbian Legal Advice (GLAD)

⌨ *Room D, 10-14 Macklin Street, Covent Garden, WC2*

☎ *Helpline 020 7831 3535 (Mon-Fri 7pm-9.30pm)*

This group of lesbian, gay and bisexual volunteer lawyers give free, confidential legal advice over the phone and can refer you to a sympathetic gay solicitor if necessary.

Gay London Policing (GALOP)

⌨ *Unit 2G, Leroy House, 436 Essex Road, N1*

☎ *020 7704 2040 Helpline (Mon 5pm-8pm, Wed 3pm-6pm, Fri noon-2pm)*

☎ *020 7704 6767*

This organisation is a gay, lesbian and bisexual anti-violence, and police monitoring charity. The help line offers support and assistance to sufferers of homophobic violence.

GayScan (Cancer Support Network)

⌨ *50 Avenue Road, London, N12*

Send a SAE for more details.

Healing Circle

⌨ *The Helios Centre, 5-9 Tavistock Place, WC1*

☎ *Greg or Mick 020 7713 7120*

🚇 *Russell Square LU*

🕐 *Mon 7.30pm*

The Healing Circle group was started in 1987 by a handful of gay men as a place to address the complexities of the gay man's lifestyle. The groups deals with fears about sexuality, illness, and releasing negative thought, with an increasing emphasis upon meditation and healing.

Healthy Gay Living Centre

⌨ *40 Borough High Street, Borough, SE1*

☎ *020 7407 3550*   ✆ *020 7407 3551*

✉ *nrg@lads.demon.co.uk*

🚇 *London Bridge BR/LU or BoroughLU*

This charity for the benefit of gay and bisexual people in need, aims to protect health, relieve poverty, sickness and distress and emphasises safe sex and the prevention of HIV.

Irish Gay Helpline

⌨ *BM Box 1GH, London, WC1N 3XX*

☎ *Helpline 020 8983 4111; Mon 7.30pm-10pm*

An information and befriending service for Irish gay men, this helpline offers an open ear, as well as information and advice.

Jewish Lesbian and Gay Helpline

⌨ *BM Jewish Helpline, London, WC1*

☎ *Helpline 020 7706 3123; Mon & Thurs 7pm-10pm*

A confidential information, support and counselling line for Jewish gays and lesbians, their families and friends.

Kairos

Kairos

🖳 *56 Old Compton Street, Soho, W1*

☎ *020 7437 6063* 📠 *020 7437 6189*

✉ *kairos@kairos-soho.demon.co.uk*

Good health for both body and mind is the idea behind Kairos, a group run by gay and lesbian people. They operate at a variety of venues across Soho, with regular events including meditations, massage, yoga and workshops.

Lesbian Al-Anon

🖳 *London Friend, 86 Caledonian Road, King's Cross, N1*

☎ *020 7837 3337; also minicom*

🚇 *King's Cross BR/LU*

🕐 *Sat 3pm-4.30pm*

A free and confidential service specifically for lesbians who have alcohol-related concerns or problems.

Lesbian and Bisexual Women's Drop-in

🖳 *170 Community Project, New Cross Road, New Cross, SE14*

☎ *Wed 10am-1pm*

🚇 *New Cross Gate/New Cross BR/LU*

An informal drop-in for friendly advice and support.

Lesbian and Gay Action in Waltham Forest (LAGA)

✉ *mail@laga.org.uk*

Offers advice, support and advocacy, as well as information on issues and rights relating to lesbians and gay men, bisexuals and transgendered people. They also run sexual diversity training and do campaign work.

Lesbian and Gay Adoption, Fostering and Parenting Network

🖳 *London Friend, 86 Caledonian Road, King's Cross, N1*

☎ *020 7837 3337*

This support group for gay men and Lesbians seeking to foster or adopt meets monthly at London Friend or in a member's home.

Lesbians at Friend on Sunday

🖳 *London Friend, 86 Caledonian Road, King's Cross, N1*

☎ *020 7837 3337; also minicom*

🚇 *King's Cross BR/LU*

🕐 *First & third Sun 6pm-8.30pm*

Non-scene social group for girls.

Lewisham Friend

☎ *Helpline 020 8690 6195 (Tues & Thurs 7.30pm-9.30pm)*

✐ *www.lewisham.com*

Part of a national organisation, this helpline offers a free and confidential telephone counselling, befriending and advice service for gays and Lesbians who have issues with either their own sexuality or that of their friends or relatives.

London Bisexual Helpline

☎ *020 8569 7500*

🕒 *Tues & Wed 7.30pm-9.30pm, Sat 9.30am-12.30pm*

Information and advice for people who think they might be bisexual.

London Friend

⌂ *86 Caledonian Road, King's Cross, N1*

☎ *020 7837 3337; also minicom*

Helpline 020 7837 3337 (daily 7.30pm-10pm)

Lesbian helpline 020 7837 2782 (Sun-Thurs 7.30pm-10pm)

🚇 *King's Cross BR/LU*

London's first gay and lesbian helpline offers free counselling for individuals and couples and a myriad of social and support groups. The switchboard gives out general information as opposed to detailed counselling. They have a small library with general lesbian and gay titles.

London Lesbian and Gay Mental Health Support Group

⌂ *35 Ashley Road, London, N19*

☎ *020 7272 6936*

🚇 *Holloway Road LU*

🕒 *Tues 10am-4.30pm; free*

Run by the Islington branch of MIND, this organisation falls between a social and a help group, with the users determining activities or topics for discussion. The group is all about offering support and friendship.

London Lesbian and Gay Switchboard

☎ *24-hour helpline 020 7837 7324*

☎ *Volunteer recruitment 020 7837 7606*

The only 24-hour gay and lesbian helpline in the world with the biggest information database in Europe taking about 70,000 calls a year. The services provides information, support and referral services to lesbians and gay men throughout the UK.

Metro Centre

- *Unit 401, 49 Greenwich High Road, Greenwich, SE10*
- *020 8265 3311 (Mon-Fri 10am-5pm)*
- *themetro@dircon.co.uk*
- *www.themetro.dircon.co.uk*
- *Greenwich BR/DLR*

The former Greenwich Lesbian and Gay Centre provides a safe, supportive space for south London lesbians, gays and bisexuals questioning or coming to terms with their sexuality. They run several groups, and offer counselling, one-to-one support, sexual health outreach, youth work and legal advice.

NORM UK

- *020 8372 1936*

A support group for men who have suffered unnecessary circumcision.

North London Line Lesbian and Gay Youth Project

- *Block G, Barnsbury Complex, Offord Road, Islington, N1*
- *020 7607 8346*
- *Highbury & Islington LU*
- *Mon-Fri 1pm-5pm; Mon-Wed 6pm-9pm*
- *£10 annual fee, or 30p per session*

A full-time lesbian and gay youth project that runs a series of under-25s gay and lesbian groups offering support and advice, as well as a place to meet other young people in a friendly and safe atmosphere.

Overeaters Anonymous

- *London Friend, 86 Caledonian Road, King's Cross, N1*
- *020 7837 3337*
- *King's Cross BR/LU*
- *Thurs 6.30pm-8.30pm*

For those who can't say no. This support group helps people with an addiction to food.

PACE (Project for Advice, Counselling and Education)

- *020 7281 3121*

PACE has been London's centre for gay and lesbian mental health advocacy for over 15 years. Among its services is an HIV-prevention programme for gay men.

Parents' Friend

✉ *c/o Wolverhampton Voluntary Services Council,*
2/3 Bell Street, Wolverhampton, WV1 3PR
☎ *01902 421 783*
🖰 *www.parentsfriend.demon.co.uk*
🕐 *Mon-Fri 7.30pm-11pm*

Parents' Friend is a national registered charity with a confidential helpline, that aims to support and educate families in understanding and accepting a lesbian/bisexual/gay loved one.

Parents Together

✉ *PO Box 464, London, SE25 4AT*
☎ *Thelma 020 8313 9629*
🕐 *Daily 10am-10pm*

Parents Together was set up to help parents deal with their feelings of anger, loss, shock or isolation, and the inability to relate to their gay son or daughter. They hold at-home meetings bi-monthly.

Phil Parkinson

☎ *Phil 020 8677 8440*

Phil Parkinson is a trained psychotherapist who offers counselling and support to help clients deal with relationships, midlife-crisis, sexual matters and low self-esteem, as well as working towards an understanding of gay spirituality. All counselling is done on an individual basis.

People First

✉ *3rd Floor, 299 Kentish Town Road, NW5*
☎ *020 7485 6660*
🚇 *King's Cross BR/LU*
🕐 *Mon-Fri 9am-5pm*

This organisation is run by people with learning disabilities, giving them the self-confidence and assertion to express their own needs. Although not specifically gay it welcomes enquiries from gays and lesbians with learning difficulties.

The Pink Practice

⌨ *BCM Pink Practice, London, WC1*

☏ *0113 242 4884*

✐ *pinkpractice.co.uk*

✐ *www.pinkpractice.co.uk/pinkprac/*

🕓 *Mon-Fri 9am-8pm*

This team of registered psychotherapists and counsellors in central London and Leeds, offer counselling for individuals, couples and families, and by e-mail for those living outside London.

Project LSD

⌨ *32 Wardour St, Soho, W1*

☏ *020 7439 0717 (Tues-Thurs 10am-1pm & 2pm-5.30pm for enquiries)*

🕓 *Thus 6.30pm-8.30pm Support Group (drop-in); Thurs 6pm-8pm Complementary Therapies (drop-in)*

Specialist drug service for lesbians, gay men and bisexuals. Confidential advice and information on drugs and drug abuse, with access to counselling, complementary therapies and treatment options.

Queer Love Quest

☏ *David 020 7388 3109*

✐ *checkin@relationshipclinic.com*

✐ *www.relationshipclinic.com*

A personal growth programme that works to find solutions to problems such as low self-esteem, co-dependent behaviour, alcohol and substance abuse and debt disorders. They also run weekly groups and monthly seminars.

Sacred Intimacy

☏ *Andy 07966 502057*

These workshops and individual session bring together tantric traditions and new work on intimacy to help enhance the life experience. Workshops cost around £70 for a whole day.

Sexual Compulsives Anonymous

⌨ *BM SCA, London, WC1N*

☏ *020 8914 7599*

This group offers a programme of recovery from compulsive sex based on the Alcoholics Anonymous's 12-step programme, by defining the problem and suggesting ways to overcome addiction. Ring for details of different groups.

volunqueer @ Kairos

Sola

☎ *020 7328 7389*

🕓 *Mon-Fri 10.30am-1pm, 2pm-4.30pm*

This confidential helpline caters for lesbian women who have been physically, sexually or emotionally abused in relationships.

Therapeia

📧 *205b Richmond Road, Twickenham, Middlesex, TW1 2NJ*

☎ *Alan 020 7284 2521*

Therapeia links you with qualified, experienced counsellors and psychotherapists in London, and work on a variety of problems.

West London Buddhist Centre

📧 *94 Westbourne Park Villas, Westbourne Park, W2*

☎ *020 7727 9382*

🚇 *Royal Oak LU*

The centre runs meditation courses which are open to all, and does have occasional courses specifically for gay men. Phone for details of current and future courses.

INTRODUCTION AGENCIES

If you are really committed to meeting the love of your life but aren't prepared to endure the sometimes harsh realities of the scene or the endless sifting through social groups, intro agencies can save time and effort. They can be expensive, but they do put themselves out to find your ideal match, and you get the chance to stipulate exactly the kind of partner you're after.

Everything and the Girl ♀

- ⌨ *Suite 28, Savant House, 63-65 Camden High Street, NW1*
- ☎ *020 7681 0954*   ✆ *020 7387 0193*
- ✎ *info@eatgirl.co.uk*
- ✎ *www.eatgirl.co.uk*
- ✆ *3 months membership £120*

A London-based intro agency for gay and bisexual women that offers a confidential, tailor-made service, for those wanting to find friendship or more – most members use the agency to establish an instant network of new friends. Before joining, applicants are given an in-depth interview, have to fill out a fun, hand-written profile and provide a photo. Once enrolled, members may then select other member's files to make contact. Women who live outside London can keep in regular telephone contact with the agency and receive profiles by post. The agency also runs a short-term membership option, which many foreign women use if they come to the UK on holiday or business.

Gay Link Intros (GLI Agency)

- ⌨ *27 Old Gloucester Street, Bloomsbury, WC1*
- ☎ *020 7627 4960*
- ✎ *www.gliagency.co.uk*
- ✆ *Annual membership £49.50 (includes access to a portfolio of 200 members and fortnightly supplements); lifetime membership £130*

Established in 1982, GLI is the country's largest agency for gay men and women seeking long-term friendships or relationships throughout Britain or abroad. Their service is completely confidential, so that only members can reveal details of his or her surname and address, and choose who they would like to meet from the exhaustive portfolios of around 200 files. Most of their members describe themselves as non-scene, straight-acting types, and are guaranteed to be genuine.

Gay Link also run Gaypen Worldwide for men seeking friends overseas (each portfolio lists 10 potential contacts and costs £20 for one, £35 for two and £45 for three).

Kenric ♀

✉ *BM Kenric, London, WC1*

☎ *01622 741213*

✍ *kenric@freenetname.co.uk*

✍ *www.kenric.co.uk*

This non-profitmaking nationwide network of lesbian and bisexual women's social organisations was founded in 1964, at a time when the sexual revolution meant attitudes towards homosexuality were becoming more tolerant. The organisation has changed considerably since the 1970s, when married members needed their application form signed by their husband, and 18-21 year olds, by a doctor or parent! Run by members for members, today Kenric organises regular social activities throughout the UK via its network of local groups for lesbian and bisexual women over 16; Kenric-affiliated groups in the London area include the North London Group, Daytime Dykes, KADS (Kent and South East London), Kingston Surbiton Group, Sappho, West London Group (Westerners), Weekenders (South London), Diversity (London's Gay Chamber Choir), Gemma, North London Metropolitan Church, Rubber Medusas and the Metro Centre in Greenwich. Events range from quiz and karaoke nights, parties, cabarets, discos and meals out. Members receive a monthly magazine with relevant articles, details of national and regional events and free-of-charge contact adverts, as well as having access to Kenric Chat, where you can chat in real time to other members, and to Kenroc, Kenric's online community where members communicate via ongoing e-mail discussions. For more information, send a SAE (min 6x4").

Out and Out

✉ *72 Old Compton Street, Soho, W1*

☎ *020 8998 8000*

✍ *www.outandout.co.uk*

❧ *Annual membership £189*

The UK's longest-established private members' club for gay men offers members the opportunity to meet other men in a relaxed and friendly atmosphere in fashionable restaurants, the theatre, opera and ballet. Around 20 people attend each event. Dinner parties start at £35, including a drinks reception and three-course meal with wine coffee and liqueurs. A host or hostess is always present to introduce people and make sure everything goes smoothly. See also Dining Groups (p.208).

Significant Others

🖃 *14 South Molton Street, Mayfair, W1*

☎/🖷 *020 7499 5939*

✐ *intro@significantothers.co.uk*

✐ *www.significantothers.co.uk*

🚇 *Bond Street LU*

💰 *Annual membership from £295 to £895*

This upmarket gay men's introduction agency deals with the romantic fancy of the professional and discerning who are looking for Mr Right in London and the Home Counties. Even their two-page questionnaire asks rigorous questions which you must slavishly justify – books you have recently read and enjoyed and what you would choose to be in a different life. After a free initial face-to-face consultation to determine whether you are right for the agency, you can choose possible partners from profiles. Their 500 members are between 25 and 65, and meet at four annual parties. First Thursday and last Thursday drinks evening in central London.

PEN PAL SCHEMES

Disabled Pen-Friend Group UK

🖃 *PO Box 42, Newton-Le-Willow, Warrington, Cheshire, WA3 2FF*

💰 *01942 269 133*

Peer By Post

🖃 *PO Box 153, Manchester, M60 1LP*

✐ *penpals@peer-support.demon.co.uk*

✐ *www.peer-support.org.uk*

The Peer Support Project provides peer support services for young lesbians, gays and bisexuals in Greater Manchester, as well as Peer By Post, a nationwide penpal service which provides young lesbians, gays and bisexuals with access to like-minded contacts.

Phoenix

🖃 *PO Box 103, Wallington, Surrey, SM6 9SJ*

In its fifth year, the Phoenix scheme caters for those who prefer more mature men. With over 600 members aged between 21 and 86, it offers monthly personal ads, regular newsletters and social events. Send SAE for details.

Postal Penfriends

🖃 *PO Box 14, Faversham, Kent*

Send a SAE for details.

LEGAL & FINANCIAL SERVICES

SOLICITORS

The law being the labyrinth that it is, you really need to have a solicitor who understands your particular needs. For example, the law does not recognise gay or lesbian relationships, and if your partner dies, the assets will not automatically come to you – so it is a good idea to draw up cohabitation contracts (or living together agreements) to provide the solid financial and legal framework that minimises areas of dispute, including property ownership, mortgage payments and wills. The following are gay firms or firms that target a gay clientele. They can deal with all your business, commercial and personal legal work, from crime and immigration, company formation and insolvency to defence against police prosecution, relationship breakdowns and adoption issues.

Aitchison Shaw
- *United House, North Road, N7*
- ☎ *020 7700 0045*
- 🖷 *020 7700 6288*

Amplett Lissimore
- *29 Westlow Street, Crystal Palace, SE19*
- ☎ *020 8771 5254*
- *103 Sydenham Road, Sydenham, SE26*
- ☎ *020 8516 7070*

Burton Woods
- *Museum House, 25 Museum Street, Bloomsbury, WC1*
- ☎ *020 7636 2448*
- 🖷 *020 7493 9241*
- ✉ *queries@burtonwoods.com*
- ✉ *www.burtonwoods.com*

David Clark & Co
- *38 Heath Street, Hampstead, NW3*
- ☎ *020 7433 1562*
- 🖷 *020 7433 1625*
- ✉ *office@davidclarkandco.freeserve.co.uk*

Anthony Gold Solicitors
- *New London Bridge House, 25 London Bridge Street, Southwark, SE1*
- ☎ *020 7940 4000*
- 🖷 *020 7378 8025*

Kaltons
- *9 White Lion Street, Islington, N1*
- ☎ *020 7278 1817*
- 🖷 *020 7278 1835*
- ✉ *lawyers@kaltons.co.uk*
- ✉ *www.kaltons.co.uk*

Andrew Keen & Co
- *121 George Lane, E18*
- ☎ *020 8989 3123*

McGlennons Solicitors
- *Park House, 158-160 Arthur Road, Wimbledon, SW19*
- ☎ *020 8946 6015*
- ✉ *mcglenn@dircon.co.uk*

Pritchard Joyce and Hinds
- *St Bride's House, 32 High Street, Beckenham, Kent, BR3*
- ☎ *020 8658 3922*
- 🖷 *020 8658 8694*

ACCOUNTANTS

The chartered accountants and registered auditors listed below cater for those who are self-employed or running a small gay or lesbian business and can see to your accounts and tax returns, book-keeping, preparation of audits, Inland Revenue investigations, cash flow and budgets, business plans and reports, and give general business advice.

David Clarke

✉ *121 Worton Road, Isleworth, Middlesex, TW7*
☎ *020 8568 0494*

KL Associates

✉ *2 Tavistock Chambers, 40 Bloomsbury Way, WC1*
☎ *020 7831 4466*

John Lester

✉ *45 Banner House, Roscoe Street, EC1*
☎ *020 7251 6798*

Nyman Libson Paul

✉ *Regina House, 124 Finchley Road, Swiss Cottage, NW3*
☎ *020 7794 5611*   ✆ *020 7431 1109*

Winter Stewart Associates

✉ *First Floor, 79-89 Lots Road, North Kensington, W10*
☎ *020 7376 5552*   ✆ *020 7376 4052*

Waterman Brown

✉ *8 Wellesley Road, Walthamstow, E17*
☎ *020 8521 4475*
☎ *01392 431 577*

FINANCIAL ADVISORS

Gay men and lesbians may need specific information to guide them through the financial jungle– life insurance premiums can be twice those of straight people regardless of HIV status or living in a monogamous relationship, and obtaining a mortgage may be difficult. Independent financial advisors can give you constructive advice on health insurance, life assurance, mortgages, pensions, investments and savings, unit trusts, PEPS, government grants, loans and setting up your own business.

Carvosso
- 3rd Floor, 40 Gerrard Street, W1
- 0800 096 9012
- www.carvosso.com

Compass
- 2nd Floor,
72 Shaftesbury Avenue, W1
- www.compassisa.co.uk
- 020 7287 9008

Independent Professional Advisors Services (IPAS)
- 25 Station Road, New Barnet, Herts, EN5 1PH
- 020 8440 8008

Lee Financial
- 30 Turnpike Link, Park Hill, East Croydon, CR0
- 020 8680 3410, 681 6050

Massow Rainbow
- 0800 328 0625
- postbox@massowrainbow.com
- www.freedompension.co.uk

Morris Sultman
- 108 High Road,
East Finchley, N2
- 020 8444 1818
- 020 8444 1663

Radford Smith
- 46 Chiswick High Road,
Chiswick, W4
- 020 8995 8351

Somerset How
- 52 Ockenden Road,
Islington, N1
- 020 7226 5584

FINANCIAL PUBLICATIONS

Pink Finance
- Compass IFA Ltd, 2nd Floor, 72 Shaftesbury Avenue, W1
- editor@pinkfinance.com
- www.pinkfinance.com
- 020 7287 9008

The UK's first gay finance magazine with specialist articles on mortgages, property, peace of mind, wealth creation, personal and business finance sections with readers' letters, best deals and useful links.

PERFORMING ARTS

They say it's queers who run the theatre – think Cameron Mackintosh, Ian McKellan, Stephen Sondheim, Alan Bennett, Jackie Clune, and just what hasn't Miriam Margoyles been in? – and there are a number of purely gay and lesbian organisations that focus on workshopping or performing gay productions, as well as a fully fledged symphony orchestra and various choirs who spread the word in full-throated rendition.

GAY THEATRE COMPANIES AND WORKSHOPS

Gay and Lesbian Amateur Dramatics (GLAD)

- *Lauderdale House, Highgate Hill, Waterlow Park, Highgate, N6*
- *020 8348 8716*
- *Highgate LU*
- *Thurs 7.30pm-10pm*
- *Membership fee*

What was a weekly drop-in for gays, bisexuals and lesbians has turned into a fully-fledged am-dram society, where boys and girls desperate to perform can do just that. Under the watchful eye of a professional performer-coach, around 5-10 budding stars workshop scenes and experiment with delivery, ending their series of classes with a public performance. The group are looking towards writing or commissioning their own material, and want to develop a musical and dance repertoire.

Homo Promos

☎ *Eric 020 7277 5014*

✎ *eric.presland@homopromos.fsnet.co.uk*

This London community-based non-profit making gay theatre company is a professional outfit with around seven core members who aim at a lesbian and gay audience. They are committed to putting on one or two plays a year by lesbian and gay playwrights, and are especially keen to work with new material. The company has performed at the Edinburgh Festival, produced a Midsummer Night play on Hampstead Heath and does a lot of charity benefits for Outrage, World AIDS Day etc. They also want to develop more in the field of musical theatre and cabaret.

Short and Girlie Theatre Company (SAG) ♀

🏢 *Drill Hall, 16 Chenies Street, Bloomsbury, WC1*

☎ *Ali 07957 666 213*

✎ *ali_bop@hotmail.com*

🕐 *Mon 7.30pm, weekly workshop*

With no other lesbian theatre company in London, founder Ali set up her own, drawing around 50 interested girls to the first workshop – most with an acting background, whether through formal training or just a lot of experience; they include writers, directors, stage managers, lighting technicians, producers, sound technicians, musicians. The group meet every week for a workshop of voice and body warm-up, a meditation/guided journey, group bonding games and improvisations to fine-tune their acting skills. The group is a co-operative with equal input from all members, including running workshops. Group decisions are made on each production, and members decide if they want to appear in it, or just attend the group workshops. SAG perform snippets of their work at the Vespa Lounge.

Youth Theatre

🏢 *Greenwich Freedom Youth, 24-24a Greens End, Woolwich, SE18*

☎ *Jamie 020 8316 4901*

🚉 *Woolwich Arsenal BR*

🕐 *Thurs 7.30pm-9.30pm* 💰 *30p per session*

Latent drama queens and dykes under 25 can indulge their performing addiction in London's only gay youth drama project. They write and design their own pieces and use rehearsal time to explore particular issues, from coming out to death. Although they do work towards a performance, members can just take part in the workshops.

VENUES

Drill Hall ♀

⌨ *16 Chenies Street, Bloomsbury, WC1*

☏ *020 7631 1353*   ✆ *020 7631 4468*

🚇 *Goodge Street LU*

🕐 *Restaurant and bar Mon-Sat 6pm-11pm, Sun 7pm-10.30pm*

London's premier gay and lesbian theatre venue is a former Victorian military drill hall that was used as the Tate Gallery's sculpture hall for a while, as well as being where Nijinsky once danced and Gay Sweatshop started up. It opened as a gay performance venue in 1981 and has achieved a reputation for innovative, daring, high-quality theatre work, including musicals, revues and drama with gay content. The auditorium seats around 200. A £400,000 Arts Council grant saw a programme of basic renovations begin in spring 2001. The Drill Hall runs various courses – anything from working with papier mâché to T'ai Chi and classical yoga – and also has various rooms for hire: three photographic darkrooms complete with equipment, a 190 square-foot craft studio and five rehearsal/meeting rooms.

Oval House Theatre

⌨ *52-54 Kennington Oval, Kennington, SE11*

☏ *020 7582 0080*

🚇 *Oval LU*

✎ *www.ovalhouse.com*

The Oval House is a long established fringe theatre, which usually has something concerning gay issues among each season's offerings, and has run a Queer Season of productions in recent years. The lesbian comedian Clare Summerskill is a regular performer here. The theatre is not only the venue for cutting-edge theatre, but runs an active education programme and gallery. The theatre has the added attraction of a bar/café (Wed-Sat 6pm–11pm).

CHOIRS AND MUSIC GROUPS

The following list is a mixture of amateur and professional choirs and orchestras which gather gay and lesbian performers together with the aim of putting on a show.

Camerata Santa Dorotea

☎ *Robin 07881 934165*

✎ *rg-p@rocketmail.com*

This string-based professional ensemble has a bias towards early Baroque music, but its repertoire takes in any classical pieces – including commissioning their own. They are flexible enough to play with anything from just a handful of musicians to a full symphonic band, relying on freelance professional players and often playing without a conductor. If you are a professional musician and interested in being involved, give them a call.

Diversity Lesbian and Gay Choir

☎ *Paul 020 7701 9833*

✎ *diversitychoir@yahoogroup.com*

🕐 *Rehearsals Thurs 7pm-9pm*

💲 *Annual membership £25, plus £2 per rehearsal*

This lesbian and gay chamber choir has a diverse repertoire from classical and opera to pop, via madrigals and barber shop, secular and sacred, as well as a certain amount of gay content. With around 20 singers, the four-part choir rehearse weekly in the Regent's Park area and perform around three times a year, usually in a church in the City. New singers, pianists, arrangers and composers are always welcome.

Gay Symphony Orchestra

☎ *Richard 020 8809 5518*

✎ *www.lgso.ndirect.co.uk*

🕐 *Rehearsals Sun 6pm-9pm*

💲 *Membership £25 per concert*

An ambitious project set up in 1996, this volunteer-only lesbian and gay symphony orchestra performs four concerts a year in St John's Church in Waterloo. They tackle full-scale orchestra works such as Mahler's First Symphony and Holst's The Planets, as well as opera galas, and their numbers average 40-50 people, swelling when the work demands. Donations and sponsorship are very much welcomed. They rehearse at ULU, usually weekly.

London Gay Men's Chorus

✉ *PO Box 21039, London, N1*
☎ *Steve 020 8981 5200*
✍ *info@glmc.org.uk*
✍ *www.lgmc.org.uk*
🕐 *Rehearsals Mon 7pm-10pm*
✇ *£20 per month, £10 unwaged*

The highest-profile and largest gay male choir has around 150 members and has performed all over the world since it was started in 1991. They put on two or three performances a year in a West End theatre, and do plenty of gay charitable gigs in-between to raise funds for gay research. Their repertoire swerves from classical and jazz to folk and pop ('Brahms to Barbie Girl' as they say), and they commission their own material from gay writers. No audition is required; rehearsals weekly in NW1. They have also set up the Friends of the London Gay Men's Chorus and organise plenty of pub crawls and parties.

Pink Singers

✉ *PO Box LB 738, London, W1*
☎ *0702 0934916*
✍ *info@pinksingers.co.uk*
✍ *www.pinksingers.co.uk*
🕐 *Rehearsals Sun 2pm-5pm*
✇ *Annual membership fee £35, £20 unwaged*

The oldest lesbian and gay chorus in Europe (established in 1983) is the highest-profile community choir in the UK. The non-auditioning Pinkies are a community choir with a 50/50 gay/lesbian split, and perform three or four times a year, with one overseas concert. There are around 50 singing members and 20 non-singers, and their non-religious repertoire takes in Abba, Queen, Cole Porter, Sondheim and original material – as *Time Out* said, "a little satire, a little politics and a lot of camp in full-throated harmonies". Although there are no formal auditions, the emphasis is on working hard and achieving a good standard. On the social side, they organise picnics, quiz evenings and nights at the pub. They've guested on Gimme Gimme Gimme and Radio 4. Weekly rehearsals close to Goodge Street tube.

POLITICAL & LOBBYING GROUPS

Since the Gay Liberation Front met at Highbury Fields in 1970 in the name of gay activism, a network of diligent underground workers dedicated to asserting the equality of the gay community fighting for legal and social recognition. But there is still a long way to go. The Sexual Discrimination (SOD) Bill promises to pave the way for equality for gays in the workplace, but the very public campaign in 1996 of four ex-service people fighting for the right to continue their jobs without prejudicial treatment has highlighted what a hypocritical notion equality is – between 1990 and 1994 alone, an alarming 309 people were expelled from the armed forces because of their sexuality.

Sister of Perpetual Indulgence

Amnesty International UK Gay, Lesbian and Bisexual and Transgender Network

- 99-119 Rosebery Avenue, Finsbury, EC1
- Nora 020 7814 6200
- rainbow@amnesty.org.uk
- www.amnesty.org.uk/action/nw/glbt.shtml

Amnesty was launched in 1961, and now has more than 1 million members and supporters in over 160 countries and territories. The GLBT Network comprises Amnesty International UK members (and affiliated groups) who share a particular interest in raising awareness of and campaigning against human rights violations based on sexual orientation. Members take part in a range of activities – campaigning, fundraising, meetings, events, information-sharing – according to their interests.

Burning Issues Group

- 50 Moundfield Road, Stoke Newington, N16
- alib@cix.compulink.co.u
- www.croydononline.org

The Burning Issues group works alongside the Library Association to ensure quality library services and stock for lesbians, gays and bisexuals by raising the profile of LGB issues in librarianship, and enabling librarians to network and share best practice. Membership is free and open to anyone interested in promoting this issue at all levels of library/information work; members come from all sectors of librarianship, including students. The group runs training days in conjunction with the Social Exclusion Action Planning Network, and has a web-based discussion list.

Campaign for Homosexual Equality (CHE)

- PO Box 342, London, WC1
- 07702 326 151   020 8743 625

CHE works to establish full legal and social equality for lesbians, gays and bisexuals. This voluntary campaigning and lobbying group began life in the 1950s as the Homosexual Law Reform Society, eventually achieving the institution of the 1967 Sexual Offenses Act, which legalised sex between two consenting adults of the same gender. The Society metamorphosed into the CHE in 1969, when it formed over 100 branches around England and Wales, which gradually splintered into small social groups. Today the Campaign still battles to change attitudes and laws that make life difficult for gays in England and Wales, with education high on their list of priorities. As it is self-funding, donations to the CHE are much appreciated.

Feminists Against Censorship ♀

📖 *BM FAC, London, WC1*

☎ *020 8552 4405*   📠 *020 8548 1591*

🖰 *www.fiawol.demon.co.uk/fac/*

🖰 *Membership: £5 (minimum donation)*

Formed in 1989 by various academics and campaigners who wanted to combat censorship deploying a feminist perspective, FAC aims to fight the fact it is used to suppress people's ideas and views, and victimise minorities. Members speak at universities, groups, to the media, and write books and articles to educate people about a truly feminist agenda. This includes discussing topics such as the elimination of restraint in media images; the removal of the powers of Customs and Excise to confiscate magazines, videos, films and other media; abolition of the Obscene Publications Acts, the Video Recordings Act, and the Clubs and Vice Squad; an accessible public forum for the discussion of vital issues such as sexism and racism; and positive and accurate sex education for young people, starting as early as possible. Send SAE for information.

Finsbury Park Action Group (FPAG)

📖 *Alexandra National House, 330 Seven Sisters Road, Finsbury Park, N4*

☎ *020 8800 2630*

🖰 *fpag.susan@virgin.net*

🖰 *www.web.ukonline.co.uk/finsbury.parker*

🚇 *Finsbury Park BR/LU*

🕐 *Wed 10am-noon: Advice Service (drop-in)*

This local regeneration project aims to improve the quality of life for everyone who lives or works in the area. They lobby for improvements, provide advice and information and promote and administer new initiatives – including setting up a Credit Union, a greening programme, and an anti-litter campaign. The advice line gives information (regardless of sexuality) about benefits, housing, homelessness, asylum-seeking and referral. The group also has an HIV/AIDS awareness arm, distributing information, red ribbons and free condoms outside Finsbury Park station on World AIDS Day.

Gay and Lesbian Humanist Association (GALHA)

⌨ *34 Spring Lane, Kenilworth, Warks, CV8 2HB*

☏/✆ *George 01926 858450*

✎ *galha@bigfoot.com*

✎ *www.visitweb.com/galha*

🚇 *Holborn LU*

☺ *Monthly meeting in Holborn*

✆ *Annual membership £17*

Founded in 1979 after Mary Whitehouse slapped a libel charge on Gay News, GALHA is a nationwide campaigning organisation for lesbian, gay and bisexual atheists and agnostics that promotes a rational humanist approach to homosexuality. It holds regular public events with speakers, discussions, socials, and arranges humanist ceremonies – baby namings, funerals and weddings – for its non-religious members. They have monthly guest speakers at Conway Hall, Red Lion Square, Holborn WC1, and a quarterly magazine with news features, reviews and letters.

International Lesbian and Gay Association (ILGA)

⌨ *81 Kolenmarkt, B 1000 Brussels, Belgium*

☏/✆ *010 322 5022471*

✎ *ilga@ilga.org*

This international federation oversees 350 local and national groups (from small collectives to city-wide associations) dedicated to achieving equal rights for lesbians, gay men, bisexuals and transgendered people throughout 80 countries. It campaigns for the repeal of discriminatory government policy, focuses on specific cases of discrimination, lobbies international organisations (such as the UN, EU, Council of Europe) for equal rights, and supports the founding of lesbian and gay support groups. ILGA has had many triumphs. It saw the World Health Organisation delete homosexuality from its International Classification of Diseases; in 1991 Amnesty International decided to accept lesbians and gay men imprisoned for their sexuality as prisoners of conscience; in 1995/96 ILGA helped set up gay and lesbian organisations in the three Baltic countries and in St Petersburg and Moscow; and in 1997, the group played a significant role in ensuring that the new European Union Treaty of Amsterdam empowers the Union to "take appropriate action to combat discrimination based on … sexual orientation". ILGA also participates in many international conferences to make the argument that the non-discrimination agenda should also cover sexual orientation. The bi-annual ILGA conference celebrates the diversity of the international community, presents achievements and collaborates on national and international projects. The organisation's World Legal Survey represents the most comprehensive data on laws affecting lesbians and gays around the world ever published.

Lesbian and Gay Coalition Against Racism (LAGCAR)

⌨ *22 c/o NAAR, 28 Commercial Street, Shoreditch, E1*

☎ *020 7247 9907*

This anti-racist organisation is part of the National Assembly Against Racism, the largest anti-racist lobbying group in Britain, and fights against unfair treatment of lesbian and gays based upon race. They address issues of asylum-seeking and immigration, and look for alliances with black and Jewish communities, trades unions and religious organisations, and women's and disabled groups.

Lesbian and Gay Employment Rights (LAGER)

⌨ *22 Unit 1G, Leroy House, 436 Essex Road, Islington, N1*

☎ *lesbians 020 7704 8066, gay men 020 7704 6066, admin/general enquiries 020 7704 2205*

📠 *020 7704 6067*

🖊 *www.lager.dircon.co.uk*

🕐 *Mon-Fri noon-4pm*

This voluntary body offers free and confidential legal advice to gay men and lesbians who experience problems at work or whilst looking for work. Although their fight against unfairness is directed mainly at helping those discriminated against on the grounds of sexuality, they also assist with issues related to race, HIV status, marital status, gender or disability. Their publications include general information sheets and reports on equal opportunities and discrimination, HIV and local authority services (all available both in braille and on tape). LAGER's caseworkers can advise you if you think your employer is treating you unfairly or if you are involved in a grievance or disciplinary procedure at work; the group can also assist you in making a claim to an industrial tribunal. LAGER also provides training and consultancy for organisations and employers. Both advice lines can be connected to minicom.

Liberal Democrats for Lesbian and Gay Action (DELGA)

⌨ *c/o Liberal Democrats, 4 Cowley Street, London, SW1*

☎ *07816 214 658*

🖊 *london.delga@delga.libdems.org*

🖊 *www.delga.libdems.org/delga*

DELGA was founded in 1987 to promote the interests of the lesbian, gay and bisexual community within the Liberal Democrats and Parliament. The party recognise that much discrimination aimed at gays and lesbians is enshrined in law, and must be changed at parliamentary level. Hence its opposition of Section 28 in the House of Commons. DELGA London Region is a campaign team focused upon London-wide issues, and meet monthly in north London. Membership is open to all non-members of other British parties.

Liberty (National Council for Civil Liberties)

🖃 *21 Tabart Street, Southwark, SE1*

☎ *Nettie 020 7403 3888*   🖎 *020 7407 5354*

🕐 *Mon-Fri 10am-5pm*

💰 *Annual membership £30*

Not the upmarket store, but the UK's foremost human rights organisation, which has spoken out on many gay and lesbian human rights issues over the past few years. It's an independent organisation that has since 1934 defended and extended the civil and political rights of people who live in Britain. Liberty irons out all types of discrimination from racial and sexual to unfairness in the justice system, including speaking out about Clause 28, pinpointing the failure of British immigration laws to recognise same-sex relationships and the fact that legislation does not protect gays sacked from their jobs, because of their sexuality. The organisation runs workshops and seminars about gay rights, with guest speakers from the community, and also gives free legal advice by letter.

LONDON MONDAY GROUP FOR HOMOSEXUAL EQUALITY –
see Social Groups (p.193)

OutRage!

PO Box 17816, London, SW14

☎ *020 8240 0222*

✍ *feedback@OutRage.org.uk*

✍ *www.outrage.org.uk*

🕐 *Thurs 7.30pm open meeting (phone for details)*

Committed to radical, non-violent direct action and civil disobedience, OutRage! is bent on fighting for equal rights for queers, including asserting queer human rights, fighting homophobic discrimination and affirming sexual freedom. And members are prepared to make themselves very unpopular in doing it. With a programme based on confronting homophobics face-to-face, this provocative, angry, voluntary activist group embarrasses and shames people – ambushing prime ministers, storming Parliament and police stations, and outing Church of England bishops – in the name of promoting public visibility of anti-gay discrimination. Some of their best stunts have raised activism to an artform – events include the Piccadilly Circus Kiss-in, an Exorcism of Homophobia, and Queer Weddings. The group distribute condoms and leaflets about homosexuality and safer sex to school pupils to combat censorship in the classroom, take up the cases of individuals suffering discrimination, provide speakers to schools and colleges, investigates and researches anti-gay discrimination, and helps organise solidarity campaigns with queers suffering persecution in other countries.

The organisation's main objectives are for an Unmarried Partners Act to give legal rights to all unwed couples, and lowering the age of consent to 14 for everyone. Ultimately, its goal is the establishment of an Equal Rights Act to protect everyone in society against all discrimination, harassment and incitement to hatred. OutRage! depends entirely on donations.

OutSideIn

✉ *PO Box 119, Orpington, Kent, BR6 9ZZ*
🖋 *www.out-side.in.org.uk*

A national charity for lesbian and gay prisoners founded in the mid 1990s to help gay and lesbian inmates who suffer verbal and physical abuse on the inside because of their sexuality.

Press for Change

✉ *BM Network, London, WC1*
🖋 *letters@pfc.org.uk*
🖋 *www.pfc.org.uk*

Press for Change is a political lobbying and educational organisation, which campaigns to achieve equal civil rights and liberties for all transgendered people in the United Kingdom, through legislation and social change. Since a divorce case in 1970 branded the transgendered as 'non-people', more than 5,000 people in the UK have successfully made the transition between genders. Press for Change was instrumental in reversing the prohibitive legislation. Today, their website is a newspaper, library and resource centre, detailing the rights campaign, as well as the legal, medical, political and social issues surrounding people it represents.

Sisters of Perpetual Indulgence

✉ *Sister Solicitation, c/o Central Station,*
37 Wharfdale Road, King's Cross, N1
🖋 *www.thesisters.org*

With their pre-Vatican II habits and catchy appellations – Mother Molesta of the Parish of the Convent of Smouldering Embers, Sister Mary Anilingus and Mother Kiss My Arse Goodbye – this order of 21st-century male and female, gay and straight nuns was set up, following the US model, to promote universal joy and the expunction of stigmatic guilt – and, more tangibly, to discuss relationships, love and safer sex. Their message of pride, happiness, equality and refusing to be treated as victims is refreshing when compared to most lobby groups' focus on oppression and shame; they state they want the gay community to 'take liberties rather than wait for freedom'. The group claim they are not sending up the church with their garb, that the benevolent symbolism of the nuns' habits will encourage people to talk more readily about safer sex and relationships; they also produce the world's only safer sex leaflet with a quiche recipe on the back, and highlight the work of outstanding members of the community through regular acts of canonisation.

Southwark Anti-Homophobic Forum

☎ 020 7525 7427

Stonewall

⌂ 46 Grosvenor Gardens, SW1

☎ 020 7881 9440   📠 020 7881 9444

✍ info@stonewall.org.uk

✍ www.stonewall.org.uk

Stonewall is the national civil rights group working for legal equality and social justice for lesbians, gay men and bisexuals – but receives no funding from local government and little support from charitable trusts, although they have received £900,000 grant from the Lottery. Set up in 1989 after Clause 28 came into being, it works towards legal protection from discrimination, legal recognition of homosexual relationships and parenting rights, raising the gay and lesbian voice to Parliament and the media – and was instrumental in bringing down the age of consent for gays. They also run the Stonewall Parenting Group for mutual support and campaigning for those with parenting problems (Sun 2pm-5pm at the Drill Hall, see p.103); the Pensions Group campaigns for equal rights under company pension law; and the Fares Fair campaigns for equal right for gay railway workers.

Tory Campaign for Homosexual Equality (TORCHE)

⌂ BM TORCHE, London, WC1

✍ torche@cableinet.co.uk

✍ www.torche.gb.org

This Tory Party gay pressure group wants to promote the interests of the gay community within the party, as well as to promote the Conservative Party in the gay community. Among its triumphs, it succeeded in having anti-gay ranter Dr Adrian Rogers expelled from the party, exposing homophobic MPs, and introducing gay themes to party conferences. It also acts as a gay Tory networking organisation, although following the departure of Ivan Massow, one wonders where the group's future lies. Annual subscription discretionary.

PUBLICATIONS

There's a good range of gay weeklies or monthly mags from the lowest-common-denominator *Boyz* to the politically driven *Pink Paper* and glossy paean *Attitude*. These are the three pillars of the gay community, *Capital Gay* and the sadly missed *Gay Gazette* having long since folded. In 1999, Millivres, publishers of *Gay Times* and *Diva*, merged with Prowler Press and became the UK's biggest gay company. There are still a lot of smaller publications which come and go – some worthy, some bizarre and some just downright silly.

+ve

⌨ *Eton House, 156 High Stret, Ruislip, Middlesex, HA4 8LJ*

☎ *01895 637878* ✎ *01895 637273*

✐ *andrewb@akitanet.co.uk*

✐ *www.howsthat.co.uk*

✎ *Distributed free throughout the UK's gay pubs, clubs and cafés on first Thursday of the month*

A monthly publication that sets out to educate the non-infected, and keep those living with HIV/AIDS abreast of new developments. There are reports on the virus from around the world, and changes in legislation that affect those living with it, as well as information on hepatitis and sexually transmitted diseases.

AIDS Education and Research Trust (AVERT)

⌨ *4 Brighton Road, Horsham, West Sussex, RH13 45BA*

☎ *01403 210202* ✎ *01403 211001*

✐ *info@avert.org*

✐ *www.avert.org*

AVERT publish information on the internet that you can download.

Attitude

⌨ *Northern and Shell Tower PLC,*
Ludgate House, 245 Blackfriars Road, SE1

☎ *020 7928 8000* ✎ *020 7922 7600*

✐ *attitude@express..co.uk*

✎ *Available from newsagents; £2.75*

The undisputed quality gay men's glossy mag is tailored to the coffee tables of professional twenty and thirtysomethings. The likes of Simon Gage, Mark Simpson and Paul Clements give their take on the gay thing in intelligent, informed editorial. It doesn't turn its back on the scene, but also looks further afield, with celebrity news and fashion pages.

Bi Community News

⌨ *BM RiBBiT, London, WC1*

✉ *bcn@bi.org*

✉ *www.bi.org/~bcn*

✆ *Available on subscription only; £8 annually (12 issues)*

Britain's only bisexual newsletter has been running for over three years
and provides monthly discussion of local and national group news and
listings, bi-relevant news, personal ads, opinion, debate, politics and
letters, as well as reviews of books, films etc. It aims to keep bisexuals in
touch, build a bigger network of community groups and to support
isolated individuals. *BCN* is published each month on the Internet, but
the latest issue is only available in paper form to subscribers. They also
organise a Bi Women's Weekend every few months.

Boyz

⌨ *Cedar House, 72 Holloway Road, London, N7*

☎ *020 7296 6000*   ✆ *020 7296 0026*

✉ *boyz@boyz.co.uk*

✉ *www.boyz.co.uk*

✆ *Distributed free throughout the UK's gay pubs, clubs and cafés on Thursdays*

The Sun for gay readers, with plenty of pictures and saucy lightweight
features on fashion, sexual advice, health, exercise, the scene and music...
and you always know there will be a nude pin-up. Since it was
launched in July 1991, *Boyz* has become the market leader in free gay
papers and is picked up by almost everyone for the listings, sex lines and
personal ads – although it is aimed at 18-35 year-olds. There's gossip
about the Madonnas and Johnny Depps of the world, razor-tongued
interviews, features, advice and reviews on music, cinema, fashion and
sex, and plenty of small ads and chat line numbers... basically everything
a gay boy needs to get by.

Diva ♀

⌨ *Millivres Ltd, Worldwide House, 116-134 Bayham Street, NW1*

☎ *020 7482 2576*   ✆ *020 7284 0329*

✉ *diva@gaytimes.co.uk*

✉ *www.gaytimes.co.uk*

✆ *Available from newsagents; £2 per issue, £24 for an annual subscription*

Founded in April, 1994, the UK's leading lesbian magazine comes out
monthly and offers a lifestyle read for all good dykes. It's crammed full
of celebrity interviews, comments on lesbian icons and culture, news,
reviews and contact ads.

Gay Times

- *Millivres Ltd, Worldwide House, 116-134 Bayham Street, London, NW1*
- *020 7482 2576   020 7284 0329*
- *info@gaytimes.co.uk*
- *www.gaytimes.co.uk*
- *Available from newsagents, £2.50*

Europe's best-selling gay and lesbian news and entertainment mag has a circulation of 57,000 and was started in 1974 under the title of *Him Exclusive*, becoming *Gay Times* in 1984. Features high-quality editorial, profiles gay celebrities, political comment, general gay news, theatre and book reviews, video reviews, and listings of pubs, clubs and groups.

GaytoZ

- *41 Cooks Road, London, SE17*
- *020 7793 7450   020 7820 1366*
- *info@gaytoz.com*
- *www.gaytoz.com*
- *Distributed free in the UK's gay pubs, clubs and cafés*

This listings directory of over 7,000 useful businesses and organisations for the lesbian, gay, bisexual and transgendered communities nationwide, includes couriers, gyms, promotion consultants, psychotherapists and trade unions, plumbers and builders, along with stained glass window-makers, interior designers, clubs, pubs and social groups. The GaytoZ website contains even more information, and includes links to gay directories around the globe.

G&L Humanist newsletter – see **G&L Humanist** (see p.109)

GBA newsletter – see **Gay Business Association** (see p.170)

NAM Publications

- *16a Clapham Common Southside, SW4*
- *020 7627 3200   020 7627 3101*
- *info@nam.org.uk*
- *www.aidsmap.com*

NAM produces the *HIV and AIDS Treatment Directory* bi-annually, the most comprehensive publication available in the UK about treatments and therapy, dealing with starting and changing treatment, body fat changes, side-effects and symptoms (£12.95 to sufferers). They also publish the *AIDS Treatment Update*, a monthly newsletter on treatments for HIV/AIDS (free to sufferers), giving info on new drugs, clinical trials and practical choices faced by people with HIV.

Now (North of Watford) UK

⌨ *All Points North Publications,*
Walk 34, Middleton Road, Leeds, LS27 8BB
☎ *08701 255 577*   ✎ *08701 298 020*
✐ *editor@nowuk.net*
✐ *www.nowuk.net*

Run by Terry George, the man behind Mr Gay UK, *Now* is a 64-page A4 full-colour magazine that tries to covers all aspects of gay life for the whole of Britain, turning away from what many see as the London bias in the gay press. The problem is that it takes on a bit much. It does have the widest distribution in the UK – at 90,000 – and is crammed with celebrity interviews, film, music, video and book reviews, arts features, travel, sport, clubbing, sex, gay news and product news... but hasn't the wit of *Boyz*.

Pink Paper

⌨ *Chronos Publishing, Cedar House, 72 Holloway Road, London, N7*
☎ *020 7296 6000*   ✎ *020 7957 0046*
✐ *editorial@pinkpaper.co.uk*
✎ *Distributed free in the UK's gay pubs & clubs, weekly (55,000 printrun)*

Launched in November 1987 as a watchdog for the gay community and record of British homosexual history, many thought the *Pink* sold out by relaunching as an A4 colour publication on sale in high-street newsagents – and promptly did an about-face when its publishers realised no-one would buy the mag. Once perceived as the intellectual, political gay newspaper, the *Pink* was considerably dumbed down in 1998 to become a 'news magazine', with less news, less discussion, less journalism, and more colour pictures. *Positive Times* was incorporated into the *Pink Paper* in 1999.

Positive Nation

⌨ *250 Kennington Lane, London, SE11*
☎ *020 7564 2121*   ✎ *020 7564 2128*
✐ *editor@positivenation.co.uk*
✐ *www.positivenation.co.uk*

By and for British HIV/AIDS sufferers (produced by the UK Coalition of People Living With HIV and AIDS; see p.80), the 20,000 copies of this intelligent, informed monthly freebie reach readers nationwide, including partners, parents, friends and family members affected by AIDS – making it the UK's No.1 HIV magazine. There are reports on treatments and research, expert interviews, international news, and self-help information on topics such as complementary therapies, exercise and supplements, as well as contact addresses and small ads. Distributed through clinics, day centres and hospitals, and by post.

QX International (Queer Xtra)

⌨ *Firststar Ltd, 2nd floor, 23 Denmark Street, London, WC2*

☎ *020 7379 7887*   ✎ *020 7379 7525*

✎ *qxmag@dircon.co.uk*

✎ *www.qxmag.co.uk*

✐ *Distributed free in London clubs, pubs and cafés*

Its motto is 'one scene, one magazine', and *QX* lives up to the pitch – its filled with images of bulging briefs and toned torsos. In a small format that's easy to read on the tube, it contains plenty of black and white photos sometimes interspersed with a bit of proper text – mainly the merits of various club nights and gay bars – and club listings, pub listings and queer contacts.

Stonewall newsletter – see **Stonewall**, p.114.

Time Out

⌨ *251 Tottenham Court Road, London, W1*

☎ *020 7813 3000*

✎ *guides@timeout.com*

✎ *www.timeout.com*

✐ *Available from newsagents, out Tuesday; £2.20*

London's weekly what's-on guide gives an exhaustive run-down of everything happening in the capital, in only the most PC of prose. It includes a good two or three page gay and lesbian section listing events, bar and club reviews, and featuring some punchy editorial.

TV/TS News

⌨ *Box 2534, London, WC1*

☎ *020 7609 1093*   ✎ *020 7609 6910*

✎ *webmaster@tv-ts.co.uk*

✎ *www.tv-ts.co.uk*

✐ *Distributed free from TV friendly venues or send a SAE to above address*

This free monthly magazine for transvestites and transsexuals, is packed full of information, with listings of TV/TS-friendly venues and clubs, special events and outings, services offered and small ads. Their website gives space to advertisers such as pubs, clubs, hairdressers, clothing shops, make-up and photographers, as well as detailing TV/TS-related news, events and support services.

PUBS & BARS

CENTRAL LONDON

79 CXR*

⌨ *79 Charing Cross Road, Soho, W1*

☎ *020 7734 0769*

🚇 *Leicester Square LU*

🕐 *Mon 1pm-2am, Tues-Sat 1pm-3am, Sun 1pm-10.30pm*

London's premier pick-up joint is so wonderfully uncoy about its role – there's no attitude or diversions here, just two floors of wall-to-wall men who are up for it. With a total capacity of around 300, the serious cruising gets going around 9pm when the lights are low and the music gets pumped up. Pub-priced drinks make for a reasonable hit on your purse, and there are games machines for the hooked.

Admiral Duncan

⌨ *54 Old Compton Street, Soho, W1*

☎ *020 7437 5300*

🚇 *Leicester Square LU*

🕐 *Mon-Sat noon-11pm, Sun noon-10.30pm*

This traditional pub has been completely refurbished since the nail bomb explosion in April 1999, but still packs in a full complement every night after work. It's neither trendy nor sleazy, just a good traditional pub with prices to match.

Bar Aquda*

⌨ *13-14 Maiden Lane, Covent Garden, WC2*

☎ *020 7557 9891*

🚇 *Charing Cross BR/LU, Covent Garden LU*

🕐 *Daily noon-late*

A trendy stylishly modern gaff for professional types, Bar Aquda's name is a pun on the name of the fish – and fittingly has a long menu of fish dishes during the day. The former Peacock (and the old Attic Bar, which is now the upstairs toilet) bills itself as a hangout for sorted boyz and girlz, and by night turns into a posey drinkery.

The Edge

The Box ♀

⌨ *32-34 Monmouth Street, Covent Garden, WC2*

☎ *020 7240 5828*

🚇 *Leicester Square LU*

🕐 *Mon-Sat 11am-11pm*

A Continental café by day, a trendy bar by night, The Box attracts a young mixed crowd who all look like they've just come out of a marketing meeting. Art on the walls, stripped wood and pavement seating: it's the closest thing to Paris we've got. There's a tasty (but pricey) selection of food until 5.30pm, when the place turns into a funky space with dim lighting and candles. Friday: Girl Friday – women-only pre-club night (8pm-11pm; free).

Brief Encounter

⌨ *42 St Martin's Lane, Covent Garden, WC2*

☎ *020 7557 9851*

🚇 *Charing Cross BR/LU*

🕐 *Mon-Sat 11am-11pm, Sun noon-10.30pm*

Brief Encounter has lost its edge in recent years. When it opened back in the late 1980s, it was the premier place in London to sample local trade, but it now reeks of the Marie Celeste, and it's all a bit seedy looking – like a New York bar circa 1982. The upstairs bar has mirrors all over the walls and a handful of punters, while the busier downstairs Basement Club Bar has a more 70s clubby ambiance – in a Scarborough kind of way.

Rocket

Candy Bar* ♀

▣ *23-24 Bateman Street, Soho, W1*

☏ *020 7437 1977*

▦ *Tottenham Court Road LU*

◷ *Mon & Tues 5pm-1am, Wed-Sat 5pm-3am, Sun 5pm-11pm;*

⊛ *Fri & Sat free £5 after 9pm, Thurs after 10pm £3*

The UK's first seven-night-a-week lesbian club-bar has moved around the corner from Carlisle Street to just a few doors down from Mildred's (see p.163), and is the premier venue for lesbians in town, attracting women of all ages, especially trendy 25-40s; gay men are allowed in as guests. The upstairs lounge has huge windows looking out onto Greek Street and is crowded out with an after-work crowd every night. Downstairs, the basement club bar is a more laid-back, funky space that hosts a karaoke night. It's all stylish, fun and lively.

Bar Code*

▣ *3-4 Archer Street, Soho, W1*

☏ *020 7734 3342*

▦ *Piccadilly Circus LU*

◷ *Mon-Sat 1pm-1am, Sun 2pm-10.30pm;*

Basement Bar Thurs-Sat 9pm-1am

Its revamp in 1998 made Bar Code even roomier and more comfortable, and extended opening hours make it even more popular. This stylish, air-conditioned venue around the corner from The Yard attracts a 30-ish unpretentious mixed gay crowd, with a lot of Muscle Marys. The basement has a DJ spinning house music for a good-sized dancefloor that gets really packed out later on.

Comptons of Soho TV

▣ *51-53 Old Compton Street, Soho, W1*

☏ *020 7479 7961*

▦ *Leicester Square/Piccadilly Circus LU*

◷ *Mon-Sat noon-11pm, Sun noon-10.30pm*

Comptons started the whole Old Compton Street gay phenomenon when it opened in the mid 1980s. It's still always packed, with a mixed age range of gay boys who like a no-frills drinking hole. Downstairs is the young crowd on the pull – and upstairs is a less cruisy refuge where you can look out over the Street and where food is served daily (noon-6pm) and a DJ spins LOUD pumping garage, house and handbag sounds (Mon-Wed, Fri & Sat from 7pm). It's all unpretentious and attitude-free – and the most profitable gay pub in the country.

The Edge*

🖃 *11 Soho Square, Soho, W1*
☎ *020 7439 1313*
✎ *www.theedge-group.co.uk*
🚇 *Tottenham Court Road LU*
🕐 *Mon-Sat 12noon-1am, Sun 12noon-10.30pm*

The Edge is a stylish haunt for West End professionals, and the best of its kind in London. It's sophisticated without being snooty, smart without being designer, arty without attitude. The three floors cater for everyone – a no-frills bar on the ground floor, a groovy lounge on the first and a more intimate café-bar on the second. Food is served until 6pm. Thursday: Open Decks – up-and-coming DJ showcase (7pm-1am).

Escape* ♀

🖃 *10 Brewer Street, Soho, W1*
☎ *020 7734 2626*
✎ *www.kudosgroup.com*
🚇 *Leicester Square/Piccadilly Circus LU*
🕐 *Mon-Sat 4pm-3am, Sun 4pm-10.30pm*

There's something sexy about Escape. Kitted out in nouveau industrial decor, the former seedy Piano Bar under Madame Jo Jo's now attracts a very mixed designer crowd. This café by day and gay dance bar at night features club events, guest DJs and regular PAs late on. The music is funky and reasonably loud, with jazz and blues during the day and house and soul at night. Trade queue-jump tickets available every Saturday night.

First Out ♀

🖃 *52 St Giles High Street, Soho, W1*
☎ *020 7240 8042*
🚇 *Tottenham Court Road LU*
🕐 *Mon-Sat 10am-11pm, Sun 11am-10.30pm*

First Out is a bit tucked away behind Centre Point Tower, but it's worth finding. A veggie café by day, serving tasty and reasonably priced tucker, First Out becomes a smoochy bar at night when the lights come down. If you can make it down the perilous staircase, the intimate basement bar is the place to be in the evening. Women-only night, Friday 8-11pm.

Freedom*

⌨ *60-66 Wardour Street, Soho, W1*

☏ *020 7734 0071*

🚇 *Leicester Square LU*

🕐 *Mon-Sat 11am-3am, Sun 11am-midnight*

Image is the word that springs to mind when it comes to Freedom. It's wall-to-wall goatee beards, square, thick-framed black glasses, designer bottled beer, cocktails at £7, and long and short drinks. That said, it's very popular with the trendy set, partly due to its late-night opening, when anyone who can get in does. The menu isn't their strength, mainly running to burgers and pizzas and an all-day breakfast, but they come into their own with ten styles of coffee. The basement sees various events, like clothes shows, launches and theatrical performances.

Glass Bar* ♀

⌨ *West Lodge, 190 Euston Road, Euston, NW1*

☏ *020 7387 6184*

🚇 *Euston BR/LU*

🕐 *Mon-Fri 5pm-till late, Sat 6pm-11.30pm*

🎟 *membership charge*

A private members women-only bar in a fabulous building in front of Euston Station. The ambiance is classy and chilled, and two bars and all-day snacks keeps the mood light. The midweek night gets very busy. Wednesday: Wednesday's Child – midweek party night with pop, indie and trash (7pm-11.30pm; £1), Saturday: smooth soul and R'n'B night.

Halfway 2 Heaven

⌨ *7 Duncannon Street, Charing Cross, WC2*

☏ *020 7321 2791*

🚇 *Charing Cross BR/LU*

🕐 *Mon-Sat noon-11pm, Sun noon-10.30pm*

A pub that prides itself on hanging onto its traditional feel in the style-conscious West End. Halfway attracts a mix of businessmen, loyal regulars and disco-boys who shun the noisier, posier venues of Soho for a chatty venue that admittedly looks a bit like a Berni inn. The ground floor is quite cruisy, while the basement bar is a large, quieter space that is good for a chinwag. It's handy for that final stagger before Charing Cross or Heaven. They also host regular karaoke and quiz nights.

Jacomos

⌨ *88-89 Cowcross Street, Clerkenwell, EC1*

☎ *020 7553 7641*

🚇 *Farringdon BR/LU*

🕐 *Mon-Fri noon-11pm*

The former He/She bar was reopened in 1998 as the smart Jacomos. During the day it's a very mixed café where nearby media people come for lunch, but in the evenings it attracts suits and workers from nearby Bart's Hospital, and boyz on their way to Turnmills. It's mostly men who come here for the comfortable surrounds – sofas, chairs and tables, stripped floors and understated designer decor – but Mondays and Wednesdays sees a good lesbian turnout. Drinks are cheaper than in the West End, with both bottled and draught beer, and food is served from noon-3pm, with jacket potatoes (£3.50-£4.50), chicken burgers and bangers and mash (£6.50).

Jonathan's

⌨ *First floor, 16 Irving Street, Leicester Square, W1*

☎ *020 7930 4770*

🚇 *Leicester Square LU*

🕐 *Mon-Sat 5pm-11pm, Sun 5pm-10.30pm* ♦ *membership fee*

Jonathan's is a flashback to the old days. For around fifty years, this private 'theatre bar' has been serving up behind closed doors to members and their guests. It's just off Leicester Square, and still has a small, loyal following of punters who all know each other, making for a chatty night out. Decor is pure queeny theatrical, with signed theatre posters and pictures of icons. There are also very cheap drinks.

The King's Arms

⌨ *23 Poland Street, Soho, W1*

☎ *020 7734 5907*

🚇 *Oxford Circus LU*

🕐 *Mon-Sat 11am-11pm, Sun noon-10.30pm*

The King's Arms is tucked away off Oxford Street, a bit of a hike from Soho. It's been around for years, and is still a traditional patterned-carpet and wood-panelling type of place, without attitude, huge plate-glass windows or designer labels. It's popular with a clony cruisy crowd, with reasonably loud music downstairs and a quieter, more relaxed bar upstairs. Several gay social groups meet here (see p.185, 189). Sunday: karaoke (7.30pm-10.30pm).

Ku Bar

⊞ *75 Charing Cross Road, Soho, W1*

☎ *020 7437 4303*

✉ *bar@ku-bar.co.uk*

🚇 *Leicester Square LU*

🕑 *Mon-Sat noon-11pm, Sun 1pm-10.30pm*

This stylish bar is popular with a sophisticated late-20s crowd and a few suits. The decor is elegant – stripped floorboards, dozens of wrought-iron candle-holders, red velvet seating and a stunning wall mosaic next to the bar. It's not really cruisy, rather very low-key and mellow. Upstairs is quieter and darker, with tables for intimate chit-chat, and yet more candles. It's open as a café throughout the day, and the menu emphasises healthy eating. Happy Hour cocktails from 4pm-7pm.

Manto Soho

Kudos

🖳 *10 Adelaide Street, Covent Garden, WC2*

☏ *020 7379 4573*

🚇 *Charing Cross BR/LU*

🕐 *Mon-Sat 11am-11pm, Sun 11am-10.30pm*

Regular décor updates ensures that Kudos stays at the front of gay chic – and packed out with muscle boys and designer denizens every night. By day a brasserie and café-bar that serves food until 6pm, the ground floor has huge plate-glass windows so customers can eye up those tottering towards Charing Cross Station – and so the world can look in and see them. Downstairs is cruisier with a large music video screen, banquettes in alcoves and attracting a lot of black, Latino and Asian men. There are exhibitions from gay artists, and regular drink promotions. If you want to skip the clubbing queues on Saturday, you can buy queue-jump tickets here for Heaven (see p.26) and the Fridge (see p.26).

Manto Soho*

🖳 *30 Old Compton Street, Soho, W1*

☏ *020 7494 2756*

✍ *www.mantogroup.com*

🚇 *Leicester Square LU*

🕐 *Mon-Sat noon-midnight, Sun noon-10.30pm;*
basement lounge bar Mon-Fri 5pm-midnight

With four floors to choose from, Mancunian Manto's is the new breed of gay bars – think Prêt à Manger meets Terence Conran. It opened in summer 2000 with a big media frenzy, and has been full of style-conscious people, straight and gay, male and female ever since. The ground floor serves food during the day and turns into an atmospheric, laid-back bar at night. The basement is a candlelit lounge with DJs from top London clubs after 9pm, and the first-floor restaurant serves from 5pm, with the ground floor bar also offering food (noon-7pm).

The Quebec*

🖳 *12 Old Quebec Street, Marble Arch, W1*

☏ *020 7629 6159*

✍ *quebec@all-man.com*

✍ *www.all-man.com*

🚇 *Marble Arch LU*

🕐 *Mon-Thurs 12noon-1am, Fri-Sat 12noon-2am, Sun 1pm-10.30pm*

Nicknamed the 'elephant's graveyard', this traditional pub behind Oxford Street has had a gay clientele since 1945. Said elephants take the form of older men with a bit of cash, out on the prowl for more nubile youngsters. The revamp in 1998 dressed the place up a bit – the ground floor is still a low-key drinking hole with a vaguely stylish traditional feel, while the basement bar opens in the evenings and has the ambiance of a dimly-lit nightclub in deepest Cumbria, with a small dance floor and men circling ready to pounce. Monday is leather night, with DJs Thursday to Sunday.

Retro Bar

🖃 *2 George Court, off the Strand, Charing Cross, WC2*

☎ *020 7321 2811*

🚇 *Charing Cross BR/LU*

🕓 *Mon-Sat 5pm-11pm, Sun 5pm-10.30pm*

In an alleyway off the Strand next to Halifax building, the old George has kept its traditional feel, despite turning itself into a shrine to 70s and 80s icons – Abba, Boy George, George Michael and the like. Beneath the beautific portraits on the walls, you can listen to classic and alternative sounds spun by DJs later on in the evening. Make the most of the pub-priced drinks, and soak up a genuinely friendly atmosphere. Upstairs is another bar with more comfortable seating and fewer people.

Rupert Street

🖃 *50 Rupert Street, Soho, W1*

☎ *020 7292 7141*

🚇 *Piccadilly Circus LU*

🕓 *Mon-Sat noon-11pm, Sun noon-10.30pm*

Style-conscious is the word for Rupert Street and the people who hang out – sorry, languish – here. It opened in 1997, closed in October 2000 for a spruce-up but emerged with the same posy formula. Attracting twentysomethings with slick hairstyles and extensive wardrobes, admittedly it does look good, with designer lighting, trademark splashes of colour on the walls and huge picture windows. There's a comfy lounge area with sofas at the back, but drinks are pricey. Food is served from noon until 5pm.

St George's Tavern

🖃 *14 Belgrave Road, Victoria, SW1*

☎ *020 7592 9911*

🚇 *Victoria BR/LU*

🕓 *Mon-Sat 11am-11pm, Sun noon-10.30pm*

On the corner of Belgrave Road behind Victoria station, this straight pub has a lesbian night in the basement, when girls get together to fight to the death over pool and a raffle. The atmosphere is friendly, and the place doesn't get too busy, so you really can work the room.

Rupert Street

Soho's Strippers

⌖ *Raymond Reveue Bar, 7-12 Walker's Court,*
off Brewer Street, Soho, W1

☎ *020 7734 1593*

🚇 *Piccadilly Circus LU*

🕐 *Sun 6pm-11pm* ✆ *£7*

Sunday's Ambient Bar at the infamous Raymond Revue Bar appeals to girls on hen nights and gay boys who like to bask in the decadence of yesteryear. It's all a bit raunchy with hunky topless waiters and male strippers who get right down to the buff – dubbed by the management as the 'greatest male strippers of the world'. And you get two bars to choose from.

The Stag*

⌖ *15 Bressenden Place, Victoria, SW1*

☎ *020 7828 7287*

🚇 *Victoria BR/LU*

🕐 *Mon-Thurs noon-midnight, Fri noon-2am, Sat 5pm-2am, Sun noon-10.30pm; charge Fri & Sat after 10.30pm*

This prefab 60s octagonal building is stuck on an off-putting plot amongst the concrete greyness of Victoria's officescape, but painted bright red – you can't miss it. Inside it looks more traditional – apart from the tinsel and streamers – with typical dim lighting, games machines and a besuited after-work crowd stopping off en route to the station. Tuesday & Sunday: night karaoke, Friday & Saturday: cabaret & DJ, Saturday: men only, Sunday: roast lunch & cabaret.

Vespa Lounge* ♀

▱ *15 St Giles High Street, Covent Garden, WC2*

☏ *020 7836 8956*

▱ *Tottenham Court Road LU*

☺ *Daily 6pm-11pm*

Opposite First Out, the Vespa hosts laid-back and friendly social nights for girls and their men friends (as guests only). The place is all soft colours, smooth edges and subtle lighting, with charty music and a funky feel. There's a small bar and a pool table. Bi Women meet here on Wednesdays at 7pm, and there are monthly Sunday comedy nights.

Village Soho

▱ *81 Wardour Street, Soho, W1*

☏ *020 7434 2124*

▱ *Leicester Square/Piccadilly Circus LU*

☺ *Mon-Sat 11.30am-11pm, Sun noon-10.30pm*

The bar that made Soho gay is a cruisy Continental-style place over two floors, with a café area and picture windows at street level. It attracts the trendy, the beautiful, the ordinary... It was refurbished in early 1996, so the ground floor bar and coffee shop has a vaguely shipwreck theme, with roughly sanded floorboards and yellowed walls. The front bar is more Prêt à Manger industrial, as is the upstairs bar. Food noon-5pm.

West Central*

▱ *29-30 Lisle Street, Soho, W1*

☏ *020 7479 7981*

▱ *Leicester Square LU*

☺ *Mon-Sat noon-11pm, Sun noon-10.30pm;*

basement Mon-Thurs 10.30pm-2am, Fri-Sat 10.30pm-3am

Gaydom takes on Chinatown! The old Polar Bear pub behind the Warner cinema complex reopened in mid-1998 as a bender venue, with three floors of men. The ground floor is no-frills, with big video screens and pub-priced drinks, while the upstairs theatre bar is plush and cosy with a non-stop soundtrack of shows and theatre divas. The basement club bar kicks off on Monday night. Friday: Shinky Shonky – retro club night with cabaret (10.30pm-3am; £5), Saturday: Fairylea – campy gay disco (9pm–3am; £5).

The Yard

57 Rupert Street, Soho, W1

020 7437 2652

Leicester Square / Piccadilly Circus LU

Mon-Sat noon-11pm, Sun noon-10.30pm; upstairs bar Mon-Sat 6pm 11pm, Sun 2pm-10.30pm

The Yard is now an institution. It may be on a dodgy street, but it's smart and stylish, and the combination of cheap drinks and relaxed atmosphere packs them in after work every night. Now that they've glassed in the front of the narrow passage, there's a sense of style about walking in, and the whole place has a more open, spacious feel. The downstairs bar is still about as welcoming as a Spanish toilet block – with hard terracotta floor tiles, harsh lighting and stark white walls – while the upstairs bar is all exposed brickwork and wooden ceiling, cigarette smoke and a few big armchairs. A bit like a barn with a drinking license. The place still attracts the same besuited, unpretentious after-work crowd, and guys around 25-35 later on. It's very media but without the poncey posturing of some other upmarket bars.

Escape

NORTH LONDON

Bar Fusion

⌨ *45 Essex Road, Islington, N1*

☎ *020 7688 2882*

🚇 *Angel LU*

🕑 *Mon-Fri 2pm-midnight, Sat-Sun 1pm-midnight*

This fun and deadly stylish café-bar is popular with young-ish professional Islington gays and lesbians, who come here for the sultry South American music and the arty, sexy ambiance. It serves up a mean coffee and light menu during the day, and turns into a chatty drinking hole come the evening.

Black Cap*

⌨ *171 Camden High Street, Camden Town, NW1*

☎ *020 7428 2721*

🚇 *Camden Town LU*

🕑 *Mon-Thurs noon-2am, Fri & Sat noon-3am, Sun noon-12.30am (cabaret bar from 7pm)*

This famous cabaret bar is London's premier drag venue, with all the big names appearing here under the watchful eye of Regina Fong. On the ground floor, the very popular cabaret bar is packed out every night with a mixed crowd who come for the entertainment and cruisy dancing to resident DJs. The quieter upstairs Shufflewick Bar is all pictures, borders, striped paper and swags, with the splendid, floodlit Fong Terrace outdoor patio. There's also a limited menu.

Blush* ♀

⌨ *8 Cazenove Road, Stoke Newington, N16*

☎ *020 7923 9202*

🚇 *Stoke Newington BR*

🕑 *Daily 5pm-midnight*

This predominantly lesbian bar-café opened in 2000 in an area that's chalking up quite a few bent venues. It's a great place – arty but not pretentious, welcoming and relaxed, with a genuinely chatty owner and punters. There's art on walls, regular bar promotions, and a relaxed, no-attitude stance. Downstairs is discreetly lit with leather sofas and chairs to chill out in, and a pool table for the more competitive. Blush's food is worth shouting about – fabulous organic, free-range creations, such as mountainous club sandwiches, tasty Greek salads and wondrous home-made cheesecakes. There's a beer garden. Wednesday: free pool all night, Friday: doubles night, Saturday: women-only, Sunday: live music.

Central Station TV*

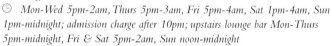

   37 Wharfdale Road, King's Cross, N1

   020 7278 3294

   www.centralstation.co.uk

   King's Cross BR/LU

   Mon-Wed 5pm-2am, Thurs 5pm-3am, Fri 5pm-4am, Sat 1pm-4am, Sun 1pm-midnight; admission charge after 10pm; upstairs lounge bar Mon-Thurs 5pm-midnight, Fri & Sat 5pm-2am, Sun noon-midnight

Since early 1992 this pub has become one of the stalwarts of gay London, and seems to have taken over where the Lesbian and Gay Centre left off as meeting place for social and sporting clubs. The pub manages to combine many facets that add up to success – it is comfortable enough to sit and talk for hours and drink real ale, there are strippers and cabaret acts every night, it's raunchy and sexy in the underground basement disco – Glory Hole celebrated its eighth birthday in 2000 (see p.36) – and the upstairs lounge bar serves food and coffee.

The Flag

   24 Crouch Hill, Crouch End, N4

   020 7272 4748

   Crouch Hill BR

   Mon-Sat noon-11pm, Sun noon-10.30pm

This friendly traditional pub is embracing the gay way by changing its name from The Racecourse to The Flag, and displays one proudly for local Crouch Enders. It's a typical traditional pub in the suburbs, with pool and darts, and the odd charity or party night.

King Edward VI*

   25 Bromfield Street, Islington, N1

   020 7704 0745

   Angel LU

   Daily noon-midnight

Joe Orton was one of the Edward's regulars back in the 1960s and the Edward still remains a favourite gaff with local guys, even though many of the buildings around it have been bulldozed for redevelopment, and the place stands in a real no-man's land. The Edward has recently been refurbished and now has two bars, rather than the bar/café arrangement of recent years. It's always quite cruisy, especially from around 9pm when it gets very busy with a sociable all-male crowd. The upstairs bar is more relaxed with video screens and quieter background music – a good alternative to the testosterone filled atmosphere of downstairs.

King William IV

⌖ *75-77 Hampstead High Street, Hampstead, NW3*

☏ *020 7435 5747*

🚇 *Hampstead LU*

🕐 *Mon-Sat noon-11pm, Sun noon-10.30pm*

Smack on Hampstead's snooty high street, the Willy is reputedly the oldest gay pub in Britain, but has been revamped to offer a more contemporary feel (without loosing its popular summer beer garden and open fires). The two separate bars (one non-smoking) are stocked by locals and people who drive over to pretend they're locals, just to bask in Hampstead's glory. The Willy does a reasonably priced four-course lunch on Sundays and is just ten minutes' walk away from the Heath.

Krystal's Bar

⌖ *97 Stoke Newington Road, Stoke Newington, N16*

☏ *020 7254 1967*

🖊 *www.krystals.org*

🚇 *Dalston Kingsland BR*

🕐 *Mon-Fri 5pm-11pm, Sat 1pm-11pm, Sun 1pm-10.30pm*

This cabaret bar on the corner of Palatine Road between Stokie and Dalston opened in mid 2000. Subtle it ain't, with chandeliers, mirror balls, flying pigs up the walls and a wall of flowers behind the bar, but you can have a laugh here. There are drag shows, karaoke and killer pool, and the regular party nights pack in 200 people. The gay/lesbian split is about equal, and punters tend to be in their mid to late twenties and upwards. Krystal's serves all-day cappuccinos and lattes. Tuesday: free pool, Saturday & Sunday: cabaret, and a monthly fancy dress ball.

Liquid Lounge*

⌖ *257-259 Pentonville Road, King's Cross, N1*

☏ *020 7724 0919*

🚇 *King's Cross BR/LU*

🕐 *Fri 6pm-2am, Sat 8pm-3am*

What was the Bell (remember the tea dances there boys?) is now a gay alternative music bar, playing a funky mix of kitsch retro music – an ideal pre-drink place before Popstarz. An outgoing, lush, louche venue that pulls in the lounging lizard crowd. Friday: Official Pre-Popstarz Piss Up – with queue-jump tickets (6pm-1am; £5, £3 before 10pm), Saturday: Miss-Shapes – gay and lesbian club with girl-oriented indie, pop, swing and alternative sounds (6pm-3am; £5, free before 8pm, £3 before 10pm).

The Londesborough

⌨ *36 Barbauld Road, Stoke Newington, N16*

☎ *020 7254 5865*

🚌 *Angel LU, then bus 73*

🕐 *Mon-Sat 3pm-midnight, Sun 3pm-10.30pm*

Discreet isn't the word for this. On a residential street, this ordinary-looking pub on the 73 bus route doesn't have a gay flag or a even a sign out advertising its presence – just a traditional Victorian façade with 'The Londesborough' written on it. Inside, local gay men and women come in equal numbers for a no-attitude, no-drugs night out. It's straight during the daytime, but by night there are regular parties, pool table, darts and pinball.

Lower Ground

⌨ *269 West End Lane, West Hampstead, NW6*

☎ *020 7431 2211*

🚌 *West Hampstead LU*

🕐 *Mon-Sat 5pm-2am, Sun noon-midnight*

This 200-capacity basement bar and club has gone through quite a few makeovers in its five-year history, and it still hasn't quite hit upon the right formula. Gay-only on Monday, mixed rest of the week.

The Oak Bar* ♀

⌨ *79 Green Lanes, Stoke Newington, N16*

☎ *020 7354 2791*

🖉 *www.oakbar.co.uk*

🚌 *Manor House LU, then bus 141 or 341*

🕐 *Mon-Thurs 5pm-midnight, Fri & Sat 5pm-2am, Sun 1pm-midnight*

This friendly women's bar welcomes mainly lesbians but also gay men from all over London to enjoy its mellow atmosphere and winning combination of live cabaret, DJs, quiz and chill-out nights. It's not mega-smart or posey, but just one big room with comfy old leather armchairs, tables and chairs and a huge TV screen showing MTV music videos or premier league matches, with a pool table completing the picture. Friday: Girl Rock – (live bands), first Saturday: Cagney & Lacy – 70s and 80s night (9pm-2am; free, £3 after 10pm), second Saturday: Saturday Beaver – (9pm-2am; £3), third Saturday: Hoppa!!! – Greek/Turkish/Arabic/Bhangra /Rai sounds (9pm-2am; £5, £3 before 10.30pm with flyer), last Saturday: Liberté (9pm-3am; free, £3 after 10pm), Sunday: karaoke with tequila slammers on the hour (8pm-midnight).

Ram Club Bar

🏠 *39 Queen's Head Street, Islington, N1*

☎ *020 7354 0576*

🚇 *Angel LU or Essex Road BR*

🕐 *Tues-Fri 3pm-11pm, Sat & Sun 1pm-11pm*

The former Ram and Teasel is still the same friendly, small, traditional gay-owned and -run pub with a name change and a lick of paint. Admittedly the ambience is now more that of a US-style bar, with dark walls, flashing lights and a background club beat, but it's still attracting a constant affable stream of locals who play pool and darts – they've even organised a darts team. Drinks are cheaper than typical Islington prices, and the management are looking into opening a conservatory. Friday: 70s and 80s, Saturday: 60s, 70s & 80s music and free buffet, Sunday lunch: free buffet, Sunday night: cabaret.

White Hart*

🏠 *51 The Hale, Tottenham, N17*

☎ *020 8808 5049*

🚇 *Tottenham Hale LU*

🕐 *Mon-Thurs 7pm-1am, Fri & Sat 7pm-2am, Sun noon-midnight*

This large Victorian pub looks a bit the worse for wear, with a handful of straight boys playing pool in the main lounge bar. At the back is a smaller, plusher gay bar, with London's most theatrically decorated cabaret stage hosting acts every night apart from Tuesday. Upstairs is a large disco bar with a good-sized crowd packing in for the classic anthems at the weekend. The pub serves up Sunday lunches. Wednesday: casting couch, Thursday: Jazz and Blues, Friday: karaoke, and Saturday: Cabaret.

SOUTH LONDON

Bar 68

⌨ *68 Brigstock Road, Thornton Heath, Surrey*

☎ *020 8665 0683*

🚇 *Thornton Heath BR*

🕐 *Mon-Fri noon-11pm, Sat-Sun 2pm-11pm*

The former Noah's Ark makes for a nice night out, with a quiet, mixed crowd who will actually chat to you in a relaxed atmosphere. Friday & Saturday: live cabaret, Sunday: karaoke and quiz night.

The Brewery Tap*

⌨ *78 Lingham Street, Stockwell, SW9*

☎ *020 7738 6683*

🚇 *Stockwell LU*

🕐 *Mon-Fri 5pm-11pm, Sat-Sun 7pm-11pm*

Opposite a hideous 1960s warehouse and between a lorry parking lot and high-rise council housing, this is deepest darkest Stockwell with warts – the Brewery Tap wins the prize for London's second worst-situated pub (after Central Station in Walthamstow). It's tacky and in need of a good sprucing up, but provides a friendly, bog-standard traditional pub for locals – everyone here seems to know each other. For boys and girls who don't grapple with image or the latest Donna Karen.

The Cock Tavern* TV

⌨ *340 Kennington Road, Kennington, SE11*

☎ *020 7735 1013*

🚇 *Kennington or Oval LU*

🕐 *Mon-Sat noon-1am, Sun noon-10.30pm*

This stylish bar next to Kennington Green is of the stripped floors, pine tables and big windows variety, and attracts an attitude-free crowd of gays and lesbians – and even straight couples. It's a very slick place – with a great sound system (but not too loud), regular theme nights (beach parties, *Grease* and *Priscilla* nights etc.), tasteful surroundings, pool table, 54 TV screens lining the walls (they've been known to host film afternoons), reasonable drink prices and regular promotions. The Gay Bikers Association meet here regularly. Food served Monday-Friday noon-3pm, Sunday roast. Monday: Divas on Video night, Tuesday: quiz, Wednesday: cheap cocktails, Thursday: Shaft – 60s, 70s, 80s night, Friday: DJ, Saturday: Camp – theme night, Sunday: karaoke.

The Crown & Anchor TV

⌂ *19 Park Road, Bromley, Kent, BR1*

☎ *020 8460 5533*

🚃 *Bromley North BR*

🕐 *Mon-Sat noon-11pm, Sun noon-10.30pm*

In a residential sidestreet close to Bromley North station, the Crown & Anchor is a good old-fashioned mixed pub where you can down a couple of pints and make new local friends. The sister pub of The Little Apple in Kennington (see p.142).

Dukes (Duke of Cambridge)* TV

⌂ *349 Kennington Lane, Vauxhall, SE11*

☎ *020 7793 0903*

🚃 *Vauxhall BR/LU*

🕐 *Mon-Tues 8pm-1am, Wed-Sat 9pm-2am, Sun 4pm-12.30am*

This big Victorian pub is the unofficial home to London's gay male chubby community. It's a bit grungy and dark and gets pretty warm late on in the evening, but the punters don't seem to mind. They tend towards the rougher, over-30 end of the market. Friday night's the big one of the week, packing in up to 400 big men for a full-on cruising session, and on other nights things generally pick up after 10.30pm. They have pinball, pool and a truly lush beer garden for use in better weather. Tuesday: Lines and Bears – line dancing, Thursday: karaoke, Friday: Chunkies – men only, Saturday: Energy – pre-club night with top DJs and cabaret/strippers (9pm-2am; £4), Sunday: BearHug – 4pm-10.30pm.

The Fort*

⌂ *131 Grange Road, Borough, SE1*

☎ *020 7237 7742*

🚃 *Elephant & Castle BR/LU*

🕐 *Mon-Fri 8pm-11pm, Sat-Sun 2pm-11pm*

The horniest venue in town is a no-holds barred cruisefest with plenty of dark and discreet corners for those intimate moments. The under-wear nights here are a sight to behold, with jocks, pouches and tangas on display, while the dress-code nights pack in a slew of up-for-it men with no inhibitions whatsoever. Monday & Tuesday: Cruise in the Dark, Wednesday: leather, rubber and uniform night, Thursday: underwear party, Friday: Cruise in the Dark, Saturday: Blackout night, Sunday: underwear party (PM), Sunday evening: Cruise in the Dark.

George & Dragon

- 2 Blackheath Hill, Greenwich, SE10
- ☎ 020 8691 3764
- Greenwich BR/DLR, then 199 bus
- 🕐 Sun-Thurs 6pm-1pm, Fri-Sat 6pm-3am

The pub prices and no-attitude atmosphere bring in the boys, but the George looks a bit down at heel – dark and gloomy, lino floors and not too many punters. But this trad boozer has its fans, who come for the cabaret four nights a week, the summer beer garden and regular strippers. Monday: karaoke, Tuesday: piano bar, Wednesday: cabaret or stripper, Thursday: quiz, Friday-Sunday: cabaret.

Gladstone Arms TV

- 64 Lant Street, Borough, SE1
- ☎ 020 7407 3962
- Borough LU
- 🕐 Mon-Fri 12noon-11pm, Sat 1pm-11pm, Sun 2pm-10.30pm

With regular theme nights, cheap drinks and an eternally friendly atmosphere, The Gladstone makes a viable alternative to the West End. One bar and two rooms, with the odd elderly local in situ who has obviously been going there for decades. It's cosy, quiet and friendly.

The Gloucester

🖼 *1 King William Walk, Greenwich, SE10*

☎ *020 8293 6131*

🚇 *Greenwich BR*

🕐 *Mon-Sat noon-11pm, Sun noon-10.30pm*

Greenwich's best gay pub was tarted up in late 1998 and has lost a bit of its appeal by buying into mainstream gay. During the day a lot of straight American tourists turn up to take a breather in their Greenwich sightseeing schedule – hope they enjoy the copies of *QX* lying around. The pub gets very crowded late in the week and at weekends, drawing a mixed age group with a lot of younger boys and locals going in groups. There's a resident DJ and regular cabaret, and food is available daily from noon until 5pm.

Goose and Carrot TV

🖼 *128 Wellesley Road, Croydon, Surrey, CR0*

☎ *020 8689 3473*

🚇 *East Croydon/West Croydon BR*

🕐 *Mon-Sat noon-11pm, Sun noon-10.30pm*

The former Horse and Jockey has been renamed and forms a welcoming mixed venue, with the basement Pink Parrot Dive Bar being exclusively gay. The pub is transvestite-friendly and provides changing facilities. There is a beer garden during the summer months.

Kazbar*

🖼 *50 Clapham High Street, Clapham, SW4*

☎ *020 7622 0070*

🚇 *Clapham Common LU*

🕐 *Mon-Fri 4pm-midnight, Sat noon-midnight, Sun noon-11.30pm*

The sister venue to Escape, Kudos and Zanzibar in Brighton, Kazbar is a stylish, friendly corner bar further down the road from the Two Brewers, and the best of the gay and lesbian venues in Clapham. The formula is similar to the rest of the Kudos group – modern decor, a good range of reasonably priced drinks and plenty of promotions. During the week it's mainly locals who hang out here, but weekends see an influx of clubgoers on their way to Substation South, the Crash Bar and the Fridge.

The Little Apple*

▨ *98 Kennington Lane, Kennington, SE11*

☏ *020 7735 2039*

🚇 *Kennington LU*

🕐 *Mon-Sat noon-11pm, Sun noon-10.30pm*

This 30s pub looks like your Aunt Ada's front room, with patterned carpet, subtle lighting and a real cosy feel. The atmosphere's good, with a chatty crowd and good lesbian and gay mix. They have a pool table and weekly competitions, and a quiz night, and there's a beer garden out back for the better weather. The one downer is it's a bit of a walk from the tube.

Man*

▨ *82 Great Suffolk Street, Borough, SE1*

☏ *020 7928 3223*

✍ *david.warrior@ukonline.co.uk*

🚇 *Borough or Southwark LU*

🕐 *Mon-Fri 8pm-1am, Sat 2pm-1am, Sun 2pm-midnight*

Formerly the notorious A-Bar, Man has a re-vamped decore but the same cruisy dress-code and attitude – in the leather, rubber, uniform and underwear areas. It's a magnet for hard, horny guys, whether skinheads, muscle boys, fetishists with tats and the like; and what goes on in the dark, moody bar is anyone's guess. The Gay Skinheads group meets here on the first and third Friday of the month (see p.192). Saturday: under-ware (2pm-8pm), followed by cruise session (8pm-1am), Sunday: under-ware (2pm-8pm), with cruise session (8pm-midnight).

Prohibition Bar*

▨ *The Greenhouse, 2a Sunny Hill Road, Streatham, SW16*

☏ *020 8677 7562*

🚇 *Streatham/Streatham Hill BR*

🕐 *Daily noon-late*

You have to ring the bell of the Greenhouse Café to be let into this very friendly tiny upstairs private drinking club (no membership charge). It's gay-owned and run – although it's straight-friendly – and attracts mainly mixed gay locals, with a few pre-clubbers dropping in. The bar is a cosy space with subdued lighting, a big menu, comfortable seating and a quadrophonic sound system playing commercial music – drinkers often get up and have a boogie in the wee hours. There's Red Stripe on draught and bar snacks, regular party nights with DJs and some entertainment laid on. Upstairs is a quiet room for chatting, as well as a minuscule room selling cards, postcards, sex aids and videos.

The Roebuck*

▣ *25 Rennel Street, Lewisham, SE13*

☏ *020 8852 1705*

🚉 *Lewisham BR*

☺ *Mon-Thurs noon-2am, Fri & Sat noon-2.30am, Sun 1pm-midnight*

💰 *Thurs-Sat admission charge to club*

You may not think Lewisham is the place for a night on the tiles, but The Roebuck packs in the locals. Lewisham's busiest gay venue is just off the High Street in a nasty 60s building. During the day the crowd is mixed, and you can sit out on the rather uninviting street munching pub food, but at night the place kicks into action when the basement bar and club, the Voltz, wakes up (see p.37).

Royal Vauxhall Tavern TV*

▣ *372 Kennington Lane, Vauxhall, SE11*

☏ *020 7582 0833*

🚉 *Vauxhall BR/LU*

☺ *Mon-Thurs 9pm-1am, Fri & Sat 9pm-2am, Sun noon-10.30pm*

This great barn of a place has been south London's premier drag venue for as far back as anyone can remember. A big, grungy Victorian pub with a large stage and dancefloor, it gets chock-a-block most nights of the week – along with Sunday lunchtime – for its top-line cabaret. The Vauxhall launched big names like Lily Savage and Adrella into the world, and as well as bursting with a friendly assortment of gay men, it holds an annual sports day on the open land out back (see p.43).

Skinners Arms* TV

▣ *60 Camberwell New Road, Camberwell, SE5*

☏ *020 7587 3891*

🖉 *www.skinnersarms.co.uk*

🚉 *Oval LU*

☺ *Tues-Thurs 9pm-2am, Fri & Sat 9pm-3am, Sun 8pm-midnight*

💰 *Fri & Sat £3 after 11pm*

This blacked-out pub looks pretty seedy, but the mixed gay and lesbian crowd who come here know how to have a good time. There's something going on here every night – from quizzes and DJs to cabaret and strippers – and it tends to pick up when the nearby Kennington pubs close their doors. There's no door charge and no attitude, just a big bar room and a smaller chill-out room with pool table. Tuesday: free pool, Wednesday: strippers, Thursday: karaoke, Friday & Saturday: cabaret then commercial handbag sounds, Sunday: karaoke.

Southern Pride* TV

⌧ *82 Norwood High Street, West Norwood, SE27*

☎ *020 8761 5200*

✎ *www.southernpride.co.uk*

🚃 *West Norwood BR*

🕐 *Mon-Thurs 7pm-2am, Fri 7pm-3am, Sat 6pm-3am, Sun noon-1am*

This cabaret bar opened its gay doors in 1997 and after a refurb in mid-2000 is quite upmarket. It's the first-choice gay venue for miles around (although, let's face it, few target Bromley for a big night out). A huge place, it has a big dancefloor, a stage and conservatory with comfy sofas and chairs, as well as a pretty patio garden with fountains and ponds.

Two Brewers* TV

⌧ *114 Clapham High Street, Clapham, SW4*

☎ *020 7498 4971*

🚃 *Clapham Common LU*

🕐 *Mon-Thurs 4pm-2am, Fri & Sat 2pm-3am, Sun noon-midnight; Tues-Thurs £2 after 11pm, Fri & Sat £3 after 9.30pm, £4 after 11pm*

Clapham's own cabaret bar and club has shed its old grungy 'Two Sewers' image, and now puts on a good show – whether in the camp Cabaret Bar or the darker, cruisier Club Bar. A lot of girls and guys come here for some of the scene's cabaret six nights a week, but The Brewers also draws a right-on crowd for its diversity of DJ mixes and cruisy atmosphere.

Ye Old Rose and Crown

⌧ *1 Crooms Hill, Greenwich, SE10*

☎ *020 8858 0154*

🚃 *Greenwich BR*

🕐 *Mon-Sat 11am-11pm, Sun noon-10.30pm*

A busy traditional pub with a good atmosphere, a mixed crowd and a gay manager, next door to Greenwich Theatre. It gets very full in the evenings with local gays and the after-theatre crowd, and it's mainly straight on weekdays. The beer is good and trad pub grub is served daily from noon to 3pm. There are occasional special nights, with parties on Valentine's Day, St David's Day and New Year's Eve.

WEST LONDON

The Champion

⌨ *1 Wellington Terrace, Bayswater Road, Bayswater, W2*

☎ *020 7243 9531*

🚇 *Notting Hill Gate LU*

🕐 *Mon-Sat noon-11pm, Sun noon-10.30pm*

With a more mature crowd, this large and friendly Victorian pub makes for an unpretentious night out. It's quite cruisy, with loud commercial music, subdued lighting and mostly standing room only. There also a courtyard garden and a small bar downstairs. Food daily (noon-8pm).

The Coleherne*

⌨ *261 Old Brompton Road, Earl's Court, SW5*

☎ *020 7244 5951*

🚇 *Earl's Court LU*

🕐 *Mon-Sat noon-11pm, Sun noon-10.30pm*

The Coleherne was done over a couple of years ago and its seedy traditional feel has been swapped for seedy high-tech ambiance. The leather scene reputedly started here, and gay men have been frequenting the place since the 1920s. It's always cruisy, with clones and uniform lovers of all ages showing off their denim, leather or tattoos, playing pool and soaking up the nightly DJ's mix.

The Penny Farthing

⌨ *135 King Street, Hammersmith, W6*

☎ *020 8600 0941*

🚇 *Hammersmith LU*

🕐 *Mon-Sat noon-11pm, Sun noon-10.30pm*

This chatty traditional pub gets busy in the evenings and features nightly drag acts, occasional themed nights and a beer garden. There are two areas – one with plush upholstered settees near the stage, and a quieter space at the back. They also offer good pub food throughout the week.

Queen's Arms

⌨ *233 Hanworth Road, Hounslow, Middlesex, TW3*

☎ *020 8230 1505*

🚇 *Hounslow BR or Hounslow Central LU*

🕐 *Mon-Fri 4pm-11pm, Sat noon-11pm, Sun noon-10.30pm*

A large, homely and friendly Victorian boozer, The Queen's Arms has nightly entertainment with regular big-name cabaret. There's a car park for those endowed with cars. Monday: karaoke, Friday-Sunday: cabaret.

Queen's Head

⌨ *27 Tryon Street, Chelsea, SW3*

☏ *020 7589 0262*

🚇 *Sloane Square LU*

🕐 *Mon-Sat 11am-11pm, Sun noon-10.30pm*

Just off the King's Road, The Queen's Head has been gay for years, and still packs in monied locals for its friendly, quiet ambiance and more mature crowd. There is no cabaret, no disco, no pool table – just a smallish, traditional pub where you can sit and chat. The two bars spill out onto the quiet side street in the warmer months. Food served Monday-Friday 11am-7pm.

Richmond Arms

⌨ *20 The Square, off Princes Street, Richmond, Surrey, TW9*

☏ *020 8940 2118*

🚇 *Richmond BR/LU*

🕐 *Fri-Sat noon-1am, Sun noon-10.30pm*

Tucked away on a small side-street behind the main road, five minutes from the station, this comfortable old pub caters to local gay men of all ages. It's very relaxed with wood panelling, sofas and small tables, flattering lighting and friendly bar staff. There's regular cabaret and other entertainment laid on.

The Rocket

⌨ *10-13 Churchfield Road, Acton, W3*

☏ *020 8992 1545*

🚇 *Acton Central BR*

🕐 *Daily 9pm-late*

⊛ *Annual membership £10, guests £2*

Opened in early 1996 just off Acton High Street, The Rocket's upstairs bar is a large room that holds around sixty boys. It's a throwback to the good old days, with marble fireplaces, comfortable leather sofas and a large dog roaming around. There's also a small stage with cabaret at the weekends. Ring the bell to enter. Oh, and there's a dark room for cruisy action.

Ted's Place

Ted's Place* TV

🖳 *305a North End Road, West Kensington, W14*

☎ *020 7385 9359*

🚇 *West Brompton LU*

🕐 *Sun-Fri 7pm-late, Thurs TV's & TS's only*

💲 *Annual membership £15*

The former Fanny's has been a private member's club since the early 1990s and serves a mixed gay/lesbian TV/TS crowd. Ring the bell to get in and descend to an intimate and friendly cabaret bar where you can wear three inches of make-up and not feel out of place.

Warwick Bar*

⌨ *294 Old Brompton Road, Earl's Court, SW5*

☎ *020 7370 1344*   ✆ *020 7370 3176*

✎ *bromptonsclub@aol.com*

✎ *www.bromptons-club.com*

🚇 *Earl's Court LU*

🕐 *Mon-Sat 8pm-2am, Sun 6.30pm-12.30am*

A small L-shaped American-style bar over the busy, cruisy Brompton's nightclub (see p.21), the Warwick gets busy later on in the evening when boys downstairs come up for a breather from the dancefloor. It's comfortable and low-key, with background music, video screens, games machines and a selection of real ale. There are strippers on Sunday and Tuesday evenings.

West Five*

⌨ *Pope's Lane, Ealing, W5*

☎ *020 8579 3266*

🚇 *South Ealing LU*

🕐 *Mon & Tues 6pm-11pm, Wed & Thurs 6pm-midnight, Fri & Sat 6pm-1am, Sun 1pm-10.30pm*

This great barn of a place gives the West End a run for its money, with six different areas – the Lounge Bar, Cabaret Lounge, pool room, central bar, the Streisand Piano Bar, and an outdoor patio with fountain. It's very friendly and attracts a big crowd at weekends for its nightly cabaret or live DJs.

EAST LONDON

The Angel Cabaret Bar

⌨ *21 Church Street, Stratford, E15*

☎ *020 8555 1148*

✎ *www.angelcabaret.com*

🚇 *Stratford BR/LU/DLR*

🕐 *Sun-Wed 7pm-midnight, Thurs 7pm-1am, Fri & Sat 7pm-2am*

This intimate local pub off the New Plaistow Road in deepest East London was revamped in late 1999 and reopened as a gay cabaret venue. There are big-name PAs, tribute bands and drag shows every night of the week, but Tuesday when you can stretch your own vocal cords with some karaoke.

The Black Horse*

   168 Mile End Road, Stepney Green, E1

   020 7790 1684

   Stepney Green LU

   Tues-Thurs 8pm-1am, Fri & Sat 8pm-3am, Sun 8pm-1am

Opposite the Genesis Cinema, The Black Horse is a high-ceilinged relaxed Victorian pub. As one of East London's first gay pubs, it became legendary for its drag. They still do a bit of glitter, with regular cabaret, karaoke and strippers. There's a pool table at the back and a huge video screen playing back-to-back music videos, and the beer is the cheapest in London. A lot of boyz start off here on their way to the White Swan.

The British Prince

   49 Bromley Street, Limehouse, E1

   020 7790 1753

   Limehouse BR/DLR

   Mon-Sat 11am-11.30pm, Sun noon-10.30pm

Just two minutes from The White Swan, this rather worn but welcoming East End local on a quiet residential street gets busiest on Friday, Saturday and Sunday nights. It's quiet and intimate with red velvet banquettes, a juke box, large-screen TV, pool table and dartboard and bar snacks on Sunday. Quiet, cosy and friendly.

Central Station Walthamstow*

   80 Brunner Road, off James Street, Walthamstow, E17

   020 8520 4836

   www.centralstation.co.uk

   St James Street Walthamstow BR

   Mon-Wed 5.30pm-1am, Thurs & Fri 5.30pm-2am,
Sat 1pm-2am, Sun 1pm-midnight

The gay pub in the most unappealing location in London, the former Artful nestles on an industrial estate next to the train line. Still, it manages to pull in a good mix of local men and women who get along well. They put on some good entertainment too, with quizzes, karaoke, regular cabaret, as well as a pool table, BBQs in the garden during summer and the occasional drink promotion.

The Coronet*

⌨ *119 The Grove, Stratford, E15*

☎ *020 8522 0811*

✉ *coronet@welcome.to*

✍ *www.coronet.com*

🚇 *Stratford BR/LU/DLR, Maryland BR*

🕐 *Mon-Thurs noon-midnight, Fri & Sat noon-3am, Sun noon-midnight*

Calling itself a 'Soho-style bar' in the East End, The Coronet is typically light and airy, but with a twist: they have cabaret, discos and comedians, as well as a strictly men-only darkroom upstairs. There are regular specialist parties, including free bar (entry charge). Monday: pool competition, Tuesday: game show, Wednesday: DJ from 9pm, Thursday: quiz, Friday: dance sounds, Saturday: pre-Trade party.

The Joiner's Arms*

⌨ *116-118 Hackney Road, Shoreditch, E2*

☎ *020 7739 9854*

🚇 *Liverpool St/Old Street LU*

🕐 *Mon-Sat 6pm-2am, Sun noon-10.30pm*

A rough-and-ready East End pub near the Columbia Road flower market, The Joiner's Arms is a reasonably quiet venue favoured by local lads during the week, picking up with the Saturday night club night, when a raunchy crowd adopts the hard dress code. Has a big central bar, with drinks standard price, old-style furnishing, a pool table, and tiny stage. Regular quiz nights, disco and cabaret; pool and food during the day. They also throw regular all-night parties from Friday right through to Sunday. Saturday: Meat – pre-Trade sportswear fetish club for leather, rubber, uniform and skinheads (10pm-4am; £5, £4 before 11.30pm).

The Olde Ship

⌨ *17 Barnes Street, York Square, Stepney, E14*

☎ *020 7790 4082*

✍ *www.welcome.to/oldship*

🚇 *Limehouse BR/DLR*

🕐 *Mon-Fri 6pm-11pm, Sat 7pm-midnight, Sun 3pm-10.30pm*

On a beautiful residential square just a couple of minutes' walk from The White Swan, The Ship is a real find. It's very much a cosy old-fashioned local with red lamps, wood panelling and frilly nets, a host of chatty regulars and a caged parrot willing to confide with passers-by. Entertainment is confined to a couple of pool tables, dartboards and games machines with Sunday cabaret. Wednesday: quiz night, Friday: 60s, 70s & 80s disco, Saturday: charty music & karaoke, Sunday: cabaret.

Royal Oak* TV

⌨ *73 Columbia Road, Bethnal Green, E2*

☎ *020 7739 8204*

🚇 *Old Street/Shoreditch LU*

🕐 *Mon-Sat 1pm-late, Sun 8am-late*

This large, old-fashioned pub in the middle of the Sunday morning flower market is real East Enders territory, with plenty of seating and sitting up at the bar chatting. It tends to be straight on Sunday mornings, mixed during the day and decidedly gay during the evenings. There's a summer beer garden and the upstairs room is also available for functions. They also have several games machines, and a pool table.

The Spiral TV

⌨ *138 Shoreditch High Street, Shoreditch, E1*

☎ *020 7613 1351*

🖃 *www.spiral-london.com*

🚇 *Old Street LU*

🕐 *Wed & Thurs 10pm-2am, Fri & Sat 10pm-4am, Sun 10pm-3.30am*

Shoreditch the new Clerkenwell? I don't think so. The Spiral stands on the high street in a no-man's land of grunge and litter. Still, it's a comfortable place with stripped floorboards, cane sofas and tables, and attracts an outrageous and flamboyant mix of people, both straight and gay. They serve a limited menu and have regular karaoke, club nights, DJs and a piano bar. Wednesday: chart sounds, Thursday: karaoke, Friday: karaoke, Saturday: commercial dance and garage, Sunday: piano bar.

The White Swan (BJs)* TV

⌨ *556 Commercial Road, Limehouse, E1*

☎ *020 7780 9870*

🚇 *Aldgate East LU or Limehouse BR/DLR*

🕐 *Mon 9pm-1am, Tues-Thurs 9pm-2am, Fri & Sat 9pm-3am, Sun 5.30pm-midnight*

Scene of Michael Barrymore's public self-outing in 1995, The White Swan has been welcoming gay boys for around fifteen years, for its regular menu of drag, strippers, dance nights and cruising. There's a big dance floor, chill-out lounge area, and two bars. The quieter main bar has a video screen, and features the weekly amateur strip night and several other nights to keep the weekday East End lads happy. The place gets very busy and cruisy at the weekend, when boys come from all over town and there's a buzzing party atmosphere, with a resident DJ playing disco, and trash music. Monday: stripper, Tuesday: cabaret, Wednesday: amateur strip night, Thursday: cabaret, Friday & Saturday: commercial and handbag sounds, Sunday: Jo Purvis' original tea dance (see p.40).

RELIGIOUS GROUPS

For gay men and women who hold firm religious beliefs but feel that it is impossible to worship in a traditional church, temple or synagogue, there are groups where you will be welcomed to worship with others in a non-judgmental, liberal atmosphere. Many of the groups also encourage discussion of faith and sexuality.

3F Group

- ▣ *Flat 8, Clements House, 135 Dalgarno Gardens, W10*
- ☏ *Drew 020 8968 4317*
- ✉ *drew@payne3f.freeserve.co.uk*
- 🚇 *Marble Arch LU*
- ☺ *Third Fri Grosvenor Chapel, 24 South Audley Street, Mayfair, W1*

This London meeting of the Lesbian and Gay Christian Movement gets together once a month to participate in a usually lively non-denominational debate. It's not overtly religious, just a place where people interested in spiritual issues can meet in a friendly space. The discussion will often touch upon gay issues in the Bible, and other contemporary issues. Around 30-40 people usually show up, and go off to a pub afterwards.

Affirmation UK

- ☏ *Michael 020 7221 4846*
- ✉ *walkerwrite@aol.com*

This social group for Mormons started up in the US in 1973, and in 1981, the UK branch started a series of social groups. Now it is more of a telephone helpline for Mormons who feel isolated or confused about their faith and sexuality, although they still sometimes meet up.

Beit Klal Yisrael

- ▣ *BKY, PO Box 1828, London, W10*
- ☏ *020 8960 5750*
- ☺ *Sat, Sun-Thurs 10am-10pm; services first & third Fri 7.30pm, second & fourth Sat 10.30am*

Established in March 1990 for Jews who feel marginalised by the mainstream Jewish community – whether due to sexuality, gender, age or outlook – BKY is associated with Reform Synagogues of Great Britain and is a member of the World Congress of Gay and Lesbian Jewish Organisations. They hold weekly services at the Unitarian Church, 112 Palace Gardens Terrace, Kensington, W8, and celebrate the major Jewish festivals. Their varied cultural programme including discussion groups, speakers, folk dancing and lesbian group events. They welcome all Jewish women and men who have issues, questions and concerns. All services are followed by a bring-and-share vegetarian meal.

Called to Be One

✉ *PO Box 24632, London,* E9

☎ *01642 465020*

Set up in 1996 by a group of Roman Catholic parents of gays and lesbians to help them through a difficult experience and provide mutual support. They are scattered all over the country and offer mainly a telephone counselling service, but can send out information and even hook people up together if they want to meet. They also publish features about how rotten the Church is to the gay community.

Changing Attitude

☎ *020 7738 1305*

✉ *changinguk@freeuk.com*

An Anglican organisation that campaigns for gay and lesbian affirmation within the Anglican Church. Their network now totals over 250 people, although membership is restricted. Contribute ideas and features to their monthly newsletter, sent free to every Bishop in the UK and every Diocesan Director of Ordinands, Social Responsibility Officer and Ministerial Training Course and Theological College Principal in England. Members are asked to exchange national and local news and information, and to offer help and support to each other. Changing Attitude are expanding their network of groups and have applied for a lottery grant to further develop their project. The organisation also publish various books about gay and lesbian Christianity.

Evangelical Fellowship for Lesbian and Gay Christians (EFLGC)

☎ *01276 24893 or 01245 252214*

✉ *info@eflgc.org.uk*

This group of lesbian, gay and bisexual people formed in 1979 to support evangelical Christians who want to explore their sexuality and confirm their faith within the Church. The Fellowship allows members to support and be supported in times of difficulty or stress, encourage one another in their faith and question their belief and sexuality. Twice a year they run residential weekend conferences with guest speakers, discussions, prayer and worship. They publish a quarterly newsletter and prayer calendar, have local gatherings and regional link persons who act as a point of contact for members, as well as links with similar groups all over the world.

Gay and Lesbian Orthodox Network (GLON)

☎ *Avraham 0777 308 6233*

✉ *andrewba@telinco.co.uk*

GLON offers a supportive environment exclusively for Orthodox members of the Jewish community, set up as a social group where like-minded people can meet and ease the sense of isolation that can sometimes be felt by people in this position. They usually have meetings once a month in a member's home or in a kosher restaurant in London, and host frequent discussion evenings about Jewish issues relevant to homosexuality. The group is also able to put people in touch with Orthodox Rabbinical authorities if they need to discuss particular aspects of their situation in detail.

Gay Spiritual Group

▨ *61 Southerton Road, Hammersmith, W6*

☎ *John 020 8846 8593*

This friendly and social group honours all forms of spirituality and meets at the Gay Spiritual Centre for socials, discussions, book readings, healing and tarot. They publish a monthly newsletter, *The Pink Path*, to keep members in touch.

Integrity

▨ *PO Box 27328, London, E15*

☎ *0845 673 6736*

✉ *info@integrityuk.org*

✉ *www.integrityuk.org*

🕐 *Second Fri and fourth Thurs*

💲 *Annual membership £15*

A friendly, safe space for lesbian, gay and bisexual evangelical Christians. National group Integrity was set up to integrate spirituality and sexuality, drawing on Pentecostal and Evangelical church culture. The group's 70 members meet twice a month, second Friday in Camden, fourth Thursday in Hampstead (contact them for details). Integrity operate a penpal scheme for the isolated and publish a bi-monthly newsletter. Their Friday night sessions comprise discussions, social nights and occasional services, as well as day trips and pub nights.

Jewish Gay and Lesbian Group

⌨ *BM JGLG, London, WC1*

☏ *020 8922 5214*

Helpline 020 7706 3123 (Mon & Wed 7pm-10pm)

✉ *info@jglg.org.uk*

✉ *www.jglg.org.uk*

✆ *Annual membership £15*

Founded in 1972, this is the longest-established Jewish gay group in the world, and attracts men and women from both religious and non-religious backgrounds to socialise and offer support. There are at least four meetings a month, with Friday night services and cinema or club outings, with an average attendance of twenty to thirty people of all ages at the Chavura. Last Tuesday: men's pub night (9pm onwards), first Wednesday: women's dinner, last Friday: Chavura service and smooze at the Montague Centre, 21 Maple Street, Mayfair, W1 (7.30pm-8.30pm).

Lesbian and Gay Christian Movement

⌨ *Oxford House, Derbyshire Street, Bethnal Green, E2*

☏ *Revd Richard Kirker 020 7739 1249*

Counselling helpline 020 7739 8134 (Wed & Sun 7pm-9.30pm)

Christian Homophobia Hotline 020 7613 1095

✆ *020 7739 1249*

✉ *lgcm@lgcm.org.uk*

✉ *www.lgcm.org.uk*

✆ *Annual membership £30, £14 unwaged*

A UK-based international charity that works for an inclusive church and combating homophobia among christians. It administers a range of local Christian groups all over the UK, arranges a national conference (see p.42) and summer retreats for meditative reflection, has an extensive Christian mail-order book list (see p.172), and runs a helpline to give counselling, advice and information to gay and lesbian Christians. They can help make arrangements for a same-sex blessing service, providing the name of a sympathetic minister or priest, and offering a certificate to commemorate the occasion.

Metropolitan Community Church

✉ *MCC Brixton, PO Box 13242, London, SW2*

☎ *020 8678 0200*

✍ *whitesmail@tesco.net*

✉ *MCC East London, 29 Dagmar Court, Manchester Road, London, E14*

☎ *020 8304 2374*

✍ *jane@mccel.demon.co.uk*

✉ *MCC North London, BM/MCC, London, WC1*

☎ *020 88020 962*

✍ *mccnl@tesco.net*

✍ *www.ufmcc.com*

The Universal Fellowship of Metropolitan Community Churches is a well structured group of Christians determined to reconcile their sexuality with the teachings of the Bible, and celebrate the integration of their spirituality and their sexuality. There are three churches in central, east and south London that organise weekly services, as well as other social events, like quizzes, discos, pub evenings and meals out. The MCC has created its own liturgical style of worship, and Orders of Service are written by a group within the church. Services are led by a man if the preacher is a woman and vice versa.

Quaker Lesbian and Gay Fellowship

✉ *Hallsfield, Cricklade, Swindon, Wilts, SN6*

☎ *020 7663 1025*

✍ *qhs@quaker.org.uk*

✍ *www.quaker.org.uk*

The 27,000 Quakers in the UK tend to be accepting of others and celebrate diversity, so there are some blessings of same-sex relationships among British Quakers. This organisation supports homosexual Quakers to accept themselves as full members of the Society of Friends.

Quest

⌨ *BM Box 2585, London, WC1*

☎ *020 7792 0234*

Linkline advice, support and information 0808 808 0234 (Fri 7pm-10pm),

✉ *quest@dircon.co.uk*

✆ *Annual membership £20*

Founded in 1973 to sustain and increase Christian belief among gay men and women, this nationwide charity for lesbian and gay Catholics offers an alternative to those who may have left the church due to its lack of understanding of homosexuality. It welcomes all into the fold, regardless of religion or sexual orientation, and provides pastoral and social support, as well as trying to educate the Catholic church about gay and lesbian issues. There are groups in all the UK's major cities, meeting in private homes and churches, and organising shared meals, concerts, retreats and social outings. The London group meets for Sunday mass once a month in a central London location, and holds other masses and general social evenings in between. They also hold an annual weekend conference on a topic of special significance for homosexual people.

Unitarian Gay Fellowship

⌨ *Mansford Street Church, 117 Mansford Street, Bethnal Green, E2*

☎ *020 7515 9609*

🚇 *Bethnal Green LU*

🕐 *Last Mon 7pm*

The UGF is a forum for gay, bisexual, lesbian and transgender people and their friends in a non-credal, non-judgmental atmosphere that welcomes Buddhists, Jews, Christians and Muslims alike, with the idea that God loves all. They meet once a month at the actively pro-gay Mansford Street Church.

Young Lesbian and Gay Christians

☎ *020 7739 8134*

Helpline 020 7739 8134 (Wed & Sun 7pm-10pm)

✉ *ylgc@appleonline.net*

✉ *www.members.aol.com/lgcm*

Run by the Lesbian and Gay Christian Movement, this group of under-30s have regular meetings to discuss Christian traditions versus sexuality, as well as to socialise and strengthen links with other groups. Confidential advice and counselling are available through the helpline, and the group's e-mail list enables contact with other YLGC's all over the country.

RESTAURANTS

What restaurant in London doesn't have at least one gay waiter or manager? These restaurants choose to specifically target the lesbian/gay (or mixed) portions of society, either because they are gay-owned, gay-run or just want to offer bent girls and boys a decent round meal.

Balans

⊞ *60 Old Compton Street, Soho, W1*

☎ *020 7437 5212*   ✆ *020 7437 5212*

⊞ *239 Old Brompton Road, Earl's Court, SW5*

☎ *020 7244 8838*   ✆ *020 7244 6226*

⊞ *187 Kensington High Street, Kensington W8*

☎ *020 7376 0115*   ✆ *020 7938 2723*

⍀ *www.balans.co.uk*

🕐 *Daily 8am-1am; Soho branch open Mon-Thurs 8am-4am,*
Fri & Sat 8am-6am, Sun 8am-1am

Fashionable and stylish, the Balans chain is the gay market leader in the capital. All branches are constantly packed out due to their subdued but modern décor, decent cuisine and vast plate-glass windows to look out of. They serve up a range of impressive sandwiches, main courses such as corn-fed chicken, grilled salmon and chicken couscous, linguine and Pad Thai noodles; and a breakfast selection of omelettes, blueberry pancakes, smoked salmon with ranch-style eggs and Cumberland sausages. Desserts typically feature summer pudding, roast peach, and baked chocolate fudge brownie cheesecakes. Very beautiful people.

Il Forno

⊞ *64 Frith Street, Soho, W1*

☎ *020 7734 4545*

🚇 *Tottenham Court Road LU*

🕐 *Daily noon-2.45pm & 6pm-10.45pm*

This gay-run café-restaurant is quite a pricey affair serving French and British nouveau cuisine, with finely cooked and presented delicacies such as snails, rabbit, duck confit, squid, mussels and beetroot tureen. It's a long and narrow place, pristine and artfully decorated, with sharp lighting and a monied 35-plus crowd.

Blades

📷 *94 Lower Richmond Road, Putney, SW15*

☎ *020 8789 0869*

🚇 *Putney Bridge BR*

🕐 *Tues-Sun noon-2.30pm & 6pm-11.30pm*

The mixed clientele of this cosy wood-panelled café-bar-restaurant come for a largely Italian menu of pastas, chicken, trout and prawns, as well as barbecued steak and lamb, soup, salmon and a choice of vegetarian dishes.

Carnevale

📷 *135 Whitecross Street, Clerkenwell, EC1*

☎ *020 7250 3452*

🚇 *Barbican/Old Street LU*

🕐 *Mon-Sat lunch & dinner*

An award-winning Mediterrean vegetarian restaurant with excellent modern cooking, a friendly atmosphere and good wine list.

The Dôme

📷 *57-59 Old Compton Street, Soho, W1*

☎ *020 7287 0770*

🚇 *Piccadilly Circus LU*

🕐 *Sun-Wed 11am-11pm, Thurs 11am-midnight, Fri-Sat 11am-1am*

This branch of the French bar and bistro chain isn't really gay, but might as well be due to its location in the hub of Gayland. It's intimate and offers a good-value two-course menu for £8.95 (noon–8pm), and a menu of Continental specialities from croque monsieur to Cajun chicken salad and teriyake salad, all reasonably priced.

Ed's Easy Diner *

📷 *12 Moor Street, Soho, W1*

☎ *020 7439 1955*

🚇 *Piccadilly Circus LU*

🕐 *Daily 11.30am-midnight*

A slice of 50s Americana, Ed's horseshoe-shaped zinc bar, high stools and jukeboxes set the scene for tuna salad, hot dogs, homemade hamburgers, shakes and fries, served by people in little white caps; celebrated its fourteenth birthday in 2001. There's also a waiters-on-wheels free delivery service around Soho.

Balans

Gallery Tea Rooms

⌧ *103 Lavender Hill, Battersea, SW11*

☎ *020 7350 2564*

🚆 *Clapham Junction BR*

🕐 *Mon-Fri 5pm-midnight; Sat-Sun 10.30am-3pm & 5pm-midnight*

The camp decoration of this gay-owned and -run restaurant and wine bar features red velvet upholstery, chandeliers, candles, tapestries and screens, with antique prints and small tables with mismatched crockery completing the scene. They serve main courses like snapper, pork and chargrilled lamb, starters like soup, pork terrine and pan-fried tiger prawns, as well as a host of cakes and desserts.

Le Gourmet

⌧ *312 King's Road, Chelsea, SW3*

☎ *020 7352 4483*

🚆 *South Kensington LU*

🕐 *Daily 6.30pm-11.30pm*

Two doors down from Osborne & Little, London's oldest gay restaurant was established in 1975, and now provides its mixed clientele with a cosy and camp setting in which to enjoy an intimate candlelit meal. The menu is cooked beautifully but is very meat-orientated, with fillet steak, venison, veal and chicken, as well as salmon, calamari, escargots, whitebait and prawns. The set menu offers two courses for around £13.

Hujo's *

⌧ *11 Berwick Street, Soho, W1*

☎ *020 7734 5144*

🚆 *Leicester Square LU*

🕐 *Mon-Sat noon-midnight*

A stylish but low-key café-restaurant in the middle of lively Berwick Street market, Hujo's is a low-key place with an ambitious, and well thought-out menu. They make the most of fresh produce from the market on their doorstep, with tasty and innovative concoctions like artichoke filled with parmesan, breadcrumbs and anchovy; grilled hake, pork rillette with salad, duck breast marinated in honey and ginger, aubergine stuffed with rice and vegetables, and Lancashire black pudding with bubble and squeak; desserts include chocolate mousse, chocolate toffee cake, fruit tart and a selection of sorbets. There is a cheap two-course matinée menu and a decent wine list.

Mildred's

⌖ *58 Greek Street, Soho, W1*

☎ *020 7494 1634*

🚇 *Leicester Square LU*

🕐 *Mon-Fri 11am-10.30pm, Sat noon-10.30pm, Sun 12.30pm-6.30pm*

The utilitarian formica tables set the tone of this dirt-cheap but perennially crowded, alternative, chatty and friendly cheap wholefood café, named after one of Joan Crawford's most celebrated characters. The two lesbians who run the place change the photocopied menus daily, but they always feature plenty of different veggie and vegan fare, with pasta, salads, a range of home-made cakes and soups, as well as a few exotic surprises such as Sag paneer with marinated olives.

The Pepper Tree

⌖ *19 Clapham Common South Side, Clapham, SW4*

☎ *020 7622 1758*

🚇 *Clapham Common LU*

🕐 *Mon noon-3pm & 6pm-10.30pm, Tues-Sat noon-3pm & 6pm-11pm, Sun noon-10.30pm*

Right opposite the Common – very handy for some – The Pepper Tree's decor makes Wagamama look cluttered. It's the same formula – bleached wood everywhere and long tables and benches you share. The taste here is Thai, with starters at £2.95 – vegetarian rolls, beancurd satay, spicy tordman; curries at £3.95 – yellow chicken, green prawn, green vegetable; noodles at £4.50 – big tum chicken, big tum prawn, big tum beef; and stir fries at £3.50-4.50 – vegetarian, prawn, beef.

Il Pinguino Ristorante

⌖ *62 Brixton Road, The Oval, SW9*

☎ *020 7735 3822*

🚇 *Oval LU*

🕐 *Tues, Wed, Fri & Sat 6pm-11pm, Sun 6pm-10.30pm*

The chef-proprietor of this simple and friendly restaurant turns out an inexpensive traditional Italian menu to a mixed clientele, with antipasti like avocado vinaigrette, whitebait and deep fried camembert; chicken, beef and fish main courses, and a range of pasta with different sauces. No credit cards accepted.

Steph's

🏠 *39 Dean Street, Soho, W1*

☎ *020 7734 5976*

🚇 *Leicester Square LU*

🕐 *Lunch Mon-Fri noon-3pm; dinner Mon-Thurs 5.30pm-11.30pm, Fri & Sat 5.30pm-midnight*

A smart, theatrical-looking restaurant (we're talking painted flamingoes and theatre posters on the walls) serving some good old-fashioned fresh British food, with dishes like roast breast of duck, lamb in red wine, cinnamon pie, and bread and butter pudding. Starters feature whiskied black pudding, Yorkshire pudding with onion, deep-fried potato skins with gravy and sour cream; main courses include tagliatelli with wild mushroom sauce, chargrilled lambchops with redcurrant sauce, chargrilled calves' liver with onions, corn-fed chicken breast on spinach, and smoked salmon with a glass of champagne; desserts are delights such as bread and butter pudding, mulled wine pudding, and tequila and lime sorbet.

Wilde About Oscar

🏠 *Philbeach Hotel, 30-31 Philbeach Gardens, Earl's Court, SW5*

☎ *020 7373 1244*

🖥 *www.philbeachhotel.freeserve.co.uk*

🚇 *Earl's Court LU*

🕐 *Mon, Wed-Sat 6pm-11pm*

Time Out proclaimed this 'probably the best gay restaurant in London', and even though it isn't at the heart of Soho, it does have a following. This elegant conservatory restaurant overlooks an English garden and you can sit outside during the summer. It's has a low-key and intimate atmosphere with subdued lighting and splendid painted wall decorations – perfect for private parties. The modern French cuisine includes reasonably priced Scotch fillet with blue cheese, breast of duck, smoked salmon, and delicious patisseries. The clientele is mainly non-residents from Thursday to Sunday, and mainly hotel guests most other nights. The first Monday of the month is transvestite night, with a buffet and changing facilities.

SAUNAS

Gay men's saunas are not just ideal for a little Norwegian-style attention to your body's largest organ – the skin – but also tend to be the sorts of places to make new friends in a short period of time. All you need is a skimpy white towel and plenty of pores to open… Strangely, lesbians don't seem to feel the need for saunas in the same way gay men do…

Chariots I

▣ *Chariots House, Fairchild Street, Shoreditch, EC2*
☎ *020 7247 5333*
✒ *www.gaysauna.co.uk*
🚇 *Liverpool Street/Old Street LU*
🕐 *Daily noon-9am*
💲 *£12*

It was already the biggest, the most palatial gay health club in Europe (25,000 square feet of pure steamy pleasure in an old car showroom), but the original Chariots had a complete refit in November 2000 to make it even bigger and better. If you make it out of the 400-locker changing room, hit one of the two 20-man sauna cabins or two 30-man steam rooms, or the huge-screen TV lounge showing adult videos, the health-food bar and 20 new restrooms, or the swimming pool, two large jacuzzis, pool table, or well-equipped gym. It's all immaculately clean and decorated with Doric columns, red velvet curtains and fountains. There's free coffee and fruit juice, towels and toiletries, as well as massage and a high-powered solarium.

Chariots II

▣ *Rear of 292 Streatham High Road, Streatham, SW16*
☎ *020 8696 0929*
✒ *www.gaysauna.co.uk*
🕐 *Mon-Thurs noon-midnight, Fri noon-Sun midnight*
💲 *£10*

The second of the Chariots sauna chain in London, this one in South London. Chariots II has a Turkish steam room, two saunas cabins, two jacuzzis, restrooms, a TV lounge/snack bar and 150 locker room capacity. There are free refreshments and high-powered sunbeds. Tuesday: BARE – for big boys, second Saturday: BARE 2000.

Chariots III

⌨ *57 Cowcross Street, Farringdon, EC1*

☎ *020 7251 5553*

✎ *www.gaysauna.co.uk*

🚇 *Farringdon BR/LU*

🕐 *Sun-Thurs 11am-11pm, Fri 11am-Sun 3am*

💷 *£8 before 4pm; £10 after 4pm and weekends*

Opposite Farringdon tube, this large sauna has a huge steam room, restrooms, TV lounge, snack bar and high-powered sun showers, along with the usual free refreshments.

The Cruise Club

⌨ *57 Camberwell Road, Camberwell, SE5*

☎ *020 7703 1100*

✎ *www.saunaclub.co.uk*

🚇 *Elephant & Castle/Kennington LU*

🕐 *Sun-Thurs noon-midnight, Fri noon- Sun 6am*

💷 *£10, concessions £8*

This 5,000-square-foot sauna has a steam room, jacuzzi, sauna room, video lounge, bar and lots of rest areas.

The Health Club TV

⌨ *800 Lea Bridge Road, Walthamstow, E17*

☎ *020 8556 8082*

🚇 *Leytonstone/Walthamstow Central*

🕐 *Daily 1pm-midnight*

💷 *£10, students £8*

A very popular east London sauna. It has been completely refurbished to provide its 3,000 air-conditioned square feet space with a steam room, sauna, jacuzzi, luxurious TV lounge, lots of rest rooms, a massage area, and free snacks and refreshments.

The Locker Room

⌨ *8 Cleaver Street, Kennington, SE11*

☎ *020 7582 6288*

🚇 *Kennington LU*

🕐 *Mon-Thurs 11am-midnight, Fri 11am-Sun midnight*

💷 *£10, £7.50 concessions, £6 before 1pm*

Opened in late 1995, The Locker Room fast proved itself a friendly place, with a large satellite TV lounge and steam room, showers, sauna, relaxation room and free light refreshments. Hairdressing, waxing and sunbed by appointment. It's busiest at weekends. On the last weekend of the month they run a £10 pass for the whole weekend.

Pacific 33

⌨ *33 Hornsey Road, Holloway, N7*

☎ *020 7609 8011*

🚇 *Holloway Road LU*

🕐 *Mon-Thurs 11am-11pm, Fri 11am-Sun 11pm*

💲 *£10, student discounts Mon-Fri*

Close to the university, this place gets busy during the late afternoon and early evening – and is open all night Friday and Saturday. It has relaxation rooms, a chill-out room, small steam room and sauna, rest room, TV lounge and coffee area with free refreshments, towels and toiletries.

Paris Gym - (see p.53)

Pleasuredrome Central

⌨ *125 Alaska Street, Waterloo, SE1*

☎ *020 7633 9194*

🚇 *Waterloo BR/LU*

🕐 *24 hours, 7 days a week*

💲 *£10*

Two minutes from Waterloo Station, this is central London's biggest and best sauna/steam complex, with 24-hour, 7-day-a-week opening. Offers two saunas, two steam rooms, spa with cabins and free refreshments.

Pleasuredrome North

⌨ *278 Caledonian Road, King's Cross, N1*

☎ *020 7607 0063*

🚇 *King's Cross BR/LU*

🕐 *Mon-Thurs noon-1am, Fri noon-Mon 1am*   💲 *£8*

After a complete refurbishment, the Pleasuredrome boasts the best sauna and steam facilities in North London. These include a three-room sauna, a large steam room, plunge pool and relaxation area with videos and free refreshments at the snack bar, along with a separate menu. There's no time limit. Those between 18 and 23 must bring proof of age.

The Portsea

⌂ *2 Portsea Place, Marble Arch, W2*

☎ *020 74023 385*

🚇 *Marble Arch LU*

🕐 *Daily noon-11pm*

💰 *£12*

This sauna and steam room is owned by the same company that runs The Sauna Bar (see above), and boasts a steamroom, sauna, rest room, video lounge and bar area with complimentary drinks. They also have massage rooms with en-suite showers and a masseur available for hire for £30 per hour.

Sailors Sauna

⌂ *572-574 Commercial Road, Limehouse, E14*

☎ *020 7791 2808*

🔗 *www.sailorsauna.co.uk*

🚇 *Limehouse BR/DLR*

🕐 *Mon-Tues, and Thurs noon-2am, Wed noon-6am, Fri noon-Mon 2am*

💰 *£10*

Close to The White Swan, this sauna has four floors in two buildings, with a large jacuzzi, sauna and steam, sunbeds, roof garden, restrooms, snack bar and TV lounge.

The Sauna Bar

⌧ *29 Endell Street, London, WC2*

☎ *020 7836 2236*

✍ *www.thesaunabar.com*

🚇 *Covent Garden LU*

🕐 *Daily noon-11.30pm*

💰 *£12*

This luxurious gay health spa has a 20–man sauna, 30–man spa, steam room, fully licensed bar, luxurious lounge area, 7 restrooms and free drinking water, hair gel, moisturiser, razors and shaving foam. There's a solarium, beautician, hair salon and holistic massage (separate charge) aromatherapy and reflexology. They also throw frequent 'special events' parties. Wednesday: drop your towel night.

Star Steam

⌧ *38 Lavender Hill, Battersea, SW11*

☎ *020 7924 2269*

🚇 *Clapham Common LU or Clapham Junction BR*

🕐 *Mon-Sat noon-midnight, Sun noon-11pm*

💰 *£11, concessions £7.50*

An old–timer, having been around since 1984, this gay sauna has Turkish baths, massage, two sauna cabins, a steam room with soft red lighting, two shower areas, a small TV lounge, six rest rooms, juice and snack bar, solarium, powertan sunbed and refreshment bar with free drinks, and free towels and toiletries. It has a full capacity of around 70.

Steamworks

⌧ *309 New Cross Road, New Cross, SE14*

☎ *020 8694 0606*

✍ *www.309.co.uk*

🚇 *New Cross or New Cross Gate BR/LU*

🕐 *Mon-Thurs 11am-11pm, Fri 11am-Sun 11pm*

💰 *£10, student discounts Mon-Fri £7*

The former Steaming@309 was London's first all-night sauna. The place is now under new management and offers a 20-man sauna and a 20-man steam room, private restrooms, shower areas, TV/relaxation area with coffee bar, and complimentary refreshments, towels and toiletries. No time restriction.

SHOPS

Gay men and women are good consumers, there's no doubt about that. A trip to Ikea, Habitat or even Sainsbury of a weekend would demonstrate that where money is to be spent, that's where we are. The following are not all necessarily gay or exclusively gay shops, but have an appeal to gays and lesbians.

Gay Business Association

- PO Box 347, Twickenham, TW1 2SN
- 0870 345 2222
- www.thecard.uk.com

The GBA was founded in 1984 and is the only UK-wide trade association that represents and promotes lesbian or gay business or those that promote products/services to the community with respect for it. Services to members include monthly networking meetings, a directory of members, a telephone referral service, a searchable database on the website and seminars. Members abide by the aims and objectives, code of practice, complaints procedure and equal opportunities policy and may use the GBA logo to promote their business.

Gay's The Word

BOOKS

Borders

⌨ *203-207 Oxford Street, London, W1*
& 120 Charing Cross Road, London, WC2
☎ *020 7292 1600*
🕐 *Mon-Sun 9am-8pm*

Borders is a new addition to book shopping in London. The shops are cool, spacious and trendy – and often the venue for a spot of cruising by female customers I noticed! Their gay and lesbian section is divided into fiction and photographers/artists and contains a good range of titles. This is the place to come for bestsellers and magazines – they have them all, in every language!

Gay Men's Press (GMP Publishers)

⌨ *PO Box 247, London, N6*
☎ *020 8341 7818* ✒ *020 8341 7467*

For 15 years, GMP has been publishing a good range of gay fiction, art and photography, travel guides and biographies; unfortunately, only the erotic visual titles on the Éditions Aubrey Walter list are sold direct by mail order. All other titles are available from Male Image (see below).

Gay Times Book Service

⌨ *283 Camden High Street, Camden Town, NW1*
☎ *020 8340 8644*

This gay and lesbian book service run by Gay Times (see p.117) prints a three-page selection of their books each month in the magazine, illustrating its extensive list of titles in the fields of health and lifestyle, history, fiction, biography and travel guides. Major credit cards accepted.

Gay's The Word

⌨ *66 Marchmont Street, Bloomsbury, WC1*
☎ *020 7278 7654*
✉ *sales@gaystheword.co.uk*
✉ *www.gaystheword.co.uk*
🚇 *Russell Square LU*
🕐 *Mon-Sat 10am-6.30pm, Sun 2pm-6pm*

Tucked away in one of Bloomsbury's backstreets, Gay's The Word is the only specifically gay and lesbian bookshop in the country, opening back in 1972. Today, it stocks a comprehensive selection of gay biographies, fiction, erotica, photographic study books, guide books and non-fiction from all over the globe. Write in for their mail-order service.

Housmans Bookshop

⌨ *5 Caledonian Road, King's Cross, N1*

☎ *020 7837 4473*

🕓 *Mon-Fri 10am-6.30pm, Sat 10am-6pm*

This is a quirky little bookshop in the centre of Kings Cross with a good range of books on gay issues and feminist literature, as well as left-wing/radical magazines and books.

Lesbian and Gay Christian Movement Mailorder

⌨ *Oxford House, Derbyshire Street, E2*

☎ *020 7739 1249*   ✒ *020 7739 1249*

✉ *lgcm@lgcm.org.uk*

The LGCM (see p.156) sells a range of Christian literature by mail-order, much of it focusing on how homosexuality relates to spirituality, and questioning, examining and ultimately embracing Christianity, with a range of books such as *Homophobia and the Bible*, *Seeking the Truth in Love*, *Homoeroticism in the Biblical World*, *Steps to Recovery from Bible Abuse* and *Aliens in the Household of God*.

Libertas

⌨ *42 Gillygate, York, YO31 7EQ*

☎ *01904 625522*

✉ *dykelife@libertas.co.uk*

A women's mail-order bookshop offering hundreds of lesbian books and videos – new releases, fiction, crime, erotica, biography, humour, magazines. There's a free 12-page mag every two months with reviews (no postage charge).

Male Image

⌨ *Dept MI, PO Box 3821, London, N5 1UY*

☎ *020 7609 3427*

✉ *www.maleimage.co.uk*

This excellent gay mail-order booklist runs the gamut of general fiction, biography, crime fiction, erotic science fiction, and horror, political and historical non-fiction, an excellent range of coffee table art and photography books, as well as erotica, travel guides, gay diaries. Accepts major credit cards.

NAT Publications

⌨ *New City Cloister, 196 Old Street, London, EC1*

☎ *020 7814 6767*   ✆ *020 7216 0111*

✍ *www.nat.org.uk*

The National AIDS Trust produces a range of mail-order publications dealing with AIDS. They also sell T-shirts featuring the World AIDS day ribbon poster and greetings cards. Cheques only.

EROTIC AND FETISH GEAR

Bob's Rubberwear *

⌨ *37 Tenbury Close, Forest Gate, E7*

☎ *020 8470 6635*

✎ *www.rubberbob.co.uk*

🚆 *Woodgrange Park BR*

This business specialises in bespoke rubberwear, and is very competitively priced. Personal callers by appointment, free catalogue with SAE.

Deviant Bespoke Rubberwear

☎ *Chris 020 7837 8546*

🕐 *By appointment*

Chris produces made-to-measure rubber clothes at reasonable prices. He doesn't run up simple shirts or trousers – you'll have to buy them off the rack – but is good for more obscure pyjamas, straight jackets, male corsets, skirts, suits and hoods. You can also commission jackets, jeans and T-shirts of more unusual design.

Expectations

⌨ *75 Great Eastern Street, Old Street, EC2*

☎ *020 7739 0292*   ✆ *020 7256 0910*

✎ *www.expectations.co.uk*

🚆 *Old Street LU*

🕐 *Mon-Fri 11am-7pm, Sat 11am-8pm, Sun noon-5pm*

This 20-year-old fetish couturier merged with Detainer in late 1995 and its now vast showroom features more nipple clamps, suspension harnesses, leather shorts and buckles than you can shake a big stick at. There's a large department of army surplus from new to very used – with camouflage trousers, used T-shirts and Air Force flying suits – dildos up to a massive 31cm, S&M equipment, and many rubber and leather clothes handmade on the premises; with a repair and alteration service also available.

Fettered Pleasures

⌨ *90 Holloway Road, N7*

☎ *020 76199 333*

✎ *www.fetteredpleasures.com*

🚆 *King's Cross BR/LU*

🕐 *Mon-Sat 11am-7pm*

This S&M specialist stocks perennial favourites such as Fetters, CB2000 and Folsom.

Sh! Women's Erotic Emporium

The Host

🏠 *45b South Lambeth Road, Vauxhall, SW8*

☎ *020 7582 2282*   📠 *020 7587 5397*

✎ *enquiries@host-rubberwear.com*

✎ *www.host-rubberwear.com*

🚇 *Vauxhall BR/LU*

🕐 *Tues-Thurs noon-8pm, Fri & Sat noon-11pm*

The so-called House of Subversive Thought is a fashion and fetish store a few doors from The Hoist club (see p.27), so it enjoys the handiest of locations. It's strictly hardcore, with an especially impressive rubberwear section – including biking and hostage gear, latex and veined latex.

Paradiso

🏠 *41 Old Compton Street, Soho, W1*

☎ *020 7287 2497*

🚇 *Leicester Square LU*

🕐 *Mon-Sat 11am-9pm*

This fetish shop sells an assortment of leather, rubber and PVC clothes for men and women, as well as lycra gear and underwear, sex toys and magazines.

Recoil.557

⌸ *The Railway Arch, Redcross Way, Southwark, SE1*

☎ *020 7378 0557*

✎ *www.dirtybastards.com*

🚇 *London Bridge BR/LU*

Suppliers of rubber gear and other little niceties.

Regulation

⌸ *17a St Albans Place, off Islington Green, Islington, N1* ③

☎ *020 7226 0665 or 020 7226 0658*

🚇 *Angel LU*

🕓 *Mon-Sat 10.30am-6.30pm, Sun noon-5pm*

This rubber, leather and PVC specialist has the UK's widest range of quality fetish gear, making and selling a good selection of rubber and leather wear, bondage gear and sex toys, as well as a good choice of gas masks. Prices start at around £8 for a pair of leather gloves and go up to £214 for an Edwardian-style rubber swimsuit with three-way all-round zip. They also have a mail-order service.

RoB

⌸ *Linton House, 24 Wells Street, W1*

☎ *020 7735 7893*   ✐ *020 637 4510*

✎ *roblondon@rob.nl*

✎ *www.rob.nl*

🚇 *Oxford Circus or Tottenham Court Road LU*

🕓 *Mon-Sat 10.30am-6.30pm, Sun noon-5pm*

Twenty-five years in Amsterdam has allowed RoB to build up a quality catalogue of over 1,000 leather and rubber products for the rough at heart. They sell everything you could desire from rubber jeans to nipple clamps and electro-stimulation apparatus.

Sh! Women's Erotic Emporium

⌸ *39 Coronet Street, Hoxton, N1*

☎ *020 7613 5458*   ✐ *020 7613 0020*

✎ *feedback@sh-womenstore.com*

✎ *www.sh-womenstore.com*

🚇 *Old Street LU*

🕓 *Mon-Sat 10am-8pm, Sunday 10am-5pm*

Proprietor Ky Hoyle makes you feel welcome, well advised (if you ask) and unembarrassed. Men can shop here should none of the women in the shop at the time object, but in the main, this is a girl thing. Sh! stock includes dildos galore, condoms, lube, vibrators, nipple clamps, magazines and 'naughty novelties'. There's also a mail-order service.

GIFTS AND SUNDRIES

Adonis Art and Antiques

- ▭ *1b Coleherne Road, Earl's Court, SW10*
- ☎ *020 7460 3888*
- ✍ *www.adonis-art.com*
- ▦ *Earl's Court LU*
- ◷ *Mon-Fri 10.30am-6.30pm, Sat 10.30am-5pm*

Britain's only art and antiques shop specialising in the naked male form, with paintings, drawings and statues with a homoerotic motif. Prices start at around £30 for a sketch and rise to thousands for an antique bronze statue or painting. The shop also stages monthly exhibitions.

American Retro

- ▭ *35 Old Compton Street, Soho, W1*
- ☎ *020 7734 3477*
- ▦ *Leicester Square/Piccadilly Circus LU*
- ◷ *Mon-Fri 10.30am-7.30pm, Sat 10.15am-7pm*

Trendy clothes – W&LT, D&G underwear and shirts, Adidas undies, Gallagher shirts and John Smedley T-shirts – kitsch gifts and greetings cards.

Clone Zone

Centaurus
- 100 Old Street, Clerkenwell, EC1
- 020 7251 3535   020 7251 3536
- info@centaurus.co.uk
- www.centaurus.co.uk
- Barbican/Old Street LU
- Mon-Sat 10am-6.30pm

This very friendly gay gallery and store stocks magazines, books, videos and DVD's from just about every producer. Centaurus also specialises in photography, with thousands of photos of hundreds of models on offer. They have a huge selection of gay magazine back issues, dating from the 1950's, a photographic studio for hire, and mail order service.

Clone Zone
- 64 Old Compton Street, Soho, W1
- 020 7287 3530
- Leicester Square LU
- 266 Old Brompton Road, Earl's Court, SW5
- 020 7373 0598
- West Brompton LU
- www.clonezone.co.uk
- Mon-Sat 11am-10.40pm, Sun 1.15pm-6.30pm

This award-winning gay multi-store has two London outlets, both featuring their hallmark selection of clothes, mags, books, greeting cards, sex toys, and club flyers. As well as the rubber and leatherwear, erotic swimwear and underwear, the company's own Flesh clothing label produces T-shirts, jackets and shirts, and has shown its collection on the *Clothes Show Live*. Their good selection of books include biographies, fiction, gay guides and photographic tomes, and there are also postcards and porn magazines.

Crusaid Shop

🖃 *17-19 Upper Tachbrook Street, Pimlico, SW1*

☎ *020 7233 8736*

🚇 *Pimlico LU*

🕒 *Mon-Sat 10.30am-5.15pm*

This charity shop is one of the best in London, and gets a great selection of designer clothes, records and CD's and books. As well as offering great bargains, the organisation raises money for HIV/AIDS.

Heals

🖃 *196 Tottenham Court Road, London, W1*

🖃 *234 Kings Road, London, SW3*

☎ *020 7636 1666*

🕒 *Mon-Wed 10am-6pm, Thurs 10am-8pm, Fri 10am-6.30pm, Sat 9.30am-6.30pm, Sun 12noon-6pm*

Heals is the business! If you want stylish contemporary home furnishings. Just about everything is priced above the average Londoners budget, but it is so worth a look anyway. Regard every purchase as a lifetime investment and you'll be OK! The staff will also happily carry goods to your car – nice touch.

Obsessions

🖃 *23 Old Brompton Road, South Kensington, SW7*

☎ *Shop info line 020 7589 0071*

🕒 *Mon-Sat 10.30am-6.30pm*

🖃 *2 Hays Galleria, Tooley Street, SE1*

☎ *020 7403 2374*

🕒 *Mon-Fri 8am-6.30pm*

🖃 *151 Cheapside, EC2*

☎ *020 7600 7410*

🕒 *Mon-Fri 9.30am-6.30pm*

Obsessions gifts and accessories chain are probably the campest shops in London, with very affordable gift ideas that go beyond the merely kitsch. Among the novelty cards, furry picture frames and washing-up gloves decorated with plastic flowers, can be found more expensive, quality gifts like silver fountain pens, manicure sets and glassware.

Positive Discounts, see p.69

Prowler

- 3-7 Brewer Street, Soho, W1
- ☎ 020 7734 4031
- 🕑 Mon-Sat 11am-10pm, Sun noon-8pm
- 283 Camden High Street, Camden Town, NW1
- ☎ 020 7284 0537
- 🕑 Mon-Sat 10am-6.30pm

This pioneering gay life and style store stocks the latest fashions, underwear, books, gifts, accessories, mags, CDs, advance club tickets, videos (including hardcore) and sex toys. They also offer a complete mail order service for books, videos and mags – call 0800 45 45 66.

MAIL-ORDER COMPANIES

Clone Zone Mail Order

▣ *Wellington House, Pollard Street East, Manchester, M40 7FS*

☎ *0800 783 7953*

The pioneers in gay shopping in London have a mail-order service with a catalogue that's a riot of videos, imported magazines from the US, uncensored novels, rubber and leatherwear, dildos and lubricant. Major credit cards accepted.

Babes-n-Horny

▣ *BCM Babes London WC1N 3XX*

☎ *020 7538 9838*

✍ *bhorny@babes-n-horny.com*

✍ *babes-n-horny.com*

This mail-order company are justly proud of their range of 32 silicone dildos in differing sizes, colours and finishes, from the £10.95 Tula model to the whopping Titus for £59.95. As its name suggests, the company is dyke friendly and was recently described by *Time Out* as offering 'the prince of dildos'.

Kiniki

▣ *Spenccroft Road, Newcastle, Staffs, ST5 9QQ*

☎ *01782 611599*   ✆ *01782 712 505*

✍ *www.kiniki.com*

This brochure and easy-to-use website features hunky models in fabulous men's underwear and swimwear in cotton, lycra, tan-through and see-through fabrics, with high and low cut briefs, thongs, g-strings and boxers. Special offers always available. UK postage just £1.50, delivery within 48 hours. Overseas 6-10 days. All major credit cards accepted.

Male Xpress

▣ *3 Broadbent Close, 20-22 Highgate High Street, N6*

☎ *mail order 0800 454566*

✍ *www.malexpress.co.uk*

Male Xpress is the UK's largest gay mail order service offering a great range of products and a quick and reliable delivery service. Their catalogue includes magazines, videos, adult toys and clothing. The website is easy to use and regularly up-dated.

New Centurion

▣ *PO Box 21528, London, E10 7XJ*

Video distributor of hard-core male porn.

Passion 8 Shop.com

⌖ *4 Kilnbeck Business Park, Beverley, E. Yorkshire, HU17 0LF*

☎ *01482 873 377*

This mail-order company deals in products calculated to increase sexual pleasure without the bias towards pornography. There is a wide range of dildos, erection maintainers, cock rings, handcuffs, penile creams and condoms in various flavours and colours, as well as vibrators, handcuffs and a variety of penis developers.

Quick and Direct

⌖ *137a Hersham Road, Walton-on-Thames, Surrey, KT12 1BR*

☎ *01932 232443* ✎ *01932 240337*

This company markets top quality condoms through the post, at around 30% of what you would otherwise pay. They sell eight different kinds of Durex and Mates, 14 different World's Best, as well as KY Jelly.

MUSIC

Trax Records

⌖ *55 Greek Street, Soho, W1*

☎ *020 7734 0795*

✄ *www.traxrecords.co.uk*

🕐 *Mon-Sat noon-7pm, Fri till 8.30pm*

Cutting edge vinyl including funky hard house, club high energy, europop, hard trance as well as merchandise.

XSF Records

⌖ *39 Berwick Street, Soho, W1*

☎ *020 7287 2496*

🕐 *Mon-Sat 11am-7pm*

Original dance vinyl, including underground funk, techno and trance.

OPTICIANS

Otto

⌖ *15 Highbury Corner, London, N5*

☎ *0207 700 7557*

🕐 *Mon-Wed 10am-6pm, Thurs 10am-8pm, Fri 10am-6.30pm, Sat 9.30am-6.30pm, Sun noon-6pm*

Otto is a very fine opticians that welcomes lesbians and gay men to their pleasant shop. The best reason to go to Otto is that once your eye test is done they have a fast lens-cutting machine; it keeps the cost of your glasses down and means you can take them away the same day. The cost of frames at Otto includes basic lenses, which is a deal you won't find anywhere else.

TATTOOS/PIERCING

Diamond Jack's Tattoo Studio
⌨ *5 Walker's Court, Soho, W1*
☎ *020 7437 0605*
🚇 *Piccadilly Circus LU*
🕐 *Mon-Sat 11am-7pm, Sun 12noon-6pm*
A friendly tattoo service in the heart of Soho.

Liquid Art Tattoo & Piercing Studio
⌨ *266 Old Brompton Road, SW5*
☎ *020 7373 0477*
🕐 *Mon-Sat 12noon-7pm*
This established studio is situated below Clone Zone.

Metal Morphosis
⌨ *10-11 Moor Street, Soho, W1*
☎ *020 7434 4554*
🚇 Leicester Square LU
🕐 *Mon-Sat 11am-7.30pm, Sun 1pm-6pm*
Trendy body piercing studio with a good selection of jewellery and a large gay/lesbian following.

Tusk Body Piercing
⌨ *1 Stukeley Street, off Drury Lane, Covent Garden, WC2*
☎ *020 7404 5999*
🚇 *Covent Garden LU*
🕐 *Mon-Sat 11.30am-7pm, Sun 12.30pm-6pm*
Professional body piercing with a free consultation.

Urban Life
⌨ *17 Hackney Road, Shoreditch, E2*
☎ *020 7729 0066*
🚇 *Bethnal Green BR/LU*
🕐 *Tues-Sat 11am-7pm*
Gay-owned and -run shop offering hair design, tattooing and body piercing.

SOCIAL GROUPS

Whether you're just starting to come to terms with your homosexuality or are finding that the scene doesn't give you the depth of relationship you're looking for, these organised groups can plug you into an instant supply of gay men and lesbians in the same area, from similar backgrounds or with the same interests as you. The groups are run by volunteers, often meeting in the privacy and safety of members' homes or on trips to gay and lesbian bars, restaurants and clubs, or even weekends away.

SPECIALIST INTEREST

Blue Haze

⌨ *BM Blue Haze, London, WC1*

✍ *ukgayinfo@aol.com or blue_haze@compuserve.com*

✍ *www.ourworld.compuserve.com/homepages/blue_haze/*

✇ *Annual membership £15*

An over-18s club set up around ten years ago for gay men who turn on to other gay men smoking – be it cigars, pipes or cigarettes. They have members aged from their 20s to their 70s and from as far afield as the USA and Australia. For London members, there are several regular social nights a week, as well as frequent parties; accommodation is provided for out-of-towners. On joining, you receive a complete set of all members details and a free post box number to contact others. The club magazine *Smoke Signals*, is filled with steamy stories, artwork and photos. First Wednesday at The Stag (8pm; see p.130), Friday & Saturday King's Arms at (8pm; see p.126), Sunday free admittance to the Hoist (9pm-1am; see p.27).

Gay Artists Group

☎ *George 020 7624 6181*

🕐 *Three times a month*

✇ *Annual membership £5, £4 per session*

This group has for almost 40 years encouraged gay artists to work together on life drawing. The twenty professional and serious amateur artists are of all abilities and standards – and include sculptors, illustrators, cartoonists, interior decorators and costume designers – and meet in members' homes for three hours to sketch a nude male model without tuition. They mounted an exhibition at Central Station in December 1995.

Gay Classic Car Group

⌨ *BM Box 5901, WC1*

☎ *David 020 7722 3094*

✍ *gccg@battenburgcake.com*

✍ *www.battenburgcake.com*

✇ *Annual membership £10 a year*

This national group was launched in 1988 for aficionados of classic cars, and most of the 320 members own at least one – albeit in varying conditions. Local regional representatives co-ordinate activities all over the country, and the group retains strong links with similar organisations worldwide. The group organises weekends away, barbecues and weekend runs into the countryside; they also publish the quarterly *Big End* newsletter.

Gay Football Supporters Network

⌨ *Box GZ, Central Station, 37 Wharfdale Road, King's Cross, N1*

☎ *Chris 020 8926 3616*

✉ *gfsn@cableinet.co.uk*

✉ *www.geocities.com/colosseum/slope/3743*

🚇 *King's Cross BR/LU*

🕐 *Last Fri 9pm*

💲 *Annual membership £10*

This national social organisation to put gay football supporters in touch with each other draws around 30-40 people to each of its monthly London sessions at Central Station. The national group meets twice yearly and there's a monthly newsletter to keep members up to date with what the regional groups are doing. It also details trips to matches, social events and contacts.

Gay and Lesbian Multiple Sclerosis Group (GLAMS)

⌨ *London Friend, 86 Caledonian Road, King's Cross, N1*

☎ *020 8882 7704*

🚇 *King's Cross BR/LU*

🕐 *Last Tues 7.30pm-9pm*

Social and support group for lesbians and gay men with MS.

Gay Vegetarians and Vegans

⌨ *BM 5700, London, WC1*

☎ *020 8690 5397*

✉ *vvgg.@freeuk.com*

✉ *www.vvgg.freeserve.co.uk*

💲 *No membership fee*

Formed in 1979 to establish a friendship network and explore vegetarianism, this national social and support group for gay, lesbian, bisexual and transgender vegetarians and vegans attracts 10-20 people of all ages. They run a calendar of regular social events, including cookery demonstrations, meals out, and a regular picnic at London Friend (see p.89).

Hathway Club

☎ *Eric 020 7277 5014*

✉ *eric.presland@homopromos.fsnet.co.uk*

🕐 *Tues monthly*

A gay crossword club! Around 10 men meet up monthly to solve cryptic puzzles together; drink wine and cook some pasta. It's not too competitive an atmosphere, and they compile the crosswords themselves, so clues can be gay-themed and often, rather risqué.

London Gay Naturists

⌨ *BM 3377, London, WC1*

☎ *Ralph or Paul 020 8802 9477*

✆ *Annual membership*

This friendly fifteen-year-old club has over 170 members countrywide who wish to shed their clothes and get closer to nature. The club offers not just day trips to nudist beaches and weekend trips staying in naturist-friendly accommodation, but also nude social events in pubs and get-togethers in private homes. The group also produces the *Naturist Beach Guide*, which details all the nude bathing sites in the UK.

MENSA Gay Special Interest Group (GaySig)

⌨ *Flat 1, 15 Shortlands Grove, Bromley, Kent, BR2*

☎ *Corinne 020 8466 5632*

✆ *Annual membership £5.50*

Twenty years old in 2001, this lively and very friendly social group for gay Mensa members has over 100 members throughout the UK. They meet monthly for lunch in a member's home, usually with a turn-out of 20-25 people, and organise further meets for cinema, theatre, meals out or weekends away. They publish a monthly newsletter and a directory of contact names. You must be a Mensa member to join.

Regard

⌨ *BM Regard, London, WC1*

☎ *020 7688 4111* ✆ *020 7688 4114*

Helpline 020 7738 6191 (Tues 7pm-9pm)

✐ *regard@dircon.co.uk*

✐ *www.regard.dircon.co.uk*

This national organisation for disabled lesbians, gay men and bisexuals works to support the rights and inclusion of all disabled people into society, and its high-profile patrons include Graham Norton, Ivan Massow and Stephen Twigg. They have a befriending service and helpline; and keep a comprehensive database with details of organisations and services for individual referrals. Their regular newsletter updates readers on new legislation that effect disabled people.

Rubber Medusas ♀

☎ *Ros 020 7727 5379*

🕐 *Tues 7.30pm at St George's Tavern in Victoria*

A bridge club for women of all ages and standards in central London, meeting weekly in St George's Tavern (see p.129). About a dozen show up for a social game, and members also take off once a year with other gay bridge groups for a weekend of gaming.

Sisterhood of Karn

☏ *07092 185781*

✍ *www.skarn@sonow.com*

🕓 *Second and fourth Wed 8pm*

Set up in 1994, this *Dr Who* (and general sci-fi) enthusiasts' club welcomes all young gay people to celebrate their passion, avoiding ridicule or awkwardness, amongst a like-minded crowd – in fact, they say it's more difficult coming out as a *Dr Who* fan than as gay. On average about 25 will turn up in the upstairs bar of The King's Arms (see p.126) twice a month. The group organise occasional outings, video nights, trips to locations and produced an all-gay *Dr Who* film.

West London Lesbian and Gay Duplicate Bridge Club

🖼 *The Running Horse, Davies Street, Mayfair, W1*

☏ *Andrew 020 7537 2481*

🚇 *Bond Street LU*

🕓 *Mon 7.30pm-11pm*

This serious but sociable duplicate pairs bridge club gathers in The Running Horse to thrash it out for supremacy. You need to know the basics as they don't encourage raw beginners. The group also organise the odd weekend away and pit themselves against other bridge clubs.

NATIONALITY-BASED GROUPS

AHBAB

✍ *www.glas.org/ahbab*

The online community for gay and lesbian Arabs throughout the world publishes news and features, and tries to bring queer Arab people together – and to promote tolerance of sexual differences. The site includes articles, poetry, recipes, classified ads and chat rooms.

Cymdeithas Gymraeg Lesbiaid a Hoywon Llundain (London Welsh Lesbian and Gay Group)

☏ *020 8881 2899*

🚇 *Leicester Square LU*

🕓 *Third Thurs 7.30pm*

💲 *Free*

If you can even come close to pronouncing this, you're in. For around ten years gay Welsh language speakers have been meeting once a month for a social night out, with occasional clubbing, theatre and cinema nights. There are around 40 people on the books altogether, and around 5-7 show up for each meeting.

DOST

📧 *c/o NAZ Project, Palingswick House, 241 King Street, Hammersmith, W6*

☎ *020 8741 1879*   📠 *020 8741 9841*

🚇 *Ravenscourt Park LU*

🕐 *First & third Wed 7.30pm; last Sat 3pm*

This social and support group for South Asians, North African and Middle Eastern men welcomes all gay and bisexual men to discuss sexual health, HIV, religion, race, racism, arranged marriages and sexuality in an informal, culturally appropriate way. Around 8-10 men turn up to each meeting and there are parties to mark cultural celebrations.

Friday Group

☎ *020 8675 6001*

🕐 *Fri 8pm*

This social and support group for black, gay and bi men meets each week in a member's home for a discussion, with up to a dozen boys showing up. They also organise nights out to pubs, the cinema, etc.

Jewish Gay and Lesbian Group – see p.156

Kiss

📧 *The NAZ Project, Palingswick House, 241 King Street, Hammersmith, W6*

☎ *020 8741 1879*

🖎 *www.planetkiss.org.uk*

🚇 *Hammersmith LU*

Part of the NAZ project, this HIV and sexual health organisation serves South Asian, Middle Eastern, African and Latin American communities, running several groups. The group runs regular social evenings for both gay men and lesbian and bi women – phone for details.

Long Yang Club

📧 *BCM Wisdom, London, WC1*

☎ *Barry 020 8391 9117*

  Recorded info 020 8397 2737

💲 *Annual membership £15, couples £20*

Started in the early 1980s for Orientals and their friends, Long Yang is now the largest group in the UK, with over 1,000 members. It's probably also the best organised one, with a professional-looking monthly magazine called *East-West*. As well as Dim Sum lunches, discos, karaoke parties and celebrations of Chinese New Year and other Asian festivals, the group host a weekly social night at the King's Arms, 68 Great Titchfield Street, Soho, W1 (Sat 8pm-11pm), and host the Tea Dance Extra disco in the Soundshaft bar at Heaven (Sun 8pm-1am).

GENERAL SOCIAL GROUPS

Able Together
☎ *Doug 01582 705257*
✉ *ableto_uk@europe.com*
🕐 *Sat noon-3pm*
A disabled gay and lesbian group that meets weekly at the Rupert Street Bar in Soho (see p.129).

BearHug
✉ *BM BearHug, London, WC1*
☎ *020 8288 9484*
✉ *secretary@bearhug.net*
✉ *www.bearhug.co.uk*
If you like your men hairy, there are over 400 members from mainly around London who can oblige. They get together for trips to art galleries, to pubs or the cinema, as well as on Sundays at 6pm for the weekly Urusus night at XXL (see p.38).

Beaumont Society
✉ *27 Old Gloucester Street, London, WC1(postal enquiries only)*
☎ *Janet 01582 732936*
    Helpline 0700 028 7878 (Tues & Thurs 7pm-11pm)
💰 *Annual membership £35*
This national organisation for cross-dressers has around 850-900 members and organises a range social events. They meet on the fourth Sunday of the month at The George in Isleworth (7pm), and the second Sunday at London Friend (7pm; see p.89), and organise nights out in between. They also publish a quarterly newsletter.

Bisexual Women's Group ♀
✉ *Vespa Lounge, 15 St Giles's High Street, Covent Garden, WC2*
☎ *Naomi 020 8768 0566*
🚇 *Tottenham Court Road LU*
🕐 *Wed 6.30pm-9pm*
A fun and friendly group for girls out to meet other girls.

Brothers and Sisters Club
☎ *020 7837 5561*   ✆ *0870 130 8719*
✉ *honsec@broandsis.org.uk*
🕐 *First Fri*
This social group for deaf and hard of hearing gay men and lesbians of all ages meets once a month in central London. Ring for details.

190

Deaf MESMAC

⌨ *1-3 Worship Street, City, EC2*

☎ *David 020 7588 3521   minicom 020 7588 3530*

Group for the hard of hearing or deaf. Ring for details of meetings.

Gay and Bisexual Men's Group

⌨ *Healthy Gay Living Centre, 40 Borough High Street, SE1*

☎ *020 7407 3550*

🚇 *Borough LU*

🕐 *Tues 6pm-8.30pm*

An ongoing open discussion group that focuses on gay and bisexual life, and which offers a good chance to meet other men off the commercial scene in a healthy and open atmosphere.

Gay and Bisexual Men's Support and Social Group (GRAB)

⌨ *Freepost ANG 2132, Brentwood, Essex, CM15 9YY*

☎ *01708 782951*

🕐 *Mon drop-in 8pm-10.30pm*

A weekly drop-in and monthly social events (pubs, clubs, theatre) for gay and bisexual men in the Barking, Dagenham, Havering and Brentwood area.

Gay Nudist Group

⌨ *BM Box 372, London, WC1*

☎ *01376 03112*

🏷 *Membership £12 (singles), £15 (couples)*

Founded in 1983, Britain's first nudist group offers men a chance to meet each other – with their clothes off. There are 250 members all over the county, the majority aged 40-60, who meet every couple of weeks in London, usually in each others' homes, for evenings of photography, body painting, massage and socials. The rules are: no clothes, no sex, bring a bottle.

Gay Rebirthing Group

⌨ *The Helios Centre, 5-9 Tavistock Place, WC1*

☎ *David 020 7388 3109*

What an Islington thing to do. Members get together and talk about their birth experience and how wonderful life is. Ring for details.

Gay Skinhead Group (GSG)

⌨ *PO Box 234, Witham, Essex, CM8*

✎ *www.public.diversity.org.uk/gay-skinheads*

✺ *Annual membership £10 (enclose SAE)*

This non-political, non-right wing befriending group for shaven-headed people (number 3 shave or less) has around 200 members all over UK, and over 50 in London. It favours a hard look, but is more about original attitudes and ideas than toughness. The group has a club night on the first and third Friday of the month at the A Bar in Borough (10pm-2am; free to members; see p.xxx), as well as arranging other meetings, weekends away and parties. *The Skinhead Nation* magazine comes out five times a year.

Gay Spiritual Group

⌨ *61 Southerton Road, Hammersmith, W6*

☎ *020 8846 8593*   ✆ *020 8563 1082*

✺ *Membership £12*

Friendly social group for gays and lesbians with weekly socials, drop-ins, discussion groups, book readings, meditation, healing and tarot readings.

Gay Young London Group

⌨ *Central Station, 37 Wharfdale Road, King's Cross, N1*

🚇 *King's Cross BR/LU*

🕐 *Mon 7.30pm-9pm*

This weekly social meeting upstairs at the King's Cross pub for 18-30-year-olds draws up to 40 young guys.

Hyde Park Gays and Sapphics

⌨ *Speakers Corner, Hyde Park, W1*

☎ *Sharley 020 8422 6498*

🚇 *Marble Arch LU*

🕐 *Sun noon*

This group was originally part of the Campaign for Homosexual Equality, set up in the early 70s to spread the word, and used to need police protection because of the amount of abuse they received. Today a small group meets at Speakers Corner come rain or shine, a couple of speakers hopping up on soap boxes to hold forth about gay rights and AIDS – and getting a lot of heckling.

Kenric – see p.95

Lesbian and Gay Conservation Volunteers (BCTV)

⌨ *80 York Way, King's Cross, N1*

☎ *020 7278 4293*

Formed in 1989 as part of the British Trust for Conservation Volunteers, the country's leading practical conservation organisation, this gay group bands together for (roughly monthly) tasks from shrub clearance and planting, coppicing and hedge-laying to dry-stone walling and bridge building. Weekend and week-long projects provide accommodation and food: all you do is provide the elbow grease.

London Bisexual Group

⌨ *London Friend, 86 Caledonian Road, King's Cross, N1*

☎ *020 7837 3337*
  Helpline Tues & Wed 020 8569 7500 (Tues & Wed)

🚇 *King's Cross BR/LU*

🕐 *Fri 8pm-10pm*

This informal social and support group for bisexual men and women meets at London Friend each week, but acts primarily as a social group with discussions, film and club nights as well as meals out.

London Monday Group (LMG)

⌨ *Central Station, 37 Wharfdale Road, King's Cross, N1*

☎ *Bob 020 7229 8272*

✎ *robertcook@kix.co.uk*

🚇 *King's Cross BR/LU*

🕐 *Mon 8.30pm-11pm*

💰 *Annual membership £10*

Set up in 1973 as the West London Group for Homosexual Equality, the LMG doesn't partake of as much campaigning these days, but still meets every Monday at Central Station for a social get-together. This group welcomes anyone but is mainly stocked with gay men of 40+ vintage. They organise an annual holiday weekend in Europe, occasional wine and cheese parties, and the popular Capital Quiz (October-March).

Network

⌨ *The Queen's Arms, 223 Hanworth Road, Hounslow, Middlesex, TW3*

🚇 *Hounslow Central LU*

🕐 *Thurs 7.30pm-11pm*

This Lesbian and bisexual social group meet at the popular West London pub (see p.146).

New Beginnings

🖾 *Central Station, 37 Wharfdale Rd, King's Cross, N1*

☎ *020 7265 9655*

🚇 *King's Cross BR/LU*

🕐 *Sat 7.45pm*

Social and discussion group for gay and bisexual people who have come out but want an alternative to the gay scene. A place to make friends without the blare of background music.

New Dykes ♀

☎ *020 8555 8186*

🚇 *East Ham LU*

🕐 *Tues 7pm-10pm*

Weekly meeting for lesbians and bisexual women 25 and under, with discussions, guest speakers and general socialising.

Shugs the Word

☎ *Sophia 07092 052238*

This book club caters for Black and Asian lesbians who have a real passion for reading and discussion. Ring for details of meetings.

Turning Point

🖾 *London Friend, 86 Caledonian Road, King's Cross, N1*

☎ *020 7833 1674*

🚇 *King's Cross BR/LU*

🕐 *Wed 7pm-9.30pm*

This London Friend group for those coming to terms with their sexuality sees a constant stream of young men in search of clarity about their ambivalent sexual feelings, featuring a different themed talk and discussion each week. Up to 50 men show up and drift off to Central Station (see p.134) afterwards.

USPCG

🖾 *PO Box 1714, Yate, Bristol, BS37 4NS*

A project that helps combat the loneliness and boredom of gay US prisoners, many of whom have no family or friends, through organising gay penpals. Write for details.

LOCALLY-BASED GROUPS

Barnet Social Group

☎ *Peter 020 8367 2930 or Robert 020 8366 6632*

☺ *Thurs; annual membership*

A well-organised local lesbian, gay and bisexual group that arranges meetings and socials four times a month, with the Icebreaker night for new members, and the Scene night to visit a pub, club or sauna. There are also non-scene trips and activity nights. Their monthly *Bugle* newsletter keeps members up to date.

Croydon Area Gay Society (CAGS)

✉ *PO Box 464, London, SE25*

☎ *Colin 020 8771 1814*

☺ *Wed 9pm*

💰 *Annual membership £10*

CAGS is a social group for gay men and women in and around Croydon. The 100 or so members attend a weekly pub night at The Goose & Carrot (see p.142) or an organised event. The monthly newsletter details their full social diary.

Ealing Gay Group

✉ *PO Box 130, Ealing, W5*

☎ *Neil 020 8998 6708*

💰 *Annual membership £4*

This social group is mainly made up of 30+ non-scene men from Ealing and other parts of West London. They usually meet in member's homes or organise pub and theatre nights at the weekend, and circulate an information sheet to members saying where events will take place.

Gay East London (GEL)

✉ *33 Romford Road, Stratford, E15*

☎ *Stephen 020 8519 5527*

🚉 *Bethnal Green BR/LU*

☺ *First and third Fri of the month 8.30pm-11pm*

💰 *£2 per meeting*

This East End gay and bisexual social group sees quite a mix of races, religions, ages, incomes and outlook, and meets twice a month, once to play board games or sit and chat, the other to hear a guest speaker talking about AIDS, legal issues or other serious topics. Between 20 and 40 people come to the meetings, and in between there are organised coffee evenings, theatre trips, stately home visits and dinner parties.

Harrow and Brent Lesbian and Gay Group

⌨ *PO Box 649, Harrow, Middlesex, HA3 0LE*

☎ *Peter 020 8908 1795*

✉ *hblgg@freeuk.com*

✉ *www.hblgg.freeuk.com*

Celebrating 30th birthday in 2001, this is London's oldest gay social group. They meet weekly at the Sports Bar, Preston Road, Wembley, and spend the evening socialising, hearing occasional speakers or making the most of the cheap bar prices. In between are quizzes, discos, sports days, barbecues, bingo nights or Sunday walks, and out of the 100 members of all ages on the books, usually 30-35 turn up to each activity.

Hounslow Lesbian and Gay Group

⌨ *PO Box 339, Hounslow, Middlesex, TW3 4PQ*

☎ *020 8577 1301*

🦑 *No membership fee*

This group has a good gay/lesbian balance, with around eighty on the mailing list. They tend to meet monthly for social evenings with a speaker or silly games in a local gay pub, or for meals out, a sauna or swimming session, and also get involved with their local borough to organise day conferences. Their mailing list keeps people up to date with upcoming activities.

Kingston and Richmond Gay Society (KRAGS)

⌨ *PO Box 158a, Surbiton, Surrey, KT6 6RS*

☎ *David 020 8397 4903*

✉ *info@krags.co.uk*

🕐 *Tues 9pm*

🦑 *Annual membership £12, couples £20*

This well-organised Kingston and Richmond gay and bisexual men's group draws 25+ men from the Kingston/Richmond/Surbiton area to a couple of events a week (some in members homes), with guest speakers, music evenings, pub and club visits, and a weekly night at The Richmond Arms (see p.147). The group has 85-90 members and on average 15 people normally show up to events.

Lewisham Gay Alliance

⌨ *c/o Voluntary Action Lewisham, 120 Rushey Green, Catford, SE6*

☎ *020 8694 2246*

Group for local lesbian and gay people. Ring for meeting details.

Magnet

⌨ *PO Box 10036, London, SE14*

☎ *Dave M 020 8854 3446 or Dave P 020 8300 4206*

✉ *magnet_social_group@hotmail.com*

💰 *Annual membership £10*

This south east London and north west Kent gay and lesbian social group was previously called Badgers but thankfully changed its name a dozen years ago. They arrange an evening or weekend event at least once a week, and alternate weekly pub nights between Bromley and Greenwich. Members receive a regular newsletter.

Marylebone and Paddington CHE Group

☎ *Terry 020 7607 4755*

🕐 *Tues 8pm*

Founded in 1957, the Marylebone and Paddington Group is made up of around thirty mature men from all over London, up to a dozen of whom meet in someone's house once a week for a coffee or drinks evening, or for organised walks during the summer. They also hold twice-yearly sales at ULU and Conway Hall to raise funds for charity.

Metroline

⌨ *The Metro Centre, Unit 401, 49 Greenwich High Road, Greenwich, SE10*

☎ *020 8265 3311* 📠 *020 8265 1645*

✉ *themetro@dircon.co.uk*

✉ *www.themetro.dircon.co.uk*

🚉 *Greenwich BR/DLR*

🕐 *Tues 1pm-4pm women's drop-in; Thurs 1pm-4pm general drop-in; first Sat: Tribe under 16s, GLB 2pm-5pm*

Lesbian, gay and bisexual people, as well as those questioning their sexuality, can use the Metro Centre's services, which include support, advice, information, events, education and training. They also offer counselling, health services, free legal advice and a meeting space for local groups, as well as drop-in sessions for those in need of support.

Octopus

⌨ *BM Box 8485, London, WC1*

☎ *020 8270 2006*

🕐 *Mon 8pm-10pm; annual membership*

This social group holds relaxed weekly socials in the homes of members in the East London/Essex area, taking in Barking, Forest Gate, Chadwell Heath and Epping. There are regular barbecues, discos and theatre trips – the group tries to provide lifts for those without transport. Many of their events have a no-smoking rule.

Out in Bromley

☎ *Lesley 020 8302 3968*

🕐 *Second and fourth Thurs 8pm*

A purely social gay and lesbian group, Out in Bromley has a good 50/50 mix of young men and women. A very friendly and well-organised group, they meet twice a month in a member's home to introduce newcomers, then run a programme of events in between.

South London Gays

📧 *PO Box 243, Wimbledon, SW19*

☎ *Philip 020 8549 0391*

💰 *Annual membership £10*

South and south west London's gay social group meets up every night of the week except Wednesday for a social evening. It's generally a 50+ group who gather for discussion nights, cinema and museum visits, days out, and regular tennis and badminton sessions.

Surrey and London Association of Gay Organisations (SLAGO)

📧 *PO Box 243, London, SW19 1XW*

☎ *01737 766651*

🖋 *www.foxearth.demon.co.uk/slago/*

The umbrella organisation for a clutch of gay and lesbian social and support groups in London and the Home Counties encourages interchange of news and ideas, and holds quarterly liaison meetings, web hosting for groups without their own web pages, a biennial conference, and a variety of combined social events.

Waltham Forest Gay and Bi Men's Group (WRAGS)

☎ *Paul 020 8478 9710*

🕐 *Tues 8pm-11pm*

The catchment area of this sociable mixed-age gay and bisexual men's group takes in Ilford, Waltham Forest, Dagenham, Romford, Walthamstow and Leytonstone, meeting every week in Ilford. When it's not holding discussions, the group hosts music and TV quizzes, picnics and other social events and trips. There are around seventy members, and on average, 15-25 normally show up.

Wim-Wim ♀

- 🏠 *Hartfields Wine Bar, Hartfields Road, SW18*
- ☎ *01483 833 966*
- 🚉 *Wimbledon BR/LU*
- 🕐 *Wed 8pm*

South west London social group for lesbians.

YOUTH (UNDER-26) GROUPS

Bexley Area Youth Group

- ☎ *Tom 020 8265 3311*
- 🕐 *Fri 7pm-9pm*

The Bexley BLAG social group is a self-run organisation for under-26s that meets once a week in Welling. There's a 60/40 mix of gay men and women, and around 15 people usually show up for tea and biscuits, a facilitated discussion, trips to pubs or guest speakers.

BreakOut in Harrow

- ☎ *020 8424 7536*
- ✎ *info@hlbgy.co.uk*

LGB group for 16-21s, with activities and social evenings in a friendly environment. Ring for meeting details.

Camden Young Lesbian and Bisexual Women's Group ♀

- ☎ *Deborah or Theresa 020 7267 8596*
- 🚉 *Kentish Town LU*

Social and support group for girls under 25. Ring for details.

Chillin' Out Drop In

- 🏠 *Unit 401, 49 Greenwich High Road, Greenwich, SE10*
- ☎ *020 8265 3311*
- ✎ *themetro@dircon.co.uk*   ✎ *www.themetro.dircon.co.uk*
- 🚉 *Greenwich BR/DLR*
- 🕐 *Sun 2pm-5pm*

Social group for south London lesbians, gays and bisexuals either coming to terms with or questioning their sexuality.

Croydon Young Lesbian, Gay and Bisexual Group

- ☎ *07071 225577*
- 🚉 *West Croydon BR*
- 🕐 *Sun 7pm-10pm*

A friendly social group for lesbian, gay men and bisexuals under 25.

Facing South

☎ *Sarah or James 020 7378 8732*

🕐 *Tues 5pm-7pm: mixed 1-to-1 drop-in, 7pm-9pm: mixed social group*

This project caters for people who either know or suspect that they are gay, lesbian or bisexual, and offers both a social group and drop-in service where young people can approach workers individually for counselling and information. The social group provides coming-out sessions, videos, outings to local gay places and clubs.

First Move

☎ *Mo 020 8205 0006*

✉ *firstmove@baeu.demon.co.uk*

A social and support group for lesbian, gay men and bisexuals under 25.

Future Perfect

☎ *020 7407 3550*

✉ *gareth@lads.demon.co.uk*

🚇 *London Bridge BR/LU*

This health and social group for gay and bisexual men under 25 runs a range of social groups and activities, as well as various courses throughout the year.

Gay Young Harrow (Freedom Youth UK)

▤ *PO Box 649, Harrow, Middlesex, HA3 0LE*

☎ *020 8908 0396 (during group hours)*

🕐 *Mon 8pm-11pm*

This local lesbian, gay and bisexual social group for under-26s meets weekly at the Preston Road Sports Centre in Harrow (ring for directions), as well as organising pub and club visits – youth workers and members turn up and decide on the night. The group also operates a penpal scheme.

Greenwich Freedom Youth

▤ *24-24a Greens End, Woolwich, SE18*

☎ *020 8316 4397*

🚇 *Woolwich Arsenal BR*

🕐 *Tues: mixed LGB night (7.30pm-10pm), Wed: women's night (7.30pm-10pm), Thurs: Freedom Youth Theatre (7.30pm-10pm)*

Lesbians, gays and bisexuals under 25 in south east London can take advantage of this social, advice and support group that meets weekly in Greenwich, with an array of discussions, workshops and social activities like bowling, theatre and cinema on offer.

Horizons at Hounslow ♀

☎ *07956 459223*

🕐 *Sun 6pm-8pm*

A social support for lesbian/bisexual/unsure women under 26. Wheelchair access.

I-dentity

✉ *c/o Hounslow Youth and Community Service, 78 St John's Road, Isleworth, Middlesex, TW7*

☎ *Lawrence 020 8742 2381*

🚇 *Turnham Green LU*

🕐 *Mon-Fri 9am-5pm, Sun 6.30pm-9pm*

This weekly social and support drop-in for gay and bisexual men under 26 offers one-to-one support, advice about housing and sexual health, and referral to various projects, as well as a programme of activities, from visiting a local pool or sauna to watching a video, discussing gay issues or going to the cinema. Around fifteen people turn up to each session in Chiswick.

Lesbian and Bisexual Women's Youth Group ♀

✉ *c/o Islington Youth Service, Education Dept, Laycock Street, Islington, N1*

☎ *020 7607 8346*

🚇 *Highbury and Islington LU*

🕐 *Tues 6pm-9pm*

Part of North London Line Lesbian and Gay Youth Project, this social and support group caters for women who are coming terms with their sexuality, or who just want to make new friends.

Lewisham Gay Young People's Group

☎ *020 8461 4112*

Local Lewisham group for under-21s. Ring for details.

London Connection Lesbian and Gay Group

✉ *12 Adelaide Street, Charing Cross, WC2*

☎ *020 7766 5550*

🚇 *Charing Cross BR/LU*

This daytime group caters for homeless and/or unemployed lesbians and gay men between 16 and 25, with a range of support and advice. Ring for times.

London Lesbian, Gay and Bisexual Teenage Group

⌧ *6-9 Manor Gardens, off Holloway Road, Holloway, N7*

☎ *020 7263 5932 (during group hours)*

⌨ *www.teenagegroup.home.ml.org*

🚇 *Archway or Holloway Road LU*

🕐 *Wed 7pm-10pm & Sun 3pm-7pm*

This safe space hosts a youth project for 16–25-year-old lesbians and gays coming to terms with their sexuality. There are discussions on HIV and coming out, one-to-one support and advice sessions, and trips out to the cinema, theatre or bowling alley. Younger members tend to come along on Sunday.

Men Out East

⌧ *ELOP, 388-392 Leyton High Road, Leyton, E10*

☎ *020 8558 0551*

🚇 *Leyton LU*

🕐 *Wed 7.30pm-10pm*

Group for gay men.

Metro Youth

⌧ *The Metro Centre, Unit 401, 49 Greenwich High Road, Greenwich, SE10*

☎ *020 8265 3311*

⌨ *themetro@dircon.co.uk*

⌨ *www.themetro.dircon.co.uk*

🚇 *Greenwich BR/DLR*

The Metro Centre (see p.90) currently runs three youth groups – Chillin' Out, a weekly social support group for young people under 26 (Sun 2pm-5pm), Tribe, which supports the under 16s (first Sat 2pm-5pm) and a drop-in for young lesbians, bisexuals and gay men (Thurs 1pm-4pm). Advice on emotional, sexual and health issues is available at each session.

The Mix

☎ *Paul 020 7267 8595*

🕐 *Tues 6.30pm-9.30pm*

Social and support group for men and women who are exploring issues of sexuality and identity in a safe space in Kentish Town. Ring from Kentish Town tube for directions.

Mosaic

☎ *Neil or Justin 020 8838 0527*

🚌 *Harlesden BR or Willesden Junction LU*

🕒 *Mon 6.30pm-9.30pm*

A place for gay and bisexual men under 25 (and those questioning their sexuality) in Brent to meet like-minded men and make friends.

MYNORS in Mitcham

☎ *Anne or Tim 020 8646 3033*

🕒 *Wed 6.30pm-9.30pm*

Social and support group for lesbians, gays and bisexuals under 21 in the Mitcham area.

Newham Out

✉ *Education Department, Little Ilford Youth Centre,*
1a Rectory Road, Manor Park, E12

☎ *Richard 020 8555 8186*

🚌 *East Ham LU*

🕒 *Mon 7pm-10pm*

This local gay and bi group for under-25s has a mixed social programme of discussions, advice sessions, and trips out to pubs and the cinema.

Newham Together

☎ *020 8555 8186*

🚌 *East Ham LU*

🕒 *Sat 3.30pm-5.30pm*

Run by the same team as the Newham Out group (see above), this is a mixed gay, bisexual and lesbian group for under-25s with an emphasis on befriending and offering a supportive atmosphere to those coming to terms with their sexuality.

North London Line Youth Project (NLL)

✉ *c/o Islington Youth Service, Education Dept, Laycock Street, Islington, N1*

☎ *020 7607 8346*

🚌 *Highbury & Islington LU*

🕒 *Mon 7pm-9pm*

A LGB project for those under 26, with activities, trips and advice/support.

North Seven Social

- Old Fire Station, 84 Mayton Street, Holloway, N7
- Douglas 020 7700 4658 (during group hours)
- Holloway Road LU
- Tues 7pm-10pm
- 40p per session

This 16–25s gay and bisexual men's social group is reliant on its members for the topics of its discussions. Regular guest speakers talk about subjects like safe sex and housing or demonstrate massage and acupuncture. Trips to the movies or a nearby gay pub are another draw, and the group also has facilities for playing pool and table tennis, and listening to music.

Notting Hill Lesbian and Gay Youth Group

- 5b Denbigh Road, Notting Hill, W11
- Dom 020 7229 3266
- Notting Hill Gate LU
- Thurs 7.30pm-10pm

This social group is for gays and lesbians under 25, or those who think they might be. There are regular guest speakers, discussions and trips to the cinema or pubs.

NRG Youth

- Michelle 020 7620 1819 (during group hours)
- nrg@lads.demon.co.uk
- Southwark LU
- Thurs 7pm-10pm

This weekly group provides socials, away from the scene, for gays, lesbians and bisexuals under 25 in Lambeth, Southwark and Lewisham, offering those confused about or coming to terms with their sexuality the chance to go out to clubs and pubs with people in the same boat. There are also information evenings exploring safer sex, and one-on-one counselling sessions. Workers meet members at the tube station.

Out on Thursday

- Ralph 0800 169 4318
- minicom 02008 846 9090 (during group hours)
- www.outonthursday.org.uk
- Thurs 6pm-10pm

An under 25s youth group for gay and bisexual men that meets in Hammersmith, with a busy programme of workshops, educational videos and one-to-one counselling and discussions revolving around families, school, relationships and sexual experiences. The organisers also encourage users to arrange outside activities like cinema visits or picnics.

Outzone

▭ *Jackson's Lane Centre, 269a Archway Road, Highgate, N6*

☎ *Pete 020 8348 1785*

✐ *www.outzone.org*

🚇 *Highgate LU*

🕐 *Wed 4pm-8pm*

Young gay and bisexual men 25 – and those who are unsure – can seek advice, information, support and make new friends in north London at this social group. They also have a full programme of events, including bowling, films and pub visits.

QT LGB Support Group

☎ *020 8427 1799 minicom 020 8427 5505*

🕐 *Fri 6pm-10pm*

Lesbians, gays and bisexuals from 16 to 25 can meet, discuss issues of sexuality and make new friends in Harrow on the Hill.

Shout!

☎ *020 8675 0306*

✐ *shout@bi.org*

🕐 *Fri 7pm-9.30pm*

South-west London social night in Balham for LGB youngsters under 26 – or those who think they might be. Social nights, discussions and trips to cinema, bowling, pubs, etc.

Staying Out Project

☎ *020 8533 2174*

🕐 *Mon: Forbidden Fruit – young men's group (7pm-9pm), Tues: Feel Free – gay and lesbian youth (4.30pm-6.30pm), Tues: Staying Out – mixed LGB group for under-26s (7pm-10pm), first Sat: Staying Out – under-17 GLB group (2pm-5pm)*

This young gay and bisexual men's group meets at a venue in Hackney to discuss their sexuality in a safe environment – members range from 11 to 25-years-old, and are often just coming to terms with sexuality. The organisation provides information, advice, support and confidential counselling on any associated issues, as well as social groups that include activities like writing, art, discussions, film-making, photography, art and sports, as well as trips to the cinema and theatre. The group is officially only open to inhabitants of Hackney, but they do take in others.

Stepping Out

⌨ *Central Station, 37 Wharfdale Road, King's Cross, N1*

🚇 *King's Cross BR/LU*

🕐 *Fri 8pm-10pm*

This weekly group for lesbians and gays between 18 and 26 meets upstairs at Central Station for a general social and support evening, and is especially good at helping people coming out.

Strength Progression Diversity (SPD)

⌨ *PO Box 12045, Waltham Forest, E4*

☏ *Al or Vicky 07889 422 854*

🚇 *Leytonstone LU*

🕐 *Mon 10am-8pm*

An affirming social group for lesbians and bisexual women under 26.

Tribe

⌨ *The Metro Centre, Unit 401, 49 Greenwich High Road, Greenwich, SE10*

☏ *020 8265 3311*

  Helpline 020 8265 3355 (Mon-Thurs 7pm-10pm)

🖱 *www.themetro.dircon.co.uk*

🚇 *Greenwich BR/DLR*

🕐 *First Sat 2pm-5pm*

Advice and support group for gay, lesbian and bisexuals under-16s.

Two to Five Club

⌨ *c/o Islington Youth Service, Education Dept, Laycock Street, Islington, N1*

☏ *020 7607 8346*

🚇 *Highbury & Islington LU*

🕐 *Wed 2pm-5pm*

Part of North London Line Lesbian and Gay Youth Project (see p.90), this general drop-in session offers advice and information to gay and bisexual men under 25 on housing, help with job applications, and employment training. There is also a typewriter and computer available. Regular workshops focus on a variety of topics, like meditation and relationship skills.

U18 Zone

☎ *020 8348 1785*

🚇 *Highgate LU*

🕐 *Thurs 4pm-8pm*

Gay and bisexual men's group in Highgate for under 18s – those who are unsure about their sexuality are also welcome.

Youth East London (YEL)

☎ *020 8552 6107*

Social and support group for young gay, lesbian and bisexual people.

Youth Out

🔲 *Pastures Youth Centre, Davies Lane, Leytonstone, E11*

☎ *020 8532 8008 (during group hours)*

🚇 *Leytonstone High Road BR or Leytonstone LU*

🕐 *Mon 7pm-10pm*

A weekly social meeting for lesbians, gays, bisexuals under 25 in the Waltham Forest area – although lesbians are in short supply. Members meet in a youth centre with a large sports hall and table tennis; sometimes the group watch videos, go to see films or a play (subsidised), there are also outside activities during the summer. It's the group themselves who decides the programme.

40+ Groups

See also:

London Monday Group (see p.193)
Gay Graduates in Greater London (GIGGLE) (see p.212)
South London Gays (see p.198)

Caffmos

🔲 *PO Box 2273, Hove, BN3 2GF*

☎ *01273 220 995*

✎ *caffmos2@aol.com*

✎ *www.members.aol.com/caffmos*

This older gentlemen's gay and bisexual site offers the more mature a chance to make friends within a safe, friendly, supportive and confidential environment, with free personal ads, senior penpals, gay forums, photo galleries and chat rooms. There are regular meetings around the country.

Libertines

☎ *Dave 01689 859806*

🚆 *Catford and Catford Bridge BR*

🕐 *Alternate Fri 8pm-9.30pm*

A friendly group for gay men over 50 in south east London that meets in Catford for relaxing coffee and chat every other Friday, and also holds various quiz nights, parties and games evenings. A quarterly newsletter keeps members in touch.

GAY DINING GROUPS
See also **Out and Out** (p.95)

Champagne Dining Club ♀

☎ *Jacky 020 8525 5656*

✉ *champagnedining@aol.com*

🕸 *Annual membership fee*

Set up for professional lesbians wanting to meet similar-minded people in civilised yet fun surroundings, this club is an excellent way for women – whether single or couples – to enhance their social diaries. The organiser arranges dinner parties, jazz evenings and trips to shows for between 10 and 50 women depending upon the event and venue. The restaurants are elegant and discreet and the meals cost around £55-75, which covers free-flowing drinks, a 3 course meal and coffee. The evenings are personally hosted by Jacky who takes care of the introductions, makes sure everything runs smoothly and that a good time is had by all.

Gay Solutions Dining Club

☎ *Marilyn 020 8363 2328*

🚆 *East Finchley LU*

🕐 *Monthly Weds 7.30pm*

🕸 *Annual membership free*

This group hosts elegant dinner parties once a month in Finchley. They meet in the restaurant bar first for introductions before moving on to the table. The group attracts professional men in their early 20s to mid 30s, and with over 60 on the books, you can find a new social circle very quickly. With under 20 people at each table, you should also get to know each other pretty well. The group have recently begun to organise weekends away and theatre trips.

FETISH & DRESS CODE CLUBS

The Boot Club

✉ *PO Box 662, Harrow, Middlesex, HA3 8HF*
✆ *020 8864 0214*
✍ *mail@thebootclub.com*
✍ *www.thebootclub.com*
✆ *Annual membership £20*

If you're turned on by men in boots of any description – shiny, dirty, well-worn, muddy, polished, DMs, army, construction, wellies, waders – then this is the club for you. In just six years this has become one of the largest boot-fetish clubs in the world, with over 200 UK members, and they host regular pub and party nights in London. Their bi-monthly newsletter *Sole Searching* gives information relevant to boot boys: contact ads, the Sole Shop for second-hand boots, a boot exchange scheme, videos for sale and discounts available in various shops. Send SAE, fax or e-mail for more information.

European Bondage Club

✉ *PO Box 9945, London, W6*
✆ *07951 259599*
✍ *ebc@greyhanky87.freeserve.co.uk*
✍ *www.members.tripod.co.uk/ebc1*

A contact club for gay men into a leather/rubber and bondage combo, EBC's 300 members hold parties in London, around the UK and in Antwerp and have a thigh-slapping good time. Members have an active social life and get discounts at Expectations, Clone Zone and the Host stores. Send SAE for further information.

Gummi Club

✉ *Gummi, BM414, London, WC1*
✍ *info@gummi.org.uk*
✍ *www.gummi.org.co.uk*
✆ *Annual membership £10*

With over 300 members nationwide, this rubber fetishists' club organises Saturday night members-only parties with a strict dress code, as well as other meets. Members are entitled to low admission rates at special nights, as well as discounts at major rubber suppliers. The group publish the bi-monthly *Rubber Sheet* newsletter for contact ads, rubber exchange and member contributions.

Kontrole

⌧ *PO Box 662, Harrow, Middlesex, HA3 8HF*

✆ *020 8864 0214*

✍ *mail@kontrole.com*

✍ *www.kontrole.com*

✺ *Annual membership £20*

Bringing masters and servants together for 'mutual benefit', Kontrole was set up for those curious about S&M role-playing – and those who are darned sure it's what they're into. In their bi-monthly magazine, the club's 160 members can express themselves and meet like-minded men through contact ads. Members receive a discount at Clone Zone, Expectations and RoB (see p.170-183).

London Reds

✍ *info@londonreds.org*

✍ *www.londonreds.org*

🕐 *First & third Wed at Crash Bar (9.30pm-2am; see p.23),*
first Fri at Brompton's (8pm-10.30pm; see p.21)

✺ *Membership £7*

Fancy a friendly fisting? London Reds can oblige. This non-profit club aims to bring together like-minded men through weekly club nights and an online contact service. They organise a handful of social events each night, along with three 'red hanky' nights at the Hoist and Crash Bar (do wear something red for easy ID). Membership brings discounts at certain outlets (Expectations, Key Largo, Prowler Press, RoB), admission to special meetings, reduced price admission to some clubs and access to the London Reds' contact web site.

Motor Sports Club London (MSC London)

⌧ *BM MSCL, London, WC1N*

☎ *John 020 8675 0521*

✍ *www.leatherbear.demon.co.uk/msc_london*

✺ *Annual membership £15*

Founded in the 1970s as part of Classic Motor Club, this started as a men-only motorcycle club but soon developed into a leather fetish social group. A monthly programme of events links the 48 clubs around Europe. The London branch organises dinners, parties, pub meetings and regular weekends away. Their *Messages* newsletter provides contacts listing.

Slosh

⊞ *PO Box 73, Harrogate, HG1 4TS*

✎ *slosh@dircon.co.uk*

✎ *www.slosh.dircon.co.uk*

This worldwide club for men – whether straight or gay – has slapstick fun with food, mud, paint, or anything else you can think of, and the 150 or so members in the UK have a whale of a time. It's basically a contact group with many organised events throughout the UK, and produces a magazine and members' directory three times a year.

SM Gays

⊞ *BM SM Gays, London, WC1*

✎ *smgays@aol.com*

✎ *www.smgays.org*

🚇 *Vauxhall BR/LU*

🕐 *Third Thurs 8pm–midnight*

💰 *Annual membership £12*

This anti-sexist, anti-fascist and anti-racist organisation, which meets at The Hoist (see p.27) acts as a non-profitmaking social and educational group for gay men interested in consensual, sexual sadomasochism. SM Gays has encouraged safe and lawful SM practices since 1981, and runs a six-week course for those interested in SM, meets once a month for a night of nut-cracking fun (attracting around 200 gay men), publishes educational guides about SM and safe sex, raises money for people with AIDS and provides speakers for events to deliver the SM message.

BUSINESS PROFESSIONALS & STUDENT GROUPS

Communications Club

⊞ *41 Cooks Road, London, SE17*

☎ *Stephen 020 7735 1592*

This group for gay male journalists, broadcasters and marketers claims that its underlying aim is to fight discrimination and homophobia in the media, but it really operates as a networking club. They meet in the West End and invite guest speakers from the gay community, such as Stonewall's Angela Mason and financial advisor Ivan Massow.

Gay Business Association

- BCM GBA, London, WC1
- 0700 225 5422   0700 232 9422
- www.gba.org.uk

This business group provides networking and social events for lesbian and gay business people. Membership is open to individuals and firms, charities and any other organisation working with the gay community.

Gay Graduates in Greater London (GIGGLE)

- Robert 020 7262 6308
- First Fri

This friendly group meets periodically in a member's home for a private drinks party, with each member bringing a bottle. The group has around 50-60 members, of varied ages and academic backgrounds.

Gay London Professionals (GLP)

- Cygnet House, 188 King's Road, Chelsea, SW3
- John or Patricia 020 7352 8228
- Green Park LU
- Tues 6pm-11pm
- Annual membership £20

Professional gay men of all ages who work in London and want to enlarge their existing circle of friends should hotfoot it down to the

GLP's weekly drinks session in stylish surroundings at The Townhouse, 3 Green Street, Mayfair, W1 every Tuesday night. Dress is smart – usually ties and suits – and the right of admission is reserved, just in case you considered being a rebel. Things get busiest at around 8pm, with Happy Hour at 6pm-7.30pm.

Lesbian and Gay Police Association (LAGPA)

⌨ *BM LAGPA, London, WC1*

☏ *070 20911 922*

✑ *info@lagpa.org.uk*

✑ *www.lagpa.org.uk*

✆ *Annual membership £15*

Formed in 1990 to provide a network for gay and lesbian plods, LAGPA works towards equal opportunities, offers advice and support for all its gay and lesbian employees, and aims to build better relations between the police and gay community. You must be fully employed in the service, although secondary membership is good for entry to social functions. There is an open committee meeting once a month at New Scotland Yard, and the regular London meetings include going out to a pub or club, a meal, disco, or some form of cabaret. The association has a fully qualified counsellor on the committee, and strict precautions are taken to prevent involuntary outing.

National Association of Teachers in Further and Higher Education

⌨ *27 Britannia Street, London, WC1*

☏ *020 7837 3636 (ask for the equality unit)*

This union offers advice, support and contacts for gay and lesbian lecturers in further and higher education.

Suit and Tie Club

⌨ *Lounge Club, The Townhouse, 3 Green Street, Mayfair, W1*

☏ *020 8374 8190*

🚇 *Marble Arch LU*

🕐 *Daily from 7.30pm*

Neatly-dressed men meet for drinks and conversation in the plush Mayfair Townhouse Club.

SPORTS & FITNESS

N o longer are gay men an ensemble of gibbering wrecks when a fast-moving ball catapults towards them; neither are lesbians purely the defence on the hockey team – the impressive number of organised bent sporting teams and societies in London indicates a more positive attitude towards sport. Most of the clubs date from the late 1980s, being set up after the ground-breaking Gay Games. For supporters groups, see Social groups p.184-213.

4 Play Squash

🖃 *Finsbury Leisure Centre, Old Street, EC1*
☏ *Paul 07958 988 277*
✎ *4playsquash@postmaster.co.uk*
🚇 *Old Street LU*
🕒 *Wed 7.30pm*

This friendly and informal gay and lesbian squash group supports a charity each year (in recent years they have raised around £8,000 for Food Chain). The group meets four times a week with around 40 (predominantly male) players turning up for a friendly game. There are two competitions a year – one in London (May), one in Gran Canaria (end October), as well as other social gatherings and trips.

Frontrunners

British Gay and Lesbian Sports Federation (Out For Sport)

✉ *PO Box 293, Harrow, Middlesex, HA1 1GA*

☎ *020 7278 3294*

This body was set up after the New York Games in June 1994 to oversee the many gay and lesbian sports groups in the UK and to provide an information base for people who want to know how to get involved. Their voluntary board is stocked with experienced sports people and supplies trophies, pays for sports clubs stalls at Pride and distributes funds to clubs around Britain. They organised a team for the 1998 Gay Games in Amsterdam, and are aiming at staging a mini Gay Games to take place in Britain. There is a £2 charge for people requesting information in writing.

British Military Fitness Training

☎ *0870 241 2517*

✉ *fitness@britmilfit.com*

✉ *www.britmilfit.com*

Want a bit of discipline in your exercise regime? Ex-Army instructors motivate men and women of all fitness levels in an outdoor session of static exercises, running and team relay. It's hard work but guaranteed to be fun – and you don't need to be a comma ndo to join. The one-hour sessions take place mornings and evenings in Clapham Common, Hyde Park, Blackheath and Battersea Park.

Dynamo Dykes

✉ *Elephant & Castle Leisure Centre, SE1*

☎ *Laura 020 7274 0453*

✉ *info@dynamodykes.org.uk*

✉ *www.dynamodykes.org.uk*

🚇 *Elephant & Castle BR/LU*

🕐 *Mon 8pm-10pm*

Britain's only out lesbian volleyball team was established in 1992, and they now have over 20 players of all levels forming three teams – Dynamo Dykes in London's Division One, and Dynamo Dykes Too in Division Two and Dynamo Dykes Free in Division Three. They are in the London Volleyball Association, and recently received a grant from the National Lottery to aid and develop further successes. They have competed in many local and international tournaments with several notable wins, and have many more tournaments planned for the future. During the volleyball season from September to April, the club trains with professional coaches at Elephant and Castle Leisure Centre.

Frontrunners

⌨ *Hyde Park, Queen Mother's Gate, W2*

☎ *Felix 020 8986 5182*

✉ *bigbutchdyke@hotmail.com*

✉ *www.frontrunners.org*

🚇 *Hyde Park Corner/South Kensington LU*

🕐 *Sat 10am, Mon 7pm, Wed 7pm*

💰 *£20 a year, £1 per session*

Started in 1974 in San Francisco, this international lesbian and gay jogging group has spread throughout the world with the London branch numbering around 150 people of all abilities. They meet up three times a week at the Princes' Gate in Hyde Park for a social run of up to six miles, then eat at a café or pub. Runners tend to be in their 30s, and around one fifth are women. There are two competitive runs a month and international meets such as the Gay Games and Euro Games, and they socialise quite a bit, with house parties, theatre and cinema trips, bowling nights and weekends away. Membership includes a monthly newsletter, 10% discount at certain running stores and free entrance to group races.

Gala Badminton

⌨ *Harrow Leisure Centre, HA1*

☎ *John 020 8952 8293*

🚇 *Harrow and Wealdstone LU*

🕐 *Sun 7pm-9pm*

Started as an offshoot of the Harrow and Brent Lesbian and Gay Group (see p.196) around 15 years ago, this mainly gay men's mixed ability badminton group was London's first, and now mainly caters to Harrow locals, attracting around 12-15 locals each week for a friendly game. They also organise a tournament at Christmas time and nights out.

Gay Birders' Club

⌨ *Deneside, Foulden Bastle, Berwick-upon-Tweed, TD15 1UL*

✉ *gay.birders@dial.pipex.com*

✉ *www.dspace.dial.pipex.com/gay.birders*

Launched in 1994 by a small group of lesbians and gays, this bird-watching society now boasts over 300 UK members across all levels of birding expertise. The group organises 60-80 outings each year to birding sites around the country and beyond – to see everything from woodlarks in Thursley Common in Surrey to the hawfinch in Northumberland and the scarlet Ibis in Trinidad. Full details of trips are published in their quarterly *Out Birding* newsletter.

Gay and Lesbian Underwater Group (GLUG)

☎ *Rupert 020 7625 5789*

🦐 *Annual membership £26*

This wittily-named club offers GLB scuba diving enthusiasts the chance to don their wetsuits and dive safely in a relaxed, non-threatening atmosphere. You do need a minimum qualification to join – PADI Open Water Diver, BSAC Club Diver, CMAS, SAA Elementary, NAUI Open Water Diver or similar. The group offers a programme of training and education, as well as organising diving trips and outings (some abroad), and meets in Central London monthly so members can fuel eachother's enthusiasm. Members receive the GLUG newsletter on a monthly basis and benefit from discounts for training/certification and for diving equipment with gay-friendly commercial companies and organisations

Gay Outdoor Club

✉ *PO Box 16124, Glasgow, G12 9YT*

☎ *Badminton: Ian 020 8802 9639, Caving: Martin 04973 204484, Climbing: Colum 020 7603 6779, Cycling: Peter 020 8747 4640, Mountaineering: Roger 01904 659544, Snowboarding: Ash 0121 373 9880, Swimming: Dave 020 8521 7567, Walks: Bob 020 8674 8367*

✍ *goc@bi.org*

✍ *www.bi.org/~goc*

This nationwide network of over 30 specialist groups was founded in 1974 and is by far the largest UK sports and social group for gay, lesbian and bisexual people, with over 1,100 members. As an umbrella organisation, it includes specialist groups – caving, climbing, tennis, swimming, cycling, summer and winter mountaineering, canoeing and snowboarding – and organises at least 20 events per month, from social gatherings to serious sports activities. Membership covers a wide age-range, with reasons for participating ranging from the purely social to the highly competitive. They are affiliated to the Ramblers' Association, the Cyclists' Touring Club and the International Gay and Lesbian Outdoor Association.

Goslings Badminton Club

⌨ *Swiss Cottage Sports Centre, Swiss Cottage, NW3*

☎ *Ian 020 8802 9639 or Andrew 01462 893410*

✉ *goslings@hotmail.com*

✉ *www.gosling.org.uk*

🚇 *Swiss Cottage LU*

🕐 *Mon & Thurs 7.50pm-10pm*　💰 *£3 entrance*

Because the Gosling Swimming Club was so popular, this badminton group was set up in 1987. Around 35-40 players – from beginners to very experienced – meet next to the Swiss Cottage sportscentre and take over the five badminton courts for a few games, then socialise afterwards in a local pub. They have regular tournaments, and participate in the international badminton tournament in July.

Goslings Cycling Club

☎ *Peter 020 8747 4640*

✉ *goslings_cycling@goslings.org.uk*

✉ *www.gosling.org.uk*

This gay and lesbian London based cycling club organises a programme of fun rides in London, in the countryside around London and beyond, tailoring the types and lengths of rides to cater for all levels of ability and interest. Members receive a bi-monthly newsletter of the ride programme, run jointly with GOC, which includes weekend trips to places like the Brecon Becons, Boulogne or Mallorca.

Goslings Swimming Club

⌨ *Oasis Sports Centre, Endell Street, Covent Garden, WC2*

☎ *Dave 020 8521 7567*

✉ *goslings@hotmail.com*

✉ *www.gosling.org.uk*

🚇 *Tottenham Court Road LU*

🕐 *Thurs 8.20pm-9.30pm*　💰 *£3 entrance*

This swimming group was founded in the mid-1970s and now meets once a week, with around 20 people showing up for a fun recreational swimming session in a private pool at the Oasis. In the summer, attendance soars up to a hundred (total membership is 120). They use the heated outdoor pool all year round in typically hardy swimmer's fashion, and socialise after each session. Open to all levels of swimming ability.

Gymnos 88

🖃 *King's Hall Leisure Centre, 39 Lower Clapton Street, Clapton, E5*

☎ *020 8985 0961 (King's Hall)*

✍ *gymnos_naturist@lycos.com*

✍ *www.angelfire.com/sports/gymnos*

🕐 *Tues & Thurs 8.45pm-10.15pm*

💰 *£2.40, day membership £1.50, full membership £18, swimming-only membership £8*

This men-only nudist swimming group has over 500 members in southeast England, and typically around 50 turn up to the weekly Tuesday swimming sessions. They train their own lifeguards, one of whom gives swimming lessons on Friday by prior arrangement. There are lanes for those who want to do lengths, but it's mostly a fun and casual get-together. There are social events almost every weekend, with private nude evenings, naturist video films, massage, sailing weekends, body painting and nude wrestling, as well as two summer holidays a year, one in the UK and one abroad. The group attracts men from 20 to 70: the swimming is more 20s-30s dominated and the social groups bring in older members. Members must be over 18 to join.

HD Walking Group (Hiking Dykes) ♀

🖃 *PO Box 3670, London, N17*

☎ *Linda 020 8695 1100 or Clare 020 7423 9388*

✍ *hikingdykes@hotmail.com*

💰 *Membership £6, £1 unwaged*

Hiking Dykes is an informal and friendly lesbian walking group who meet up a couple of times a month for a gentle one-day walk at the weekend (5-12 miles,with refreshment stops!), usually about an hour's train ride from London. Send off membership money for a full list of the walks for the year.

Irons Golf Society

☎ *Martin 020 8780 9409 or 07966 456 553*

🕐 *Sun, March-Nov*

This gay and lesbian golfing group has around 40 members (the majority being men) and play weekly or more often during the warmer months. They organise at least three golfing getaways a year – so far to places like Ireland, Bournemouth and South Carolina in the states – and put members in touch with others in their area so they can play when they want. You don't need a handicap or to belong to a golf club to join.

Ishigaki Ju-jitsu Club

☎ *Simon 020 7739 8442 or Pauline 020 8286 1071*

✉ *simple@dircon.co.uk*

✉ *www.ishigaki.org.uk*

🕑 *Tues 7.30pm-9.30pm Finsbury Leisure Centre basement, Old Street, EC1; Thurs 7.30pm-9.30pm & Sat 3.30pm-5.30pm Oasis Sports Centre badminton hall, Endell Street, Covent Garden, WC2*

💰 *£5, annual membership £27.50 (includes insurance)*

The Japanese art of self-defence (Ishigaki means 'stone wall' in Japanese) will not only protect you from attackers by enabling you to use their force against them, but is also an excellent way of keeping fit, improving confidence and relieving frustration. These martial arts classes of 25-30 men and women feature all ages and abilities, from black belt to complete beginners – you are paired up with someone of similar ability and don't have to be hugely fit. Women make up a third of the class, and half the black belts. Even though the class is very focused and committed, they do find time to go to the pub after each session.

KB Kickboxing ♀

☎ *Kelly 07881 957977*

✉ *kelly@kbkickboxing.co.uk*

✉ *www.kbkickboxing.co.uk*

🕑 *Classes take place at the Drill Hall, Bloomsbury, (see p.103) and Juno's Fitness Centre, 1 Broad Yard, off Turnmill Street, Farringdon, EC1*

💰 *10-week course £60*

This fusion of boxing, kung fu, karate and ancient arts of self-defence strengthens and conditions every muscle in your body, and follows the syllabus up to black belt standard. After a 15-minute warm-up, the class uses focus mitts and hand-held kick shields, and there is the opportunity spar with protective gear. There is also a weekly women-only class on Monday night.

King's Cross Steelers

▭ *East London RFC*

☎ *Chris 020 7476 6647*

✉ *secretary@kxsrfc.com*

✉ *www.kxsrfc.com*

🕑 *Mon & Wed practice at (7.30pm-9pm)*

💰 *Annual membership £25*

London's first gay rugby team plays competitively at league level – a triumph over the namby-pamby image of gay boys. They have set up two Union Code-following teams: the first XV is for committed and experienced players, while the second XV acts as a training and development squad, and for those who cannot commit to training or league games. The team is a member of the Surrey County Rugby Football Union and Rugby Football Union, and offer two student bursaries a year for promising players in full or part-time adult education. They also have regular social events and tour nationally and overseas.

Lesbian and Gay Karate Club (Fudoshinkai Karate England)

🖳 *Fitness Exchange, Cutlers Gardens, Devonshire Square, EC2*
Lambs Health & Fitness, Clubs Passage, off Chiswell Street, EC2
☎ *Kevin 07711 793 416*
✍ *kevin@fudoshinkai.freeserve.co.uk*
✍ *www.fudoshinkai.freeserve.co.uk/glglinks.htm*
🚇 *Covent Garden LU*
☺ *Mon, Tues, Wed and Thurs 7.30pm-9pm*

The lesbian and gay instructors teach traditional Shotokan Karate with the backing of the Amateur Martial Association AMA and the English Karate Governing Body EKGB, and are headed by a Fifth Dan Black Belt Karate instructor. Students are typically committed to their sport, and work towards passing grading examinations, as well as increasing fitness, strength and flexibility, self-confidence and discipline. At the moment, membership consists of novice and intermediate/advanced students. Although the instructors and the majority of the members are gay, this is a gay friendly, rather than exclusively gay club. Visitors are welcome.

London Spikers Volleyball Club

☎ *Richard 020 7237 4578*
✍ *ssvc@hotmail.com*
☺ *Sun Afternoons (Sept-Apr) Bethnal Green Sports Centre, E1 (beginners); Sun Afternoons (May-Aug) Hyde Park, near Speaker's Corner, W1 (beginners)*

The UK's only gay men's volleyball club started up in 1995 and received a lottery grant. They take their game seriously – they meet in London at least twice a week (and on the beach in Bournemouth some weekends), have four teams playing in the London Volleyball Association leagues and enter a lot of gay tournaments in Europe and further afield. The club is open to all volleyball players of any standard, and provides professional coaching.

Out to Swim

Outriggers

☎ *Blair 020 8450 4214*

✉ *orionrc@amazon122.demon.co.uk*

✉ *www.outriggers.org*

Outriggers, or Orion RC, is a gay and lesbian rowing club based on the Thames at Hammersmith and affiliated to the Amateur Rowing Association. In 1998, its second year, it won medals in seven rowing events at the Gay Games in Amsterdam. It has built up over 40 active rowing members, but is still looking for male and female rowers of all standards. They assure that you don't need to be highly athletic or fit, just reasonably tall, willing to train and the fitness you need will come.

Out to Swim

🖃 *BM Swim, London, WC1*

☎ *07808 295 349 Alistair*

✉ *www.outtoswim.org*

🕔 *Tues 7pm-8pm Queen Mother Sports Centre, Vauxhall Bridge Road, SW1;*
Wed 8pm-9pm Kentish Town Pool; Thurs 7pm-8pm (women-only 8pm-9pm)
Oasis Sports Centre, Endell Street, Covent Garden, WC2; Sun 4pm-5pm ULU

💰 *Annual membership £50*

This fitness and competitive swimming club for lesbians, gay men and their friends meets four days a week and offers five training sessions with qualified coaches and pool lanes for different abilities. Out of the 140 total membership, around 30-40 people show up to each session. Some swimming ability is needed, but coaches are there to improve technique. Swimmers compete locally, nationally and internationally – one Out to Swim member set a new European record in 1994's Gay Games. They're not only fit but sociable, arranging plenty of barbecues, day trips to the seaside and meals.

Rainbow Raiders Softball Team

⌨ *Regent's Park, NW1*
☎ *Peter 07970 237705*
✐ *rainbowraiders@hotmail.com*
✐ *www.rainbowraiders.com*
🚇 *Regent's Park LU*
✺ *Annual membership £35*

This gay and lesbian softball team plays in the publishing league and competes for the London Softball Federation Cup. They have a mixed team, as well as separate men's and women's teams, and play recreation softball to a decent standard – they won the regionals in 2000 and came third in the nationals, as well as attending the Gay Games in Amsterdam and the Sydney games. They practice from March to September in Regent's Park, and provide all equipment and training.

Sailing and Cruising Association

⌨ *BM Sailing, London, WC1*
☎ *Reggie 020 7207 2885*
✐ *www.gaysailing.org.uk*
🕐 *Fortnightly Tues 7.30pm at The Edge (see p.124)*
✺ *Annual membership £12*

The Gay Sailing Club and Gay and Lesbian Windsurfing Club amalgamated to form this group of over 200 (mostly male) members who like to get wet. They meet up fortnightly during the season (March–August) to set up meets at weekends, whether dinghy racing, yacht sailing, canal trips or charters – or in the case of the windsurfers on reservoirs around London. You don't have to have sailing experience or equipment to join, as members are of all abilities from beginners to yacht master instructors, and the club matches up people with or without equipment. They are affiliated to clubs in the US and France, so they arrange meets abroad. The monthly *Newsbuoy* club newsletter appears every 2-3 months and gives a full membership list.

Saint Gabriel's Badminton Club

⌨ *St Gabriel's Church Hall, Lupus Street, Pimlico, SW1*

☎ *Mark 020 7976 6805*

✉ *stgay@hotmail.com*

✉ *www.pete.ndo.co.uk/stgabs.htm*

🕐 *Wed 7.30pm-9.30pm*

✎ *Membership £25, £3 per practice*

This men's badminton club takes its game seriously, with one team in the first division, the other in the second. There are 14 committed members who compete all around Europe, have weekends away to take on other teams, and go away for a yearly two-week holiday together.

Snowboyz

☎ *01843 298030 or 0845 3344 356*

✉ *ski@snowboyz.com*

✉ *www.snowboyz.com*

In a beautiful mountain chalet – complete with stone fireplaces, spectacular terraces, fantastic views, door-to-door ski-ing and bars only minutes away – this holiday company welcomes gay male skiers as house guests in the famous Les Arcs ski domain in the high French Alps. The area has 110 lifts, over 200kms of marked runs and vast off-piste potential, and the company has experienced skiing 'Snowboyz' who take care of coaching. They throw lively dinner parties six nights a week, tended by a four-star chef. Expect to pay around £400 per person per week, including twin room, 3/4 board, drinks, local transfers, service and entertainment – but not airfares.

Stonewall Football Club ♀

⌨ *c/o Central Station, 37 Wharfdale Road, Kings Cross, N1*

☎ *020 7565 4254*

✉ *info@stonewallfc.org*

✉ *www.stonewallfc.org*

This gay football club comprises four squads of differing standards – the flagship team London Lions, second league London Apprentices and London Wreckers, and women's team London Lionesses – and have twice topped the International Gay and Lesbian Football Association World Championship (in 1995 and 2000). They organise games each week, with two 11-a-side matches on Sundays in Regent's Park, and two five-a-side games each Thursday on an astroturf pitch in north London. They also arrange social activities from time to time, with pub and club nights and paintball fights, and tours abroad every year to Europe and North America. Ring first for details and times. See also Football Supporters Network, p.186.

Tennis London International

⌨ *36 Prince George Road, Stoke Newington, N16*

☎ *020 7739 5567*

✎ *tennislondon@bigfoot.com*

✎ *www.maiko.demon.co.uk/tennis*

🚇 *Shepherd's Bush LU*

🕐 *Sun Westway Tennis Centre, W12 (5pm-9pm)*

The UK's biggest lesbian and gay tennis group – also one of the biggest in Europe – organises the Tennis London International Tournament and promotes gay and lesbian fraternity in sport. They meet up every weekend and play on three indoor courts, have around 70 male and female members, run leagues and accept beginners. It's strictly social tennis for the first hour on Sunday, then becomes more competitive. They are especially keen on promoting women's tennis.

Yoga Classes for Gay Men

⌨ *Helios Centre, 5-9 Tavistock Place, WC1*

☎ *David 020 7625 4521*

✎ *www.gayyogalondon.com*

🚇 *Russell Square LU*

🕐 *Fri 6.30pm (intermediate; 2hrs £7); Sun 7pm (beginners; 1.5 hours £6)*

A qualifed yoga instructor teaches the physical and mental discipline of yoga to groups of up to 16 gay men, developing flexibility, strength, stamina and relaxation. The group is sociable and often meet up for a meal.

Yoga – see also Kairos (p.88)

Yoga for Gay Men

⌨ *The Factory, 407 Hornsey Road, Archway, N19*

☎ *020 7272 1122*

✎ *www.tangolondon.com*

🚇 *Archway LU*

🕐 *Mon 8pm-9.30pm, Wed 7.45pm-9pm, Thurs 10.15am-noon,*
Sun noon-1.30pm

💰 *£7 per class*

There are regular yoga classes for men in this dance and fitness centre – catering for complete beginners to the more experienced. Membership includes free use of the sauna and fitness classes.

TAXIS

There are a handful of gay and lesbian taxi companies that make snogging the love of your life or your latest pick-up on the back seat an easy exercise – a lot of straight women also use the service as they know they can guarantee getting to their front door without being propositioned or molested. Some of the cab companies also offer luxury cars, with one devoted solely to offering clients a glimpse of the high life from the back of a stretch limo.

Freedom Cars

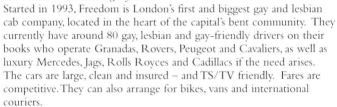

⌨ *2nd Floor, 52 Wardour Street, Soho, W1*

☏ *020 7278 7654*

✍ *www.connected.co.uk/get/freedom*

Started in 1993, Freedom is London's first and biggest gay and lesbian cab company, located in the heart of the capital's bent community. They currently have around 80 gay, lesbian and gay-friendly drivers on their books who operate Granadas, Rovers, Peugeot and Cavaliers, as well as luxury Mercedes, Jags, Rolls Royces and Cadillacs if the need arises. The cars are large, clean and insured – and TS/TV friendly. Fares are competitive. They can also arrange for bikes, vans and international couriers.

Q Cars

⌨ *46 New Park Road, Streatham Hill, SW2*

☏ *020 8671 0011 or 020 7622 0011*

Started in July 1995, this 24-hour south London-based cab company now has 20 cars, all with gays and lesbians and some post and pre-op TSs behind the wheel. They prefer to pick up in south London.

Rainbow Cars

⌨ *28 Wilcox Road, Wandsworth, SW8*

☏ *Ken 020 7622 1863   Mob 0802 755092*

This 24-hour radio-controlled gay cab service operates a fleet of 25 cabs – including Granadas, Orions, limos and a Bentley – and has already scooped up the Heaven, GAY, London Lighthouse, Reflex and Positive Place contracts. Not all the drivers are gay, just good at their jobs and able to get you to your front door in one piece.

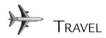

TRAVEL

I t's true that lesbians and gays flock to Lesbos, Barcelona and Mykonos, but there is a handful of gay-operated travel agents that can take us further afield and cater for our 'special needs'.

Alternative Holidays

⌨ *PO Box 16393, London, SE1*

☏ *020 7701 7040* ✆ *020 7708 5668*

✍ *info@alternative-holidays.com*

✍ *www.alternative-holidays.com*

This fully bonded gay male travel agency concentrates on two major holiday experiences for the gay market. During the summer they have a holiday to Otranto in Italy at a comfortable Club Med location. In the winter they organise the annual European Gay Ski Week which takes place at a number of European resorts and has a good deal of après Ski events for those more interested in a socialising than improving their ski technique.

D Tours

⌨ *59 Rupert Street, Soho, W1*

☏ *020 7837 3323*

✍ *info@dtours.co.uk*

This is the premier incoming tour operator for gay men and lesbians travelling to Britain.

@home around the world

⌨ *PO Box 19518, Battersea, SW11*

☏ *Ken Russell 020 7564 3739*

✍ *london@homearoundtheworld.com*

✍ *www.london@homearoundtheworld.com*

This company has offices in London, Paris, New York, San Francisco and Sydney, and organises home exchanges for members, and a worldwide hosting or guesting service for likeminded people. Free colour brochure.

JA Travel

✉ *PO Box 6602, London, N20*

☎ *Tony 020 8361 8026*

The businessmen's choice of travel organiser, JA Travel provides a flights and hotel booking service, with confidentiality and discretion foremost in their mind.

Man Around

✉ *89 Wembley Park Drive, Wembley, Middlesex, HA9 8HS*

☎ *020 8902 7177*   ✆ *020 8903 7357*

✎ *manaround@aol.com*

✎ *www.manaround.com*

Fully-bonded independent gay-run travel company Man Around has been running ten years and merged with Sensations Holidays in 1999 to create Europe's largest gay tour operator. Man Around's gay or gay-friendly holidays include the world's most sought-after gay destinations, whether a whole package or just accommodation or flights. Things on offer include city breaks to Amsterdam, New York, Barcelona and Paris; holidays to Gran Canaria, Ibiza, the Algarve and Florida; the RSVP gay cruises; trips to Sydney's Mardi Gras festival; vacations to Fiji's six-star Man Friday resort; opera in Verona and Lake Garda tour; 7-night Thailand and Malaysia tour; wine tasting in South Africa... They have also launched several lesbian holiday packages. Flights go from most UK airports and there are group reductions.

Respect Holidays

✉ *74 Haverstock Hill, Belsize Park, NW3*

☎ *020 7485 8855*   ✆ *020 7267 7766*

✎ *info@respect-holidays.co.uk*

✎ *www.respect-holidays.co.uk*

Brochure requests: brochures@respect-holidays.co.uk

The world's only ABTA and ATOL-licensed gay holiday company has packages at gay and gay-friendly hotels and apartments in Ibiza, Mallorca, Mykonos, Sitges, Gran Canaria, Torremolinos and the Algarve, with many exclusive properties.

Sensations

✉ *89 Wembley Park Drive, Wembley, Middlesex, HA9 8HS*

☎ *Tel: 020 8900 0809*

✎ *Website: www.sensationsholidays.com*

Sensations and Man Around merged in 1999 to form Europe's biggest gay and lesbian holiday company. See main entry for further details.

Map 1
SOHO & COVENT GARDEN

PUBS & BARS
1 Admiral Duncan
2 Bar Aquda
3 Bar Code
4 The Box
5 Brief Encounter
6 Candy Bar
7 Compton's of Soho
8 The Edge
9 Escape
10 First Out

CLUBS
24 79 CXR
25 Café de Paris
26 The Clinic
27 The Depot
28 Form
29 Heaven
30 T2 Bar
31 London Astoria

11 Freedom Café
12 Halfway 2 Heaven
13 Jonathans
14 King's Arms
15 Ku Bar
16 Kudos
17 Manto Soho
18 Retro Bar
19 Rupert Street
20 Vespa Lounge
21 Village Soho
22 West Central/
   Underground West Central Bar
23 The Yard

32 Madame Jo Jo's
33 The Rock
34 The Tube
35 Twenty Three Club
36 Velvet Room

CAFÉS & RESTAURANTS
37 Balans
38 The Dome
39 Ed's Easy Diner
40 Hujo's
41 Il Forno
42 Mildred's
43 Steph's
44 Costa Coffee
45 Old Compton Café
46 Patisserie Valerie

GYMS & SAUNAS
47 Oasis Sports Centre
48 The Sauna Bar
49 Soho Athletic Club

SHOPS & SERVICES
50 American Retro
51 Clone Zone
52 Freedom Cars
53 Kairos
54 Metal Morphosis
55 Accomodation Outlet
56 Paradiso
57 Prowler
58 Silvermoon Women's Bookshop
59 Trax Records
60 XSF Records

Map 2
EARL'S COURT

PUBS & BARS
1   The Coleherne
2   Warwick Bar

CLUBS
2   Bromptons

SHOPS & SERVICES
8   Adonis Arts & Antiques
9   Basement Project
10   Clone Zone
11   Liquid Art Tattoo & Piercing Studio
12   Streetwise Youth

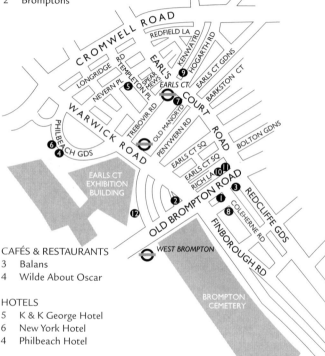

CAFÉS & RESTAURANTS
3   Balans
4   Wilde About Oscar

HOTELS
5   K & K George Hotel
6   New York Hotel
4   Philbeach Hotel

GYMS
7   Earl's Court Gym

Map 3
ISLINGTON & KING'S CROSS

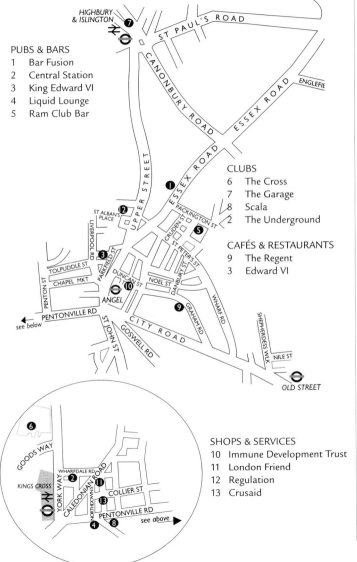

PUBS & BARS
1 Bar Fusion
2 Central Station
3 King Edward VI
4 Liquid Lounge
5 Ram Club Bar

CLUBS
6 The Cross
7 The Garage
8 Scala
2 The Underground

CAFÉS & RESTAURANTS
9 The Regent
3 Edward VI

SHOPS & SERVICES
10 Immune Development Trust
11 London Friend
12 Regulation
13 Crusaid

233

Map 4
KENNINGTON & VAUXHALL

PUBS & BARS
1   The Cock Tavern
2   Dukes (The Duke of Cambridge)
3   The Little Apple
4   Royal Vauxhall Tavern
5   The Skinners Arms

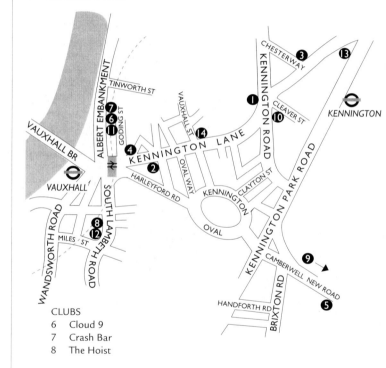

CLUBS
6   Cloud 9
7   Crash Bar
8   The Hoist

GYMS & SAUNAS
9   The Cruise Club
10 The Locker Room
11 Paris Gym

SHOPS & SERVICES
12 The Host
13 Mainliners
14 UK Coalition of People
    Living with HIV and AIDS

Index

Order Form

The following titles are also available from Metro Publications:

Please send your order along with a cheque made payable to Metro Publications to the address below.
Postage is free, please allow 14 days for delivery.

Metro Publications,
PO Box 6336, London N1 6PY
e-mail: metro@dircon.co.uk
www.metropublications.com

or contact our Credit Card Order Line:

Order line: 020 8533 0922 (Visa/Mastercard/Switch)
Open: 9am–6pm; Mon–Fri

Gay & Lesbian London
Author: Graham Parker
£7.99, 260pp, 40 b/w photos, 4 Maps
ISBN 1-902910-09-5

Gay & Lesbian London includes reviews of all the social clubs, political organizations, health services, restaurants and night clubs to help gay men and woman enjoy the Capital. The book is essential for exploring the Capital's gay scene.

The London Market Guide
2nd edition
Authors: Andrew Kershman & Ally Ireson
£5.99, 192pp, 40 b/w photos,
80 Maps
ISBN 1-902910-04-4

The London Market Guide contains all the essential information needed to explore London's 70 street markets including maps, photos, travel information, consumer tips, over 90 cafés and full contact details for those wanting to get a stall.

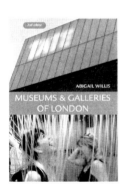

Museums & Galleries of London
2nd edition
Author: Abigail Willis
£8.99, 288pp, 60 b/w photos,
3 Area Maps & 8 Floor plans
ISBN 1-9029-10-079

This is the first guide to combine detailed reviews of all the museums and galleries of London with listings of the city's commercial galleries, archives and details of London's many art degree shows

The Guide to Cookery Courses
Cooking & Wine Schools, Courses &
Holidays Throughout The British Isles &
Further Afield (2nd edition)
Author: Eric Treuille
£7.99, 210pp, 10 b/w photos
ISBN 1-902910-05-2

The Guide to Cookery Courses has been
updated and expanded to provide a
comprehensive listing of the cookery and
wine courses in the British Isles and
further afield.

Taste of London
Author: Jenny Linford
£6.99, 144pp, 42 b/w photos
ISBN 0-9522914-7-9

A Taste of London contains over 80
cosmopolitan recipes, many of them
recommended by Londoners of diverse
ethnic origin and using all the ingredients
to be found in the Capital, from dried
porcini mushrooms to root ginger and
lemon grass. The book also contains a
glossary of cooking ingredients.

Food Lovers' London
Author: Jenny Linford
£6.99, 160pp, 40 b/w photos
ISBN 1-902910-03-6

Food Lovers' London contains all the information a London foodie needs to start cooking any of the thirteen nationalities of cuisine featured. Each cuisine has a glossary of ingredients and reviews of all London's best food shops and eating places, as well as a brief history of the people and culture that gave rise to the food.

Book Lovers' London
Author: Lesley Reader
£7.99, 192pp, 30 b/w photos
ISBN 0-9522914-4-4

This is a complete guide to London's bookshops (both new, second-hand and antiquarian), as well as all the best book-related markets, charity shops, auctions and bookfairs.